SIMPLE
SUCCESS

Simple Success Guides

SIMPLE SUCCESS

How to Prosper in Good Times and Bad

Napoleon Hill, Joseph Murphy,
Florence Scovel Shinn,
Elbert Hubbard, Peter B. Kyne,
Arnold Bennett, Emmet Fox

ST. MARTIN'S
ESSENTIALS
NEW YORK

Published in the United States by St. Martin's Essentials, an imprint of St. Martin's Publishing Group

INTRODUCTION. Copyright © 2023 by Joel Fotinos. All rights reserved. Printed in the United States of America. For information, address St. Martin's Publishing Group, 120 Broadway, New York, NY 10271.

www.stmartins.com

The Library of Congress Cataloging-in-Publication Data is available upon request.

ISBN 978-1-250-88781-8 (trade paperback)
ISBN 978-1-250-88782-5 (ebook)

Our books may be purchased in bulk for promotional, educational, or business use. Please contact your local bookseller or the Macmillan Corporate and Premium Sales Department at 1-800-221-7945, extension 5442, or by email at MacmillanSpecialMarkets@macmillan.com.

The Game of Life and How to Play It was first published in 1925.
Foreword copyright © 2020 by Joel Fotinos.
The material in *Let Ambition Be Your Master and Other Works* was first published from 1915 to 1937.
Introduction copyright © 2022 by Joel Fotinos.
The Golden Key was first published in 1867. Introduction copyright © 2022 by Joel Fotinos.
How to Attract Money was first published in 1955. Introduction copyright © 2023 by Joel Fotinos.
How to Live on 24 Hours a Day was first published in 1908. Foreword copyright © 2020 by Joel Fotinos.
The Go-Getter was first published in 1921. Foreword copyright © 2020 by Joel Fotinos.
A Message to Garcia was first published in 1899.

First St. Martin's Essentials Edition: 2023

10 9 8 7 6 5 4 3 2 1

This edition seeks to faithfully reproduce the original publications of the author's works and so has maintained the original spelling and grammar throughout, with only minor alterations for clarity or content.

CONTENTS

INTRODUCTION

"The journey of a thousand miles begins with a single step."
—Lao Tzu

Welcome to *Simple Success*. The quote above from Lao Tzu is both uncomplicated and profound—your journey not only begins with a single step but is made up of a series of steps. Some steps will be small, some will be big, but each one will take you farther.

Think of *Simple Success* as a series of steps for your journey. This book is not made up of one book but rather several small books that, together, create a powerful path to life's success. Similarly, you'll find that success in your life is not made up of one action, or one idea, or any one thing—but rather a series of actions, ideas, and help.

Each of these books was originally published years ago, some over a century ago. And yet the truths they each teach are timeless and can help us in today's world. How is that possible? I think each author tapped into an evergreen principle or truth, applied those principles to their own life, and then turned around and taught them to others. That's how every generation has always gone further than those before them, by taking the best of the past and then applying that best to their own future.

We originally published these six books individually, in our collection of Simple Success Guides at St. Martin's Essentials, each with an introduction by me that is specific to that book (and which are left intact in this volume). However, at a certain point, it became clear that the books *together* create a unique and powerful roadmap that can speak to today's readers.

And now you are holding this book in your hands. Might I make a suggestion to make your reading of this book more personal and fruitful? If so, I would say to read the books on three levels. First, read the book literally. These books contain ideas, stories, and principles that can create a more positive experience in life. Second, read the book with the understanding that while the principles may be timeless, the stories might be of their time. The language and stories and examples might be dated. Take the dated material and translate it in your mind to modern equivalents. If one of the authors gives an example that involves something that is not of our time, then pause and try to come up with our modern counterpart. Don't discard powerful ideas merely because they are cloaked in examples of a distant past.

And third, read the book, noticing which ideas stand out to you. I believe that since you are holding this book, there are ideas contained within that can benefit you greatly. Pay attention as you read to both the things that speak to you deeply and those things you think don't apply to you—both are valuable and can teach you where you are most comfortable and which ideas might challenge you to grow bigger than you ever dreamed.

It's up to you now. Enjoy, and allow these ideas—which have already collectively helped millions—now help you. I often say in my introductions that we are each responsible for our own lives. Books like this can help inspire the best versions of ourselves and keep us moving in positive directions. Success may be simple, but it's not always easy. Dig deep and move forward, one step at a time. Before you know it, you'll have gone ten thousand miles . . .

—*Joel Fotinos*

FLORENCE SCOVEL SHINN

The Game of Life and How to Play It

Contents

Foreword

Life is difficult. Everything seems so hard. I'm always broke. I'll never find my soul mate. Work is a grind. Nothing ever seems to work out for me.

These are only some of the many negative thoughts that can run rampant through our minds. Many people can relate to the idea that life doesn't seem to turn out the way we thought it would . . . or hoped it would.

But is that true? Or is that just what we tell ourselves? Is it possible that we make life so much more difficult than it needs to be? And . . . is it even remotely possible that life can be fun? Even a game?

That is the premise of Florence Scovel Shinn's classic masterpiece, *The Game of Life and How to Play It*. Published in 1925, *The Game of Life and How to Play It* has never been out of print, and over the years has sold millions of copies. Originally self-published by the author after no publisher would accept it, the book has gone on to influence people from all walks of life, from business leaders to students, to spiritual teachers such as Louise Hay, Norman Vincent Peale, and Emmet Fox.

When a book continues to inspire readers nearly a century after original publication, it generally means that the ideas in the book are universal and applicable. That is absolutely true for *The Game of Life and How to Play It*. The book contains simple-yet-powerful advice for living a positive life. In fact, Shinn shows how we can turn our life into a game, and turn our minds into power attractors of abundance at every turn, in every area of our lives.

Filled with stories from the author's life as well as the lives of her many students, *The Game of Life and How to Play It* also contains instructions on changing our viewpoint from one of limitation and negativity to that of possibility and positivity. She also shows how affirmations can yield powerful effects, and even gives us exercises to use.

Shinn used these ideas and practices in her own life. Born in New Jersey in 1871, Shinn became an artist, book and magazine illustrator, and even an actress in New York City. Divorced and living on her own in Manhattan, Shinn became interested in New Thought teachings, and eventually became a popular spiritual teacher. It is from these experiences that she wrote her books. *The Game of Life and How to Live It* was the one that captured the attention of millions over the years, and continues to change readers' lives to this day.

As you read this book, be prepared to see your life in a new way. Shinn is clear that we have a choice in how we perceive and live our lives. Not only that, but that we have a responsibility to elevate our attitudes and thoughts, which will in turn change every area in our life. She doesn't leave room for doubt, complaints, or procrastination. Follow the positive ideas in this book, and see positive effects ripple in your life as well.

—*Joel Fotinos*

The Game

Most people consider life a battle, but it is not a battle, it is a game.

It is a game, however, which cannot be played successfully without the knowledge of spiritual law, and the Old and the New Testaments give the rules of the game with wonderful clearness. Jesus Christ taught that it was a great game of *Giving and Receiving*.

"Whatsoever a man soweth that shall he also reap." This means that whatever man sends out in word or deed, will return to him; what he gives, he will receive.

If he gives hate, he will receive hate; if he gives love, he will receive love; if he gives criticism, he will receive criticism; if he lies he will be lied to; if he cheats he will be cheated. We are taught also, that the imaging faculty plays a leading part in the game of life.

"Keep thy heart (or imagination) with all diligence, for out of it are the issues of life." (Prov. 4:23.)

This means that what man images, sooner or later externalizes in his affairs. I know of a man who feared a certain disease. It was a very rare disease and difficult to get, but he pictured it continually and read about it until it manifested in his body, and he died, the victim of distorted imagination.

So we see, to play successfully the game of life, we must train the imaging faculty. A person with an imaging faculty trained to image only good, brings into his life "every righteous desire of his heart"—health, wealth, love, friends, perfect self-expression, his highest ideals.

The imagination has been called, *"The Scissors of The Mind,"* and it is ever cutting, cutting, day by day, the pictures man sees there, and sooner or later he meets his own creations in his outer world. To train the imagination successfully, man must understand the workings of his mind. The Greeks said: "Know Thyself."

There are three departments of the mind, the *subconscious, conscious and superconscious.* The subconscious, is simply power, without direction. It is like steam or electricity, and it does what it is directed to do; it has no power of induction.

Whatever man feels deeply or images clearly, is impressed upon the subconscious mind, and carried out in minutest detail.

For example: a woman I know, when a child, always "made believe" she was a widow. She "dressed up" in black clothes and wore a long black veil, and people thought she was very clever and amusing. She grew up and married a man with whom she was deeply in love. In a short time he died and she wore black and a sweeping veil for many years. The picture of herself as a widow was impressed upon the subconscious mind, and in due time worked itself out, regardless of the havoc created.

The conscious mind has been called mortal or carnal mind.

It is the human mind and sees life as it *appears to be.* It sees death, disaster, sickness, poverty and limitation of every kind, and it impresses the subconscious.

The *superconscious* mind is the God Mind within each man, and is the realm of perfect ideas.

In it, is the *"perfect pattern"* spoken of by Plato, *The Divine Design;* for there is a *Divine Design* for each person.

"There is a place that you are to fill and no one else can fill, something you are to do, which no one else can do."

There is a perfect picture of this in the *superconscious mind.*

It usually flashes across the conscious as an unattainable ideal—
"something too good to be true."

In reality it is man's true destiny (or destination) flashed to him
from the Infinite Intelligence which is *within himself.*

Many people, however, are in ignorance of their true des-
tinies and are striving for things and situations which do not
belong to them, and would only bring failure and dissatisfaction
if attained.

For example: A woman came to me and asked me to "speak
the word" that she would marry a certain man with whom she was
very much in love. (She called him A. B.)

I replied that this would be a violation of spiritual law, but that
I would speak the word for the right man, the "divine selection,"
the man who belonged to her by divine right.

I added, "If A. B. is the right man you can't lose him, and if
he isn't, you will receive his equivalent." She saw A. B. frequently
but no headway was made in their friendship. One evening she
called, and said, "Do you know, for the last week, A. B. hasn't
seemed so wonderful to me." I replied, "Maybe he is not the divine
selection—another man may be the right one." Soon after that, she
met another man who fell in love with her at once, and who said
she was his ideal. In fact, he said all the things that she had always
wished A. B. would say to her.

She remarked, "It was quite uncanny."

She soon returned his love, and lost all interest in A. B.

This shows the law of substitution. A right idea was substituted
for a wrong one, therefore there was no loss or sacrifice involved.

Jesus Christ said, "Seek ye first the Kingdom of God and his
righteousness; and all these things shall be added unto you," and
he said the Kingdom *was within man.*

The Kingdom is the realm of *right ideas,* or the divine pattern.

Jesus Christ taught that man's words played a leading part in the game of life. "By your words ye are justified and by your words ye are condemned."

Many people have brought disaster into their lives through idle words.

For example: A woman once asked me why her life was now one of poverty and limitation. Formerly she had a home, was surrounded by beautiful things and had plenty of money. We found she had often tired of the management of her home, and had said repeatedly, "I'm sick and tired of things—I wish I lived in a trunk," and she added: "Today I am living in that trunk." She had spoken herself into a trunk. The subconscious mind has no sense of humor and people often joke themselves into unhappy experiences.

For example: A woman who had a great deal of money, joked continually about "getting ready for the poorhouse."

In a few years she was almost destitute, having impressed the subconscious mind with a picture of lack and limitation.

Fortunately, the law works both ways, and a situation of lack may be changed to one of plenty.

For example: A woman came to me one hot summer's day for a "treatment" for prosperity. She was worn out, dejected and discouraged. She said she possessed just eight dollars in the world. I said, "Good, we'll bless the eight dollars and multiply them as Jesus Christ multiplied the loaves and the fishes," for He taught that *every man* had the power to bless and to multiply, to heal and to prosper.

She said, "What shall I do next?"

I replied, "Follow intuition. Have you a 'hunch' to do anything, or to go anywhere?" Intuition means, intuition, or to be taught from within. It is man's unerring guide, and I will deal more fully with its laws in a following chapter.

The woman replied: "I don't know—I seem to have a 'hunch' to go home; I've just enough money for carfare." Her home was in a distant city and was one of lack and limitation, and the reasoning mind (or intellect) would have said: "Stay in New York and get work and make some money." I replied, "Then go home—never violate a hunch." I spoke the following words for her: *"Infinite Spirit open the way for great abundance for——. She is an irresistible magnet for all that belongs to her by divine right."* I told her to repeat it continually also. She left for home immediately. In calling on a woman one day, she linked up with an old friend of her family.

Through this friend, she received thousands of dollars in a most miraculous way. She has said to me often, "Tell people about the woman who came to you with eight dollars and a hunch."

There is always *plenty on man's pathway;* but it can only be *brought into manifestation* through desire, faith or the spoken word. Jesus Christ brought out clearly that man must make the *first move.*

"Ask, and it shall be given you, seek, and ye shall find, knock, and it shall be opened unto you." (Mat. 7:7.)

In the Scriptures we read:

"Concerning the works of my hands, command ye me."

Infinite Intelligence, God, is ever ready to carry out man's smallest or greatest demands.

Every desire, uttered or unexpressed, is a demand. We are often startled by having a wish suddenly fulfilled.

For example: One Easter, having seen many beautiful rose-trees in the florists' windows, I wished I would receive one, and for an instant saw it mentally being carried in the door.

Easter came, and with it a beautiful rose-tree. I thanked my friend the following day, and told her it was just what I had wanted.

She replied, "I didn't send you a rose-tree, I sent you lilies!"

The man had mixed the order, and sent me a rose-tree simply because I had started the law in action, and *I had to have a rose-tree.*

Nothing stands between man and his highest ideals and every

desire of his heart, but doubt and fear. When man can "wish without worrying," every desire will be instantly fulfilled.

I will explain more fully in a following chapter the scientific reason for this and how fear must be erased from the consciousness. It is man's only enemy—fear of lack, fear of failure, fear of sickness, fear of loss and a feeling of *insecurity on some plane.* Jesus Christ said: "Why are ye fearful, oh ye of little faith?" (Mat. 8:26.) So we can see we must substitute faith for fear, for fear is only inverted faith; it is faith in evil instead of good.

The object of the game of life is to see clearly one's good and to obliterate all mental pictures of evil. This must be done by impressing the subconscious mind with a realization of good. A very brilliant man, who has attained great success, told me he had suddenly erased all fear from his consciousness by reading a sign which hung in a room. He saw printed, in large letters this statement—*"Why worry, it will probably never happen."* These words were stamped indelibly upon his subconscious mind, and he has now a firm conviction that only good can come into his life, therefore only *good can manifest.*

In the following chapter I will deal with the different methods of impressing the subconscious mind. It is man's faithful servant but one must be careful to give it the right orders. Man has ever a silent listener at his side—his subconscious mind.

Every thought, every word is impressed upon it and carried out in amazing detail. It is like a singer making a record on the sensitive disc of the phonographic plate. Every note and tone of the singer's voice is registered. If he coughs or hesitates, it is registered also. So let us break all the old bad records in the subconscious mind, the records of our lives which we do not wish to keep, and make new and beautiful ones.

Speak these words aloud, with power and conviction: "I now smash and demolish (by my spoken word) every untrue record in my subconscious mind. They shall return to the dust-heap of their native nothingness, for they came from my own vain imaginings. I now make my perfect records through the Christ within—The records of *Health, Wealth, Love and perfect self-Expression."* This is the square of life, *The Game completed.*

In the following chapters, I will show how man can *change* his *conditions by changing his words.* Any man who does not know the power of the word, is behind the times.

"Death and Life are in the power of the tongue."
(Prov. 18:21.)

The Law of Prosperity

*"Yea, the Almighty shall be thy defense and
thou shalt have plenty of silver."*

One of the greatest messages given to the race through the scriptures is that God is man's supply and that man can release, *through
his spoken word,* all that belongs to him by divine right. He must,
however, have *perfect faith in his spoken word.*

Isaiah said, "My word shall not return unto me void, but shall
accomplish that where unto it is sent." We know now, that words
and thoughts are a tremendous vibratory force, ever moulding man's
body and affairs.

A woman came to me in great distress and said she was to be
sued on the fifteenth of the month for three thousand dollars. She
knew no way of getting the money and was in despair.

I told her God was her supply, and *that there is a supply for every
demand.*

So I spoke the word! I gave thanks that the woman would receive
three thousand dollars at the right time in the right way. I told her
she must have perfect faith, and act her *perfect faith.* The fifteenth
came but no money had materialized.

She called me on the 'phone and asked what she was to do.

I replied, "It is Saturday, so they won't sue you today. Your part is to act rich, thereby showing perfect faith that you will receive it by Monday." She asked me to lunch with her to keep up her courage. When I joined her at a restaurant, I said, "This is no time to economize. Order an expensive luncheon, act as if you have already received the three thousand dollars."

"All things whatsoever ye ask in prayer, *believing,* ye shall receive." "You must act as if you *had already received.*" The next morning she called me on the 'phone and asked me to stay with her during the day. I said "No, you are divinely protected and God is never too late."

In the evening she 'phoned again, greatly excited and said, "My dear, a miracle has happened! I was sitting in my room this morning, when the door-bell rang. I said to the maid: 'Don't let anyone in.' The maid however, looked out the window and said, 'It's your cousin with the long white beard.'

"So I said, 'Call him back. I would like to see him.' He was just turning the corner, when he heard the maid's voice, and *he came back.*

"He talked for about an hour, and just as he was leaving he said, 'Oh, by the way, how are finances?'

"I told him I needed the money, and he said, 'Why, my dear, I will give you three thousand dollars the first of the month.'

"I didn't like to tell him I was going to be sued. What shall I do? I won't *receive it till* the first of the month, and I must have it tomorrow." I said, "I'll keep on 'treating.'"

I said, "Spirit is never too late. I give thanks she has received the money on the invisible plane and that it manifests on time." The next morning her cousin called her up and said, "Come to my office this morning and I will give you the money." That afternoon, she had three thousand dollars to her credit in the bank, and wrote checks as rapidly as her excitement would permit.

If one asks for success and prepares for failure, he will get the situation he has prepared for. For example: A man came to me asking me to speak the word that a certain debt would be wiped out.

I found he spent his time planning what he would say to the man when he did not pay his bill, thereby neutralizing my words. He should have seen himself paying the debt.

We have a wonderful illustration of this in the Bible, relating to the three kings who were in the desert, without water for their men and horses. They consulted the prophet Elisha, who gave them this astonishing message:

"Thus saith the Lord—Ye shall not see wind, neither shall ye see rain, yet make this valley full of ditches."

Man must prepare for the thing he has asked for, *when there isn't the slightest sign of it in sight.*

For example: A woman found it necessary to look for an apartment during the year when there was a great shortage of apartments in New York. It was considered almost an impossibility, and her friends were sorry for her and said, "Isn't it too bad, you'll have to store your furniture and live in a hotel." She replied, *"You needn't feel sorry for me, I'm a superman, and I'll get an apartment."*

She spoke the words: *"Infinite Spirit, open the way for the right apartment."* She knew there was a supply for every demand, and that she was "unconditioned," working on the spiritual plane, and that "one with God is a majority."

She had contemplated buying new blankets, when "the tempter," the adverse thought or reasoning mind, suggested, "Don't buy the blankets, perhaps, after all, you won't get an apartment and you will have no use for them." She promptly replied (to herself): "I'll dig my ditches by buying the blankets!" So she prepared for the apartment—acted as though she already had it.

She found one in a miraculous way, and it was given to her although there were over *two hundred other applicants.*

The blankets showed active faith.

It is needless to say that the ditches dug by the three kings in the desert were filled to over-flowing. (Read, II Kings.)

Getting into the spiritual swing of things is no easy matter for the average person. The adverse thoughts of doubt and fear surge from the subconscious. They are the "army of the aliens" which must be put to flight. This explains why it is so often, "darkest before the dawn."

A big demonstration is usually preceded by tormenting thoughts.

Having made a statement of high spiritual truth one challenges the old beliefs in the subconscious, and "error is exposed" to be put out.

This is the time when one must make his affirmations of truth repeatedly, and rejoice and give thanks that he has already received. "Before ye call I shall answer." This means that "every good and perfect gift" is already man's awaiting his recognition.

Man can only receive what he sees himself receiving.

The children of Israel were told that they could have all the land they could see. This is true of every man. He has only the land within his own mental vision. Every great work, every big accomplishment, has been brought into manifestation through holding to the vision, and often just before the big achievement, comes apparent failure and discouragement.

The children of Israel when they reached the "Promised Land," were afraid to go in, for they said it was filled with giants who made them feel like grasshoppers. "And there we saw the giants and we were in our own sight as grasshoppers." This is almost every man's experience.

However, the one who knows spiritual law, is undisturbed by appearance, and rejoices while he is "yet in captivity." That is, he holds to his vision and gives thanks that the end is accomplished, he has received.

Jesus Christ gave a wonderful example of this. He said to his disciples: "Say not ye, there are yet four months and then cometh the harvest? Behold, I say unto you, lift up your eyes and look on the fields; for they are ripe already to harvest." His clear vision pierced the "world of matter" and he saw clearly the fourth dimensional world, things as they really are, perfect and complete in Divine Mind. So man must ever hold the vision of his journey's end and demand the manifestation of that which he has already received. It may be his perfect health, love, supply, self-expression, home or friends.

They are all finished and perfect ideas registered in Divine Mind (man's own superconscious mind) and must come through him, not to him. For example: A man came to me asking for treatments for success. It was imperative that he raise, within a certain time, fifty-thousand dollars for his business. The time limit was almost up, when he came to me in despair. No one wanted to invest in his enterprise, and the bank had flatly refused a loan. I replied: "I suppose you lost your temper while at the bank, therefore your power. You can control any situation if you first control yourself." "Go back to the bank," I added, "and I will treat." My treatment was: "You are identified in love with the spirit of everyone connected with the bank. Let the divine idea come out of this situation." He replied, "Woman, you are talking about an impossibility. Tomorrow is Saturday; the bank closes at twelve, and my train won't get me there until ten, and the time limit is up tomorrow, and anyway they won't do it. It's too late." I replied, "God doesn't need any time and is never too late. With Him all things are possible." I added, "I don't know anything about business, but I know all about God." He replied: "It all sounds fine when I sit here listening to you, but when I go out it's terrible." He lived in a distant city, and I did not hear from him for a week, then came a letter. It read: "You were right. I raised the money, and will never again doubt the truth of all that you told me."

I saw him a few weeks later, and I said, "What happened? You evidently had plenty of time, after all." He replied, "My train was late, and I got there just fifteen minutes to twelve. I walked into the bank quietly and said, 'I have come for the loan,' and they gave it to me without a question."

It was the last fifteen minutes of the time allotted to him, and Infinite Spirit was not too late. In this instance the man could never have demonstrated alone. He needed someone to help him hold to the vision. This is what one man can do for another.

Jesus Christ knew the truth of this when he said: "If two of you shall agree on earth as touching anything that they shall ask, it shall be done for them of my Father which is in heaven." One gets too close to his own affairs and becomes doubtful and fearful.

The friend or "healer" sees clearly the success, health or prosperity, and never wavers, because he is not close to the situation.

It is much easier to "demonstrate" for someone else than for one's self, so a person should not hesitate to ask for help, if he feels himself wavering.

A keen observer of life once said, "no man can fail, if some one person sees him successful." Such is the power of the vision, and many a great man has owed his success to a wife, or sister or a friend who "believed in him" and held without wavering to the perfect pattern!

The Power of the Word

---

*"By thy words thou shalt be justified,
and by thy words thou shalt be condemned."*

A person knowing the power of the word, becomes very careful of his conversation. He has only to watch the reaction of his words to know that they do "not return void." Through his spoken word, man is continually making laws for himself.

I knew a man who said, "I always miss a car. It invariably pulls out just as I arrive."

His daughter said: "I always catch a car. It's sure to come just as I get there." This occurred for years. Each had made a separate law for himself, one of failure, one of success. This is the psychology of superstitions.

The horseshoe or rabbit's foot contains no power, but man's spoken word and belief that it will bring him good luck creates expectancy in the subconscious mind, and attracts a "lucky situation." I find however, this will not "work" when man has advanced spiritually and knows a higher law. One cannot turn back, and must put away "graven images." For example: Two men in my class had had great success in business for several months, when suddenly everything "went to smash." We tried to analyze the situation, and I found, instead of making their affirmations and looking to God for success and prosperity, they had each bought a "lucky monkey." I said: "Oh I see, you have been trusting in the lucky monkeys instead of God." "Put away the lucky monkeys and call on the law of forgiveness," for man has power to forgive or neutralize his mistakes.

They decided to throw the lucky monkeys down a coalhole, and all went well again. This does not mean, however, that one should throw away every "lucky" ornament or horseshoe about the house, but he must recognize that the power back of it is the one and only power, God, and that the object simply gives him a feeling of expectancy.

I was with a friend, one day, who was in deep despair. In crossing the street, she picked up a horseshoe. Immediately, she was filled with joy and hope. She said God had sent her the horseshoe in order to keep up her courage.

It was indeed, at that moment, about the only thing that could have registered in her consciousness. Her hope became faith, and she ultimately made a wonderful demonstration. I wish to make the point clear that the men previously mentioned were depending on the monkeys, alone, while this woman recognized the power back of the horseshoe.

I know, in my own case, it took a long while to get out of a belief that a certain thing brought disappointment. If the thing happened, disappointment invariably followed. I found the only way I could make a change in the subconscious, was by asserting, "There are not two powers, there is only one power, God, therefore, there are no disappointments, and this thing means a happy surprise." I noticed a change at once, and happy surprises commenced coming my way.

I have a friend who said nothing could induce her to walk under a ladder. I said, "If you are afraid, you are giving in to a belief in two powers, Good and Evil, instead of one. As God is absolute, there can be no opposing power, unless man makes the false of evil for himself. To show you believe in only One Power, God, and that there is no power or reality in evil, walk under the next ladder you see." Soon after, she went to her bank. She wished to open her box in the safe-deposit vault, and there stood a ladder on her pathway. It was impossible to reach the box without passing under the ladder. She quailed with fear and turned back. She could not face the lion on her pathway. However, when she reached the street, my words rang in her ears and she decided to return and walk under it. It was a big moment in her life, for ladders had held her in bondage for years. She retraced her steps to the vault, and the ladder was no longer there! This so often happens! If one is willing to do a thing he is afraid to do, he does not have to.

It is the law of nonresistance, which is so little understood.

Someone has said that courage contains genius and magic. Face a situation fearlessly, and there is no situation to face; it falls away of its own weight.

The explanation is, that fear attracted the ladder on the woman's pathway, and fearlessness removed it.

Thus the invisible forces are ever working for man who is always "pulling the strings" himself, though he does not know it. Owing to the vibratory power of words, whatever man voices, he begins to attract. People who continually speak of disease, invariably attract it.

After man knows the truth, he cannot be too careful of his words. For example: I have a friend who often says on the 'phone, "Do come to see me and have a fine old-fashioned chat." This "old-fashioned chat" means an hour of about five hundred to a thousand destructive words, the principal topics being loss, lack, failure and sickness.

I reply: "No, I thank you, I've had enough old-fashioned chats in my life, they are too expensive, but I will be glad to have a new-fashioned chat, and talk about what we want, not what we don't want." There is an old saying that man only dares use his words for three purposes, to "heal, bless or prosper." What man says of others will be said of him, and what he wishes for another, he is wishing for himself.

"Curses, like chickens, come home to roost."

If a man wishes someone "bad luck," he is sure to attract bad luck himself. If he wishes to aid someone to success, he is wishing and aiding himself to success.

The body may be renewed and transformed through the spoken word and clear vision, and disease be completely wiped out of the consciousness. The metaphysician knows that all disease has a mental correspondence, and in order to heal the body one must first "heal the soul."

The soul is the subconscious mind, and it must be "saved" from wrong thinking.

In the twenty-third psalm, we read: "He restoreth my soul." This means that the subconscious mind or soul, must be restored with the right ideas, and the "mystical marriage" is the marriage of the soul and the spirit, or the subconscious and superconscious mind. They must be one. When the subconscious is flooded with the perfect ideas of the superconscious, God and man are one. "I and the Father are one." That is, he is one with the realm of perfect ideas; he is the man made in God's likeness and image (imagination) and is given power and dominion over all created things, his mind, body and affairs.

It is safe to say that all sickness and unhappiness come from the violation of the law of love. A new commandment I give unto you, "Love one another," and in the Game of Life, love or good-will takes every trick.

For example: A woman I know, had, for years an appearance of a terrible skin disease. The doctors told her it was incurable, and she was in despair. She was on the stage, and she feared she would soon have to give up her profession, and she had no other means of support. She, however, procured a good engagement, and on the opening night, made a great "hit." She received flattering notices from the critics, and was joyful and elated. The next day she received a notice of dismissal. A man in the cast had been jealous of her success and had caused her to be sent away. She felt hatred and resentment taking complete possession of her, and she cried out, "Oh God don't let me hate that man." That night she worked for hours "in the silence."

She said, "I soon came into a very deep silence. I seemed to be at peace with myself, with the man, and with the whole world. I continued this for two following nights, and on the third day I found I was healed completely of the skin disease!" In asking for love, or good will, she had fulfilled the law, ("for love is the fulfilling of the law") and the disease (which came from subconscious resentment) was wiped out.

Continual criticism produces rheumatism, as critical, inharmonious thoughts cause unnatural deposits in the blood, which settle in the joints.

False growths are caused by jealousy, hatred, un-forgiveness, fear, etc. Every disease is caused by a mind not at ease. I said once, in my class, "There is no use asking anyone 'What's the matter with you?' we might just as well say, 'Who's the matter with you?'" Unforgiveness is the most prolific cause of disease. It will harden arteries or liver, and affect the eye-sight. In its train are endless ills.

I called on a woman, one day, who said she was ill from having eaten a poisoned oyster. I replied, "Oh, no, the oyster was harmless, you poisoned the oyster. What's the matter with you?" She answered, "Oh about nineteen people." She had quarrelled with nineteen people and had become so inharmonious that she attracted the wrong oyster.

Any inharmony on the external, indicates there is mental inharmony. "As the within, so the without."

Man's only enemies are within himself. "And a man's foes shall be they of his own household." Personality is one of the last enemies to be overcome, as this planet is taking its initiation in love. It was Christ's message—"Peace on Earth, good will towards man." The enlightened man, therefore, endeavors to perfect himself upon his neighbor. His work is with himself, to send out goodwill and blessings to every man, and the marvelous thing is, that if one blesses a man he has no power to harm him.

For example: A man came to me asking to "treat" for success in business. He was selling machinery, and a rival appeared on the scene with what he proclaimed, was a better machine, and my friend feared defeat. I said, "First of all, we must wipe out all fear, and know that God protects your interests, and that the divine idea must come out of the situation. That is, the right machine will be sold, by the right man, to the right man." And I added, "Don't hold one critical thought towards that man. Bless him all day, and be willing not to sell your machine, if it isn't the divine idea." So he went to the meeting, fearless and nonresistant, and blessing the other man. He said the outcome was very remarkable. The other man's machine refused to work, and he sold his without the slightest difficulty. "But I say unto you, love your enemies, bless them that curse you, do good to them that hate you, and pray for them which spitefully use you and persecute you."

Goodwill produces a great aura of protection about the one who sends it, and "No weapon that is formed against him shall prosper." In other words, love and goodwill destroy the enemies within one's self, therefore, one has no enemies on the external!

"There is peace on earth for him who sends goodwill to man!"

The Law of Nonresistance

"Resist not evil. Be not overcome of evil,
but overcome evil with good."

Nothing on earth can resist an absolutely nonresistant person.

The Chinese say that water is the most powerful element, because it is perfectly nonresistant. It can wear away a rock, and sweep all before it.

Jesus Christ said, "Resist not evil," for He knew in reality, there is no evil, therefore nothing to resist. Evil has come of man's "vain imagination," or a belief in two powers, good and evil.

There is an old legend, that Adam and Eve ate of "Maya the Tree of Illusion," and saw two powers instead of one power, God.

Therefore, evil is a false law man has made for himself, through psychoma or soul sleep. Soul sleep means, that man's soul has been hypnotized by the race belief (of sin, sickness and death, etc.) which is carnal or mortal thought, and his affairs have out-pictured his illusions.

We have read in a preceding chapter, that man's soul is his subconscious mind, and whatever he feels deeply, good or bad, is outpictured by that faithful servant. His body and affairs show forth what he has been picturing. The sick man has pictured sickness, the poor man, poverty, the rich man, wealth.

People often say, "why does a little child attract illness, when it is too young even to know what it means?"

I answer that children are sensitive and receptive to the thoughts of others about them, and often out-picture the fears of their parents.

I heard a metaphysician once say, "If you do not run your subconscious mind yourself, someone else will run it for you."

Mothers often, unconsciously, attract illness and disaster to their children, by continually holding them in thoughts of fear, and watching for symptoms.

For example: A friend asked a woman if her little girl had had the measles. She replied promptly, "not yet!" This implied that she was expecting the illness, and, therefore, preparing the way for what she did not want for herself and child.

However, the man who is centered and established in right thinking, the man who sends out only good-will to his fellow-man, and who is without fear, cannot be *touched or influenced by the negative thoughts of others*. In fact, he could then receive only good thoughts, as he himself, sends forth only good thoughts.

Resistance is Hell, for it places man in a "state of torment."

A metaphysician once gave me a wonderful recipe for taking every trick in the game of life, it is the acme of nonresistance. He gave it in this way; "At one time in my life, I baptized children, and of course, they had many names. Now I no longer baptize children, but I baptize events, but *I give every event the same name*. If I have a failure I baptize it success, in the name of the Father, and of the Son and of the Holy Ghost!"

In this, we see the great law of transmutation, founded on nonresistance. Through his spoken word, every failure was transmuted into success.

For example: A woman who required money, and who knew the spiritual law of opulence, was thrown continually in a business-way, with a man who made her feel very poor. He talked lack and limitation and she commenced to catch his poverty thoughts, so she disliked him, and blamed him for her failure. She knew in order to demonstrate her supply, she must first feel that she *had received—a feeling of opulence must precede its manifestation.*

It dawned upon her, one day, that she was resisting the situation, and seeing two powers instead of one. So she blessed the man and baptized the situation "Success"! She affirmed, "As there is only one power, God, this man is here for my good and my prosperity" (just what he did not seem to be there for). Soon after that she met, *through this man,* a woman who gave her for a service rendered, several thousand dollars, and the man moved to a distant city, and faded harmoniously from her life. Make the statement, "Every man is a golden link in the chain of my good," for all men are God in manifestation, *awaiting the opportunity given by man, himself, to serve the divine plan of his life.*

"Bless your enemy, and you rob him of his ammunition." His arrows will be transmuted into blessings.

This law is true of nations as well as individuals. Bless a nation, send love and good-will to every inhabitant, and it is robbed of its power to harm.

Man can only get the right idea of nonresistance, through spiritual understanding. My students have often said: "I don't want to be a door-mat." I reply "when you use nonresistance with wisdom, no one will ever be able to walk over you."

Another example: One day I was impatiently awaiting an important telephone call. I resisted every call that came in and made no out-going calls myself, reasoning that it might interfere with the one I was awaiting.

Instead of saying, "Divine ideas never conflict, the call will come at the right time," leaving it to Infinite Intelligence to arrange, I commenced to manage things myself—I made the battle mine, not God's and remained tense and anxious. The bell did not ring for about an hour, and I glanced at the 'phone and found the receiver had been off that length of time, and the 'phone was disconnected. My anxiety, fear and belief in interference, had brought on a total eclipse of the telephone. Realizing what I had done, I commenced blessing the situation at once; I baptized it "success," and affirmed, "I cannot lose any call that belongs to me by divine right; I am under *grace, and not under law.*"

A friend rushed out to the nearest telephone, to notify the Company to reconnect.

She entered a crowded grocery, but the proprietor left his customers and attended to the call himself. My 'phone was connected at once, and two minutes later, I received a very important call, and about an hour afterward, the one I had been awaiting.

One's ships come in over a calm sea.

So long as man resists a situation, he will have it with him. If he runs away from it, it will run after him.

For example: I repeated this to a woman one day, and she replied, "How true that is! I was unhappy at home, I disliked my mother, who was critical and domineering; so I ran away and was married—but I married my mother, for my husband was exactly like my mother, and I had the same situation to face again." "Agree with thine adversary quickly."

That means, agree that the adverse situation is good, be undisturbed by it, and it falls away of its own weight. "None of these things move me," is a wonderful affirmation.

The inharmonious situation comes from some inharmony within man himself.

When there is, in him, no emotional response to an inharmonious situation, it fades away forever, from his pathway.

So we see man's work is ever with himself.

People have said to me, "Give treatments to change my husband, or my brother." I reply, "No, I will give *treatments to change you;* when you change, your husband and your brother will change."

One of my students was in the habit of lying. I told her it was a failure method and if she lied, she would be lied to. She replied, "I don't care, I can't possibly get along without lying."

One day she was speaking on the 'phone to a man with whom she was very much in love. She turned to me and said, "I don't trust him, I know he's lying to me." I replied, "Well, you lie yourself, so someone has to lie to you, and you will be sure it will be just the person you want the truth from." Some time after that, I saw her, and she said, "I'm cured of lying."

I questioned: "What cured you?"

She replied: "I have been living with a woman who lied worse than I did!"

One is often cured of his faults by seeing them in others.

Life is a mirror, and we find only ourselves reflected in our associates.

Living in the past is a failure method and a violation of spiritual law.

Jesus Christ said, "Behold, now is the accepted time." "Now is the day of Salvation."

Lot's wife looked back and was turned into a pillar of salt.

The robbers of time are the past and the future. Man should bless the past, and forget it, if it keeps him in bondage, and bless the future, knowing it has in store for him endless joys, but live *fully in the now.*

For example: A woman came to me, complaining that she had no money with which to buy Christmas gifts. She said, "Last year was so different; I had plenty of money and gave lovely presents, and this year I have scarcely a cent."

I replied, "You will never demonstrate money while you are pathetic and live in the past. Live fully in the *now,* and *get ready to give Christmas presents.* Dig your ditches, and the money will come." She exclaimed, "I know what to do! I will buy some tinsel twine, Christmas seals and wrapping paper." I replied, "Do that, and the *presents will come and stick themselves to the Christmas seals.*"

This too, was showing financial fearlessness and faith in God, as the reasoning mind said, "Keep every cent you have, as you are not sure you will get any more."

She bought the seals, paper and twine, and a few days before Christmas, received a gift of several hundred dollars. Buying the seals and twine had impressed the subconscious with expectancy, and opened the way for the manifestation of the money. She purchased all the presents in plenty of time.

Man must live suspended in the moment.

"Look well, therefore, to this Day! Such is the salutation of the Dawn."

He must be spiritually alert, ever awaiting his leads, taking advantage of every opportunity.

One day, I said continually (silently), "Infinite Spirit, don't let me miss a trick," and something very important was told to me that evening. It is most necessary to begin the day with right words.

Make an affirmation immediately upon waking.

For example:

"Thy will be done this day! Today is a day of completion; I give thanks for this perfect day, miracle shall follow miracle and wonders shall never cease."

Make this a habit, and one will see wonders and miracles come into his life.

One morning I picked up a book and read, "Look with wonder at that which is before you!" It seemed to be my message for the day, so I repeated again and again, "Look with wonder at that which is before you."

At about noon, a large sum of money, was given me, which I had been desiring for a certain purpose.

In a following chapter, I will give affirmations that I have found most effective. However, one should never use an affirmation unless it is absolutely satisfying and convincing to his own consciousness, and often an affirmative is changed to suit different people.

For example: The following has brought success to many:

"I have a wonderful work, in a wonderful way, I give wonderful service, for wonderful pay!"

I gave the first two lines to one of my students, and she added the last two.

It made a *most powerful statement,* as there should always be perfect payment for perfect service, and a rhyme sinks easily into the subconscious. She went about singing it aloud and soon did receive wonderful work in a wonderful way, and gave wonderful service for wonderful pay.

Another student, a business man, took it, and changed the word work to business.

He repeated, "I have a wonderful business, in a wonderful way, and I give wonderful service for wonderful pay." That afternoon he made a forty-one-thousand-dollar deal, though there had been no activity in his affairs for months.

Every affirmation must be carefully worded and completely "cover the ground."

For example: I knew a woman, who was in great need, and made a demand for work. She received a great deal of work, but was never paid anything. She now knows to add, "wonderful service for wonderful pay."

It is man's divine right to have plenty! More than enough!

"His barns should be full, and his cup should flow over!" This is God's idea for man, and when man breaks down the barriers of lack in his own consciousness, the Golden Age will be his, and every righteous desire of his heart fulfilled!

The Law of Karma and the Law of Forgiveness

Man receives only that which he gives. The Game of Life is a game of boomerangs. Man's thoughts, deeds and words, return to him sooner or later, with astounding accuracy.

This is the law of Karma, which is Sanskrit for "Comeback." "Whatsoever a man soweth, that shall he also reap."

For example: A friend told me this story of herself, illustrating the law. She said, "I make all my Karma on my aunt, whatever I say to her, some one says to me. I am often irritable at home, and one day, said to my aunt, who was talking to me during dinner. *'No more talk, I wish to eat in peace.'*"

"The following day, I was lunching with a woman with whom I wished to make a great impression. I was talking animatedly, when she said: *'No more talk, I wish to eat in peace!'*"

My friend is high in consciousness, so her Karma returns much more quickly than to one on the mental plane.

The more man knows, the more he is responsible for, and a person with a knowledge of Spiritual Law, which he does not practice, suffers greatly, in consequence. "The fear of the Lord (law) is the beginning of wisdom." If we read the word Lord, law, it will make many passages in the Bible much clearer.

"Vengeance is mine, I will repay, saith the Lord" (law). It is the law which takes vengeance, not God. God sees man perfect, "created in his own image," (imagination) and given "power and dominion."

This is the perfect idea of man, registered in Divine Mind,

awaiting man's recognition: for man can only be what he sees himself to be, and only attain what he sees himself attaining.

"Nothing ever happens without an on-looker" is an ancient saying.

Man sees first his failure or success, his joy or sorrow, before it swings into visibility from the scenes set in his own imagination. We have observed this in the mother picturing disease for her child, or a woman seeing success for her husband.

Jesus Christ said, "And ye shall know the truth and the truth shall make you free."

So, we see freedom (from all unhappy conditions) comes through knowledge—a knowledge of Spiritual Law.

Obedience precedes authority, and the law obeys man when he obeys the law. The law of electricity must be obeyed before it becomes man's servant. When handled ignorantly, it becomes man's deadly foe. *So with the laws of Mind!*

For example: A woman with a strong personal will, wished she owned a house which belonged to an acquaintance, and she often made mental pictures of herself living in the house. In the course of time, the man died and she moved into the house. Several years afterwards, coming into the knowledge of Spiritual Law, she said to me: "Do you think I had anything to do with that man's death?" I replied: "Yes, your desire was so strong, everything made way for it, but you paid your Karmic debt. Your husband, whom you loved devotedly, died soon after, and the house was a white elephant on your hands for years."

The original owner, however, could not have been affected by her thoughts had he been positive in the truth, nor her husband, but they were both under Karmic law. The woman should have said (feeling the great desire for the house), "Infinite Intelligence, give me the right house, equally as charming as this, the house *which is mine by divine right.*"

The divine selection would have given perfect satisfaction and brought good to all. The divine pattern is the only safe pattern to work by.

Desire is a tremendous force, and must be directed in the right channels, or chaos ensues.

In demonstrating, the most important step is the *first step, to "ask aright."*

Man should always demand only that which is his by *divine right.*

To go back to the illustration: Had the woman taken this attitude: "If this house, I desire, is mine, I cannot lose it, if it is not, give me its equivalent," the man might have decided to move out, harmoniously (had it been the divine selection for her) or another house would have been substituted. Anything forced into manifestation through personal will, is always "ill-got," and has "ever bad success."

Man is admonished, "My will be done not thine," and the curious thing is, man always gets just what he desires when he does relinquish personal will, thereby enabling Infinite Intelligence to work through him.

"Stand ye still and see the salvation of the Lord" (law).

For example: A woman came to me in great distress. Her daughter had determined to take a very hazardous trip, and the mother was filled with fear.

She said she had used every argument, had pointed out the dangers to be encountered, and forbidden her to go, but the daughter became more and more rebellious and determined. I said to the mother, "You are forcing your personal will upon your daughter, which you have no right to do, and your fear of the trip is only attracting it, for man attracts what he fears." I added, "Let go, and take your mental hands off; *put it in God's Hands, and use this statement*:" "I put this situation in the hands of Infinite Love and

Wisdom; if this trip is the Divine plan, I bless it and no longer resist, but if it is not divinely planned, I give thanks that it is now dissolved and dissipated." A day or two after that, her daughter said to her, "Mother, I have given up the trip," and the situation returned to its "native nothingness."

It is learning to "stand still," which seems so difficult for man. I have dealt more fully with this law in the chapter on nonresistance.

I will give another example of sowing and reaping, which came in the most curious way.

A woman came to me saying, she had received a counterfeit twenty-dollar bill, given to her at the bank. She was much disturbed, for, she said, "The people at the bank will never acknowledge their mistake."

I replied, "Let us analyze the situation and find out why you attracted it." She thought a few moments and exclaimed: "I know it, I sent a friend a lot of stagemoney, just for a joke." So the law had sent her some stagemoney, for it doesn't know anything about jokes.

I said, "Now we will call on the law of forgiveness, and neutralize the situation."

Christianity is founded upon the law of forgiveness—Christ has redeemed us from the curse of the Karmic law, and the Christ within each man is his Redeemer and Salvation from all inharmonious conditions.

So I said: "Infinite Spirit, we call on the law of forgiveness and give thanks that she is under grace and not under law, and cannot lose this twenty dollars which is hers by divine right."

"Now," I said, "Go back to the bank and tell them, fearlessly, that it was given you, there by mistake."

She obeyed, and to her surprise, they apologized and gave her another bill, treating her most courteously.

So knowledge of the Law gives man power to "rub out his mistakes." Man cannot force the external to be what he is not.

If he desires riches, he must be rich first in consciousness.

For example: A woman came to me asking treatment for prosperity. She did not take much interest in her household affairs, and her home was in great disorder.

I said to her, "If you wish to be rich, you must be orderly. All men with great wealth are orderly—and order is heaven's first law." I added, "You will never become rich with a burnt match in the pincushion."

She had a good sense of humor and commenced immediately, putting her house in order. She rearranged furniture, straightened out bureau drawers, cleaned rugs and soon made a big financial demonstration—a gift from a relative. The woman, herself, became made over, and keeps herself keyed-up financially, by being ever watchful of the *external and expecting prosperity, knowing God is her supply.*

Many people are in ignorance of the fact that gifts and things are investments, and that hoarding and saving invariably lead to loss.

"There is that scattereth and yet increaseth; and there is that withholdeth more than is meet, but it tendeth to poverty."

For example: I knew a man who wanted to buy a fur-lined overcoat. He and his wife went to various shops, but there was none he wanted. He said they were all too cheap-looking. At last, he was shown one, the salesman said was valued at a thousand dollars, but which the manager would sell him for five-hundred dollars, as it was late in the season.

His financial possessions amounted to about seven hundred dollars. The reasoning mind would have said, "You can't afford to spend nearly all you have on a coat," but he was very intuitive and never reasoned.

He turned to his wife and said, "If I get this coat, I'll make a ton of money!" So his wife consented, weakly.

About a month later, he received a ten-thousand-dollar commission. The coat made him feel so rich, it linked him with success and prosperity; without the coat, he would not have received the commission. It was an investment paying large dividends!

If man ignores these leadings to spend or to give, the same amount of money will go in an uninteresting or unhappy way.

For example: A woman told me, on Thanksgiving Day, she informed her family that they could not afford a Thanksgiving dinner. She had the money, but decided to save it.

A few days later, someone entered her room and took from the bureau drawer the exact amount the dinner would have cost.

The law always stands back of the man who spends fearlessly, with wisdom.

For example: One of my students was shopping with her little nephew. The child clamored for a toy, which she told him she could not afford to buy.

She realized suddenly that she was seeking lack, and not recognizing God as her supply!

So she bought the toy, and on her way home, picked *up, in the street, the exact amount of money she had paid for it.*

Man's supply is inexhaustible and unfailing when fully trusted, but faith or trust must precede the demonstration. "According to your faith be it unto you." "Faith is the substance of things hoped for, the evidence of things not seen—" for faith holds the vision steady, and the adverse pictures are dissolved and dissipated, and "in due season we shall reap, if we faint not."

Jesus Christ brought the good news (the gospel) that there was a higher law than the law of Karma—and that that law transcends the law of Karma. It is the law of grace, or forgiveness. It is the law which *frees man from the law of cause and effect—the law of consequence. "Under grace, and not under law."*

We are told that on this plane, man reaps where he has not sown; the gifts of God are simply poured out upon him. "All that the Kingdom affords is his." This continued state of bliss awaits the man who has overcome the race (or world) thought.

In the world thought there is tribulation, but Jesus Christ said: "Be of good cheer; I have overcome the world."

The world thought is that of sin, sickness and death. He saw their absolute unreality and said sickness and sorrow shall pass away and death itself, the last enemy, be overcome.

We know now, from a scientific standpoint, that death could be overcome by stamping the subconscious mind with the conviction of eternal youth and eternal life.

The subconscious, being simply power without direction, *carries out orders without questioning.*

Working under the direction of the superconscious (the Christ or God within man) the "resurrection of the body" would be accomplished.

Man would no longer throw off his body in death, it would be transformed into the "body electric," sung by Walt Whitman, for Christianity is founded upon the forgiveness of sins and "an empty tomb."

Casting the Burden

Impressing the Subconscious

When man knows his own powers and the workings of his mind, his great desire is to find an easy and quick way to impress the subconscious with good, for simply an intellectual knowledge of the Truth will not bring results.

In my own case, I found the easiest way is in "casting the burden."

A metaphysician once explained it in this manner. He said, "The only thing which gives anything weight in nature, is the law of gravitation, and if a boulder could be taken high above the planet, there would be no weight in that boulder; and that is what Jesus Christ meant when he said: 'My yoke is easy and my burden is light.'"

He had overcome the world vibration, and functioned in the fourth dimensional realm, where there is only perfection, completion, life and joy.

He said: "Come to me all ye that labor and are heavy laden, and I will give you rest." "Take my yoke upon you, for my yoke is easy and my burden is light."

We are also told in the fifty-fifth Psalm, to "cast thy burden upon the Lord." Many passages in the Bible state that the *battle is God's* not man's and that man is always to *"stand still"* and see the *Salvation of the Lord*.

This indicates that the superconscious mind (or Christ within) is the department which fights man's battle and relieves him of burdens.

We see, therefore, that man violates law if he carries a burden, and a burden is an adverse thought or condition, and this thought or condition has its root in the subconscious.

It seems almost impossible to make any headway directing the subconscious from the conscious, or reasoning mind, as the reasoning mind (the intellect) is limited in its conceptions, and filled with doubts and fears.

How scientific it then is, to cast the burden upon the superconscious mind (or Christ within) where it is "made light," or dissolved into its "native nothingness."

For example: A woman in urgent need of money, "made light" upon the Christ within, the superconscious, with the statement, "I cast this burden of lack on the Christ (within) and I go free to have plenty!"

The belief in lack was her burden, and as she cast it upon the Superconscious with its belief of plenty, an avalanche of supply was the result.

We read, "The Christ in you the hope of glory."

Another example: One of my students had been given a new piano, and there was no room in her studio for it until she had moved out the old one. She was in a state of perplexity. She wanted to keep the old piano, but knew of no place to send it. She became desperate, as the new piano was to be sent immediately; in fact, was on its way, with no place to put it. She said it came to her to repeat, "I cast this burden on the Christ within, and I go free."

A few moments later, her 'phone rang, and a woman friend asked if she might rent her old piano, and it was moved out, a few minutes before the new one arrived.

I knew a woman, whose burden was resentment. She said, "I

cast this burden of resentment on the Christ within, and I go free, to be loving, harmonious and happy." The Almighty superconscious, flooded the subconscious with love, and her whole life was changed. For years, resentment had held her in a state of torment and imprisoned her soul (the subconscious mind).

The statement should be made over and over and over, sometimes for hours at a time, silently or audibly, with quietness but determination.

I have often compared it to winding-up a victrola. We must wind ourselves up with spoken words.

I have noticed, in "casting the burden," after a little while, one seems to see clearly. It is impossible to have clear vision, while in the throes of carnal mind. Doubts and fear poison the mind and body and imagination runs riot, attracting disaster and disease.

In steadily repeating the affirmation, "I cast this burden on the Christ within, and go free," the vision clears, and with it a feeling of relief, and sooner or later comes *the manifestation of good, be it health, happiness or supply.*

One of my students once asked me to explain the "darkness before the dawn." I referred in a preceding chapter to the fact that often, before the big demonstration "everything seems to go wrong," and deep depression clouds the consciousness. It means that out of the subconscious are rising the doubts and fears of the ages. These old derelicts of the subconscious rise to the surface, *to be put out.*

It is then, that man should clap his cymbals, like Jehoshaphat, and give thanks that he is saved, even though he seems surrounded by the enemy (the situation of lack or disease). The student continued, "How long must one remain in the dark" and I replied, "until one *can see in the dark,*" and *"casting the burden enables one to see in the dark."*

In order to impress the subconscious, active faith is always essential.

"Faith without works is dead." In these chapters I have endeavored to bring out this point.

Jesus Christ showed active faith when "He commanded the multitude to sit down on the ground," before he gave thanks for the loaves and the fishes.

I will give another example showing how necessary this step is. In fact, active faith is the bridge, over which man passes to his Promised Land.

Through misunderstanding, a woman had been separated from her husband, whom she loved deeply. He refused all offers of reconciliation and would not communicate with her in any way.

Coming into the knowledge of Spiritual law, she denied the appearance of separation. She made this statement: "There is no separation in Divine Mind, therefore, I cannot be separated from the love and companionship which are mine by divine right."

She showed active faith by arranging a place for him at the table every day; thereby impressing the subconscious with a picture of his *return*. Over a year passed, but she never wavered, and *one day he walked in.*

The subconscious is often impressed through music. Music has a fourth dimensional quality and releases the soul from imprisonment. It makes wonderful things seem *possible, and easy of accomplishment!*

I have a friend who uses her victrola, daily, for this purpose. It puts her in perfect harmony and releases the imagination.

Another woman often dances while making her affirmations. The rhythm and harmony of music and motion carry her words forth with tremendous power.

The student must remember also, not to despise the "day of small things."

Invariably, before a demonstration, come "signs of land."

Before Columbus reached America, he saw birds and twigs

which showed him land was near. So it is with a demonstration; but often the student mistakes it for the demonstration itself, and is disappointed.

For example: A woman had "spoken the word" for a set of dishes. Not long afterwards a friend gave her a dish which was old and cracked.

She came to me and said, "Well, I asked for a set of dishes, and all I got was a cracked plate."

I replied, "The plate was only signs of land. It shows your dishes are coming—look upon it as birds and seaweed," and not long afterwards the dishes came.

Continually "making-believe," impresses the subconscious. If one makes believe he is rich, and makes believe he is successful, in "due time he will reap."

Children are always "making believe," and "except ye be converted, and become as little children, ye shall not enter the Kingdom of Heaven."

For example: I know of a woman who was very poor, but no one could make her *feel poor*. She earned a small amount of money from rich friends, who constantly reminded her of her poverty, and to be careful and saving. Regardless of their admonitions, she would spend all her earnings on a hat, or make someone a gift, and be in a rapturous state of mind. Her thoughts were always centered on beautiful clothes and "rings and things," but without envying others.

She lived in the world of the wondrous, and only riches seemed real to her. Before long she married a rich man, and the rings and things became visible. I do not know whether the man was the "Divine Selection," but opulence had to manifest in her life, as she had imaged only opulence.

There is no peace or happiness for man, until he has erased all fear from the subconscious.

Fear is misdirected energy and must be redirected, or transmuted into Faith.

Jesus Christ said, "Why are ye fearful, O ye of little faith?" "All things are possible to him that believeth."

I am asked, so often by my students, *"How can I get rid of fear?"* I reply, *"By walking up to the thing you are afraid of."*

"The lion takes its fierceness from your fear."

Walk up to the lion, and he will disappear; run away and he runs after you.

I have shown in previous chapters, how the lion of lack disappeared when the individual spent money fearlessly, showing faith that God was his supply and therefore, unfailing.

Many of my students have come out of the bondage of poverty, and are now bountifully supplied, through losing all fear of letting money go out. The subconscious is impressed with the truth that *God is the Giver and the Gift;* therefore as one is one with the Giver, he is one with the Gift. A splendid statement is, "I now thank God the Giver for God the Gift."

Man has so long separated himself from his good and his supply, through thoughts of separation and lack, that sometimes, it takes dynamite to dislodge these false ideas from the subconscious, and the dynamite is a big situation.

We see in the foregoing illustration, how the individual was freed from his bondage by *showing fearlessness.*

Man should watch himself hourly to detect if his motive for action is fear or faith.

"Choose ye this day whom we shall serve," fear or faith.

Perhaps one's fear is of personality. Then do not avoid the people feared; be willing to meet them cheerfully, and they will either prove "golden links in the chain of one's good," or disappear harmoniously from one's pathway.

Perhaps one's fear is of disease or germs. Then one should be fearless and undisturbed in a germ-laden situation, and he would be immune.

One can only contract germs while vibrating at the same rate as the germ, and fear drags men down to the level of the germ. Of course, the disease laden germ is the product of carnal mind, as all thought must objectify. Germs do not exist in the superconscious or Divine Mind, therefore are the product of man's "vain imagination."

"In the twinkling of an eye," man's release will come when he realizes *there is no power in evil.*

The material world will fade away, and the fourth dimensional world, the "World of the Wondrous," will swing into manifestation.

"And I saw a new heaven, and a new earth—and there shall be no more death, neither sorrow nor crying, neither shall there be any more pain; for the former things are passed away."

Love

Every man on this planet is taking his initiation in love. "A new commandment I give unto you, that ye love one another." Ouspensky states, in "Tertium Organum," that "love is a cosmic phenomenon," and opens to man the fourth dimensional world, "The World of the Wondrous."

Real love is selfless and free from fear. It pours itself out upon the object of its affection, without demanding any return. Its joy is in the joy of giving. Love is God in manifestation, and the strongest magnetic force in the universe. Pure, unselfish love *draws to itself its own;* it does not need to seek or demand. Scarcely anyone has the faintest conception of real love. Man is selfish, tyrannical or fearful in his affections, thereby losing the thing he loves. Jealousy is the worst enemy of love, for the imagination runs riot, seeing the loved one attracted to another, and invariably these fears objectify if they are not neutralized.

For example: A woman came to me in deep distress. The man she loved had left her for other women, and said he never intended to marry her. She was torn with jealousy and resentment and said she hoped he would suffer as he had made her suffer; and added, "How could he leave me when I loved him so much?"

I replied, "You are not loving that man, you are hating him," and added, *"You can never receive what you have never given. Give a perfect love and you will receive a perfect love.* Perfect yourself on this man. Give him a perfect, *unselfish* love, demanding nothing in return, do not criticise or condemn, and *bless him wherever he is.*"

She replied, "No, I won't bless him unless I know where he is!"

"Well," I said, "that is not real love."

"When you *send out real love,* real love will return to you, either from this man or his equivalent, for if this man is not the divine selection, you will not want him. As you are one with God, you are one with the love which belongs to you by divine right."

Several months passed, and matters remained about the same, but she was working conscientiously with herself. I said, "When you are no longer disturbed by his cruelty, he will cease to be cruel, as you are attracting it through your own emotions."

Then I told her of a brotherhood in India, who never said, "Good morning" to each other. They used these words: *"I salute the Divinity in you."* They saluted the divinity in every man, and in the wild animals in the jungle, and they were never harmed, for they *saw only God in every* living thing. I said, "Salute the divinity in this man, and say, 'I see your divine self only. I see you as God sees you, perfect, made in His image and likeness.'"

She found she was becoming more poised, and gradually losing her resentment. He was a Captain, and she always called him "The Cap."

One day, she said, suddenly, *"God bless the Cap wherever he is."*

I replied: "Now, that is real love, and when you have become a 'complete circle,' and are no longer disturbed by the situation, you will have his love, or attract its equivalent."

I was moving at this time, and did not have a telephone, so was out of touch with her for a few weeks, when one morning I received a letter saying, "We are married."

At the earliest opportunity, I paid her a call. My first words were, "What happened?"

"Oh," she exclaimed, "a miracle! One day I woke up and all

suffering had ceased. I saw him that evening and he asked me to marry him. We were married in about a week, and I have never seen a more devoted man."

There is an old saying: *"No man is your enemy, no man is your friend, every man is your teacher."*

So one should become impersonal and learn what each man has to teach him, and soon he would learn his lessons and be free.

The woman's lover was teaching her selfless love, which every man, sooner or later, must learn.

Suffering is not necessary for man's development; it is the result of violation of spiritual law, but few people seem able to rouse themselves from their "soul sleep" without it. When people are happy, they usually become selfish, and automatically the law of Karma is set in action. Man often suffers loss through lack of appreciation.

I knew a woman who had a very nice husband, but she said often, "I don't care anything about being married, but that is nothing against my husband. I'm simply not interested in married life."

She had other interests, and scarcely remembered she had a husband. She only thought of him when she saw him. One day her husband told her he was in love with another woman, and left. She came to me in distress and resentment.

I replied, "It is exactly what you spoke the word for. You said you didn't care anything about being married, so the subconscious worked to get you unmarried."

She said, "Oh yes, I see. People get what they want, and then feel very much hurt."

She soon became in perfect harmony with the situation, and knew they were both much happier apart.

When a woman becomes indifferent or critical, and ceases to be an inspiration to her husband, he misses the stimulus of their early relationship and is restless and unhappy.

A man came to me dejected, miserable and poor. His wife was

interested in the "Science of Numbers," and had had him read. It seems the report was not very favorable, for he said, "My wife says I'll never amount to anything because I am a two."

I replied, "I don't care what your number is, you are a perfect idea in divine mind, and we will demand the success and prosperity which are *already planned* for you by that Infinite Intelligence."

Within a few weeks, he had a very fine position, and a year or two later, he achieved a brilliant success as a writer. No man is a success in business unless he loves his work. The picture the artist paints for love (of his art) is his greatest work. The pot-boiler is always something to live down.

No man can attract money if he despises it. Many people are kept in poverty by saying: "Money means nothing to me, and I have a contempt for people who have it."

This is the reason so many artists are poor. Their contempt for money separates them from it.

I remember hearing one artist say of another, "He's no good as an artist, he has money in the bank."

This attitude of mind, of course, separates man from his supply; he must be in harmony with a thing in order to attract it.

Money is God in manifestation, as freedom from want and limitation, but it must be always kept in circulation and put to right uses. Hoarding and saving react with grim vengeance.

This does not mean that man should not have houses and lots, stocks and bonds, for "the barns of the righteous man shall be full." It means man should not hoard even the principal, if an occasion arises, when money is necessary. In letting it go out fearlessly and cheerfully he opens the way for more to come in, for God is man's unfailing and inexhaustible supply.

This is the spiritual attitude towards money and the great Bank of the Universal never fails!

We see an example of hoarding in the film production of

"Greed." The woman won five thousand dollars in a lottery, but would not spend it. She hoarded and saved, let her husband suffer and starve, and eventually she scrubbed floors for a living.

She loved the money itself and put it above everything, and one night she was murdered and the money taken from her.

This is an example of where "love of money is the root of all evil." Money in itself, is good and beneficial, but used for destructive purposes, hoarded and saved, or considered more important than love, brings disease and disaster, and the loss of the money itself.

Follow the path of love, and all things are added, *for God is love,* and *God is supply;* follow the path of selfishness and greed, and the supply vanishes, or man is separated from it.

For example; I knew the case of a very rich woman, who hoarded her income. She rarely gave anything away, but bought and bought and bought things for herself.

She was very fond of necklaces, and a friend once asked her how many she possessed. She replied, "Sixty-seven." She bought them and put them away, carefully wrapped in tissue paper. Had she used the necklaces it would have been quite legitimate, but she was violating "the law of use." Her closets were filled with clothes she never wore, and jewels which never saw the light.

The woman's arms were gradually becoming paralyzed from holding on to things, and eventually she was considered incapable of looking after her affairs and her wealth was handed over to others to manage.

So man, in ignorance of the law, brings about his own destruction.

All disease, all unhappiness, come from the violation of the law of love. Man's boomerangs of hate, resentment and criticism, come back laden with sickness and sorrow. Love seems almost a lost art, but the man with the knowledge of spiritual law knows it must be regained, for without it, he has "become as sounding brass and tinkling cymbals."

For example: I had a student who came to me, month after month, to clean her consciousness of resentment. After a while, she arrived at the point where she resented only one woman, but that one woman kept her busy. Little by little she became poised and harmonious, and one day, all resentment was wiped out.

She came in radiant, and exclaimed "You can't understand how I feel! The woman said something to me and instead of being furious I was loving and kind, and she apologized and was perfectly lovely to me.

"No one can understand the marvelous lightness I feel within!"

Love and good-will are invaluable in business.

For example: A woman came to me, complaining of her employer. She said she was cold and critical and knew she did not want her in the position.

"Well," I replied, "Salute the Divinity in the woman and send her love."

She said "I can't; she's a marble woman."

I answered, "You remember the story of the sculptor who asked for a certain piece of marble. He was asked why he wanted it, and he replied, 'because there is an angel in the marble,' and out of it he produced a wonderful work of art."

She said, "Very well, I'll try it." A week later she came back and said, "I did what you told me to, and now the woman is very kind, and took me out in her car."

People are sometimes filled with remorse for having done someone an unkindness, perhaps years ago.

If the wrong cannot be righted, its effect can be neutralized by doing some one a kindness *in the present.*

"This one thing I do, forgetting those things which are behind and reaching forth unto those things which are before."

Sorrow, regret and remorse tear down the cells of the body, and poison the atmosphere of the individual.

A woman said to me in deep sorrow, "Treat me to be happy and joyous, for my sorrow makes me so irritable with the members of my family that I keep making more Karma."

I was asked to treat a woman who was mourning for her daughter. I denied all belief in loss and separation, and affirmed that God was the woman's joy, love and peace.

The woman gained her poise at once, but sent word by her son, not to treat any longer, because she was "so happy, it wasn't respectable."

So "mortal mind" loves to hang on to its griefs and regrets.

I knew a woman who went about bragging of her troubles, so, of course, she always had something to brag about.

The old idea was if a woman did not worry about her children, she was not a good mother.

Now, we know that mother-fear is responsible for many of the diseases and accidents which come into the lives of children.

For fear pictures vividly the disease or situation feared, and these pictures objectify, if not neutralized.

Happy is the mother who can say sincerely, that she puts her child in God's hands, and *knows* therefore, that he is divinely protected.

For example: A woman awoke suddenly, in the night, feeling her brother was in great danger. Instead of giving in to her fears, she commenced making statements of Truth, saying, "Man is a perfect idea in Divine Mind, and is always in his right place, therefore, my brother is in his right place, and is divinely protected."

The next day she found that her brother had been in close proximity to an explosion in a mine, but had miraculously escaped.

So man is his brother's keeper (in thought) and every man

should know that the thing he loves dwells in "the secret place of the most high, and abides under the shadow of the Almighty."

"There shall no evil befall thee, neither shall any plague come nigh thy dwelling."

"Perfect love casteth out fear. He that feareth is not made perfect in love," and "Love is the fulfilling of the Law."

Intuition or Guidance

*"In all thy ways acknowledge Him
and He shall direct thy paths."*

There is nothing too great of accomplishment for the man who knows the power of his word, and who follows his intuitive leads. By the word he starts in action unseen forces and can rebuild his body or remold his affairs.

It is, therefore, of the utmost importance to choose the right words, and the student carefully selects the affirmation he wishes to catapult into the invisible.

He knows that God is his supply, that there is a supply for every demand, and that his spoken word releases this supply.

"Ask and ye shall receive."

Man must make the first move. "Draw nigh to God and He will draw nigh to you."

I have often been asked just how to make a demonstration.

I reply: "Speak the word and then do not do anything until you get a definite lead." Demand the lead, saying, "Infinite Spirit, reveal to me the way, let me know if there is anything for me to do."

The answer will come through intuition (or hunch); a chance remark from someone, or a passage in a book, etc., etc. The answers are sometimes quite startling in their exactness. For example: A woman desired a large sum of money. She spoke the words: "In-finite Spirit, open the way for my immediate supply, let all that is mine by divine right now reach me, in great avalanches of abun-dance." Then she added: "Give me a definite lead, let me know if there is anything for me to do."

The thought came quickly, "Give a certain friend" (who had helped her spiritually) "a hundred dollars." She told her friend, who said, "Wait and get another lead, before giving it." So she waited, and that day met a woman who said to her, "I gave some-one a dollar today; it was just as much for me, as it would be for you to give someone a hundred."

This was indeed an unmistakable lead, so she knew she was right in giving the hundred dollars. It was a gift which proved a great investment, for shortly after that, a large sum of money came to her in a remarkable way.

Giving opens the way for receiving. In order to create activity in finances, one should give. Tithing or giving one-tenth of one's income, is an old Jewish custom, and is sure to bring increase. Many of the richest men in this country have been tithers, and I have never known it to fail as an investment.

The tenth-part goes forth and returns blessed and multiplied. But the gift or tithe must be given with love and cheerfulness, for "God loveth a cheerful giver." Bills should be paid cheerfully; all money should be sent forth fearlessly and with a blessing.

This attitude of mind makes man master of money. It is his to obey, and his spoken word then opens vast reservoirs of wealth.

Man, himself, limits his supply by his limited vision. Some-times the student has a great realization of wealth, but is afraid to act.

The vision and action must go hand in hand, as in the case of the man who bought the fur-lined overcoat.

A woman came to me asking me to "speak the word" for a

position. So I demanded: "Infinite Spirit, open the way for this woman's right position." Never ask for just "a position"; ask for the right position, the place already planned in Divine Mind, as it is the only one that will give satisfaction.

I then gave thanks that she had already received, and that it would manifest quickly. Very soon, she had three positions offered her, two in New York and one in Palm Beach, and she did not know which to choose. I said, "Ask for a definite lead."

The time was almost up and was still undecided, when one day, she telephoned, "When I woke up this morning, I could smell Palm Beach." She had been there before and knew its balmy fragrance.

I replied: "Well, if you can smell Palm Beach from here, it is certainly your lead." She accepted the position, and it proved a great success. Often one's lead comes at an unexpected time.

One day, I was walking down the street, when I suddenly felt a strong urge to go to a certain bakery, a block or two away.

The reasoning mind resisted, arguing, "There is nothing there that you want."

However, I had learned not to reason, so I went to the bakery, looked at everything, and there was certainly nothing there that I wanted, but coming out I encountered a woman I had thought of often, and who was in great need of the help which I could give her.

So often, one goes for one thing and finds another.

Intuition is a spiritual faculty and does not explain, but simply *points the way.*

A person often receives a lead during a "treatment." The idea that comes may seem quite irrelevant, but some of God's leadings are "mysterious."

In the class, one day, I was treating that each individual would receive a definite lead. A woman came to me afterwards, and said: "While you were treating, I got the hunch to take my furniture out of storage and get an apartment." The woman had come to be treated for health. I told her I knew in getting a home of her own, her health would improve, and I added, "I believe your trouble, which is a congestion, has come from having things stored away. Congestion of things causes congestion in the body. You have violated the law of use, and your body is paying the penalty."

So I gave thanks that *"Divine order was established in her mind, body and affairs."*

People little dream of how their affairs react on the body. There is a mental correspondence for every disease. A person might receive instantaneous healing through the realization of his body being a perfect idea in Divine Mind, and, therefore, whole and perfect, but if he continues his destructive thinking, hoarding, hating, fearing, condemning, the disease will return.

Jesus Christ knew that all sickness came from sin, but admonished the leper after the healing, to go and sin no more, lest a worse thing come upon him.

So man's soul (or subconscious mind) must be washed whiter than snow, for permanent healing; and the metaphysician is always delving deep for the "correspondence."

Jesus Christ said, "Condemn not lest ye also be condemned."

"Judge not, lest ye be judged."

Many people have attracted disease and unhappiness through condemnation of others.

What man condemns in others, he attracts to himself.

For example: A friend came to me in anger and distress, because her husband had deserted her for another woman. She condemned the other woman, and said continually, "She knew he was a married man, and had no right to accept his attentions."

I replied, "Stop condemning the woman, bless her, and be through with the situation, otherwise, you are attracting the same thing to yourself."

She was deaf to my words, and a year or two later, became deeply interested in a married man, herself.

Man picks up a live-wire whenever he criticises or condemns, and may expect a shock.

Indecision is a stumbling-block in many a pathway. In order to overcome it, make the statement, repeatedly, *"I am always under direct inspiration; I make right decisions, quickly."*

These words impress the subconscious, and soon one finds himself awake and alert, making his right moves without hesitation. I have found it destructive to look to the psychic plane for guidance, as it is the plane of many minds and not "The One Mind."

As man opens his mind to subjectivity, he becomes a target for destructive forces. The psychic plane is the result of man's mortal thought, and is on the "plane of opposites." He may receive either good or bad messages.

The science of numbers and the reading of horoscopes, keep man down on the mental (or mortal) plane, for they deal only with the Karmic path.

I know of a man who should have been dead, years ago, according to his horoscope, but he is alive and a leader of one of the biggest movements in this country for the uplift of humanity.

It takes a very strong mind to neutralize a prophecy of evil. The student should declare, "Every false prophecy shall come to naught; every plan my Father in heaven has not planned, shall be dissolved and dissipated, the divine idea now comes to pass."

However, if any good message has ever been given one, of coming happiness, or wealth, harbor and expect it, and it will manifest sooner or later, through the law of expectancy.

Man's will should be used to back the universal will. "I will that the will of God be done."

It is God's will to give every man, every righteous desire of his heart, and man's will should be used to hold the perfect vision, without wavering.

The prodigal son said: "I will arise and go to my Father."

It is, indeed, often an effort of the will to leave the husks and swine of mortal thinking. It is so much easier, for the average person, to have fear than faith; *so faith is an effort of the will.*

As man becomes spiritually awakened he recognizes that any external inharmony is the correspondence of mental inharmony. If he stumbles or falls, he may know he is stumbling or falling in consciousness.

One day, a student was walking along the street condemning someone in her thoughts. She was saying, mentally, "That woman is the most disagreeable woman on earth," when suddenly three boy scouts rushed around the corner and almost knocked her over. She did not condemn the boy scouts, but immediately called on the law of forgiveness, and "saluted the divinity" in the woman. Wisdom's ways are ways of pleasantness and all her paths are peace.

When one has made his demands upon the Universal, he must be ready for surprises. Everything may seem to be going wrong, when in reality, it is going right.

For example: A woman was told that there was no loss in divine mind, therefore, she could not lose anything which belonged to her; anything lost, would be returned, or she would receive its equivalent.

Several years previously, she had lost two thousand dollars. She had loaned the money to a relative during her lifetime, but the relative had died, leaving no mention of it in her will. The woman was resentful and angry, and as she had no written statement of the transaction, she never received the money, so she determined to deny the loss, and collect the two thousand dollars from the Bank of the Universal. She had to begin by forgiving the woman, as resentment and unforgiveness close the doors of this wonderful bank.

She made this statement, "I deny loss, there is no loss in Divine Mind, therefore, I cannot lose the two thousand dollars, which belong to me by divine right." *"As one door shuts another door opens."*

She was living in an apartment house which was for sale; and in the lease was a clause, stating that if the house was sold, the tenants would be required to move out within ninety days.

Suddenly, the landlord broke the leases and raised the rent. Again, injustice was on her pathway, but this time she was undisturbed. She blessed the landlord, and said, "As the rent has been raised, it means that I'll be that much richer, for God is my supply."

New leases were made out for the advanced rent, but by some divine mistake, the ninety days clause had been forgotten. Soon after, the landlord had an opportunity to sell the house. On account of the mistake in the new leases, the tenants held possession for another year.

The agent offered each tenant two hundred dollars if he would vacate. Several families moved; three remained, including the woman. A month or two passed, and the agent again appeared. This time he said to the woman, "Will you break your lease for the sum of fifteen hundred dollars?" It flashed upon her, "Here comes the two thousand dollars." She remembered having said to friends in the house, "We will all act together if anything more is said about leaving." So her *lead* was to consult her friends.

These friends said: "Well, if they have offered you fifteen hundred they will certainly give two thousand." So she received a check for two thousand dollars for giving up the apartment. It was certainly a remarkable working of the law, and the apparent injustice was merely opening the way for her demonstration.

It proved that there is no loss, and when man takes his spiritual stand, he collects all that is his from this great Reservoir of Good.

"I will restore to you the years the locusts have eaten."

The locusts are the doubts, fears, resentments and regrets of mortal thinking.

These adverse thoughts, alone, rob man; for "No man gives to himself but himself, and no man takes away from himself, but himself."

Man is here to prove God and "to bear witness to the truth," and he can only prove God by bringing plenty out of lack, and justice out of injustice.

"Prove me now herewith, saith the Lord of hosts, if I will not open you the windows of heaven, and pour out a blessing, that there shall not be room enough to receive it."

Perfect Self-Expression
or the Divine Design

"No wind can drive my bark astray
nor change the tide of destiny."

There is for each man, perfect self-expression. There is a place which he is to fill and no one else can fill, something which he is to do, which no one else can do; it is his destiny!

This achievement is held, a perfect idea in Divine Mind, awaiting man's recognition. As the imaging faculty is the creative faculty, it is necessary for man to see the idea, before it can manifest.

So man's highest demand is for the *Divine Design of his life.*

He may not have the faintest conception of what it is, for there is, possibly, some marvelous talent, hidden deep within him.

His demand should be: *"Infinite Spirit, open the way for the Divine Design of my life to manifest; let the genius within me now be released; let me see clearly the perfect plan."*

The perfect plan includes health, wealth, love and perfect self-expression. This is the *square of life,* which brings perfect happiness. When one has made this demand, he may find great changes taking place in his life, for nearly every man has wandered far from the Divine Design.

I know, in one woman's case, it was as though a cyclone had struck her affairs, but readjustments came quickly, and new and wonderful conditions took the place of old ones.

Perfect self-expression will never be labor; but of such absorbing interest that it will seem almost like play. The student knows, also, as man comes into the world financed by God, the *supply* needed for his perfect self-expression will be at hand.

Many a genius has struggled for years with the problem of supply, when his spoken word, and faith, would have released quickly, the necessary funds.

For example: After the class, one day, a man came to me and handed me a cent.

He said: "I have just seven cents in the world, and I'm going to give you one; for I have faith in the power of your spoken word. I want you to speak the word for my perfect self-expression and prosperity."

I "spoke the word," and did not see him again until a year later. He came in one day, successful and happy, with a roll of yellow bills in his pocket. He said, "Immediately after you spoke the word, I had a position offered me in a distant city, and am now demonstrating health, happiness and supply."

A woman's perfect self-expression may be in becoming a perfect wife, a perfect mother, a perfect home-maker and not necessarily in having a public career.

Demand definite leads, and the way will be made easy and successful.

One should not visualize or force a mental picture. When he demands the Divine Design to come into his conscious mind, he will receive flashes of inspiration, and begin to see himself making some great accomplishment. This is the picture, or idea, he must hold without wavering.

The thing man seeks is seeking him—*the telephone was seeking Bell!*

Parents should never force careers and professions upon their children. With a knowledge of spiritual Truth, the Divine Plan could be spoken for, early in childhood, or prenatally.

A prenatal treatment should be: "Let the God in this child have perfect expression; let the Divine Design of his mind, body and affairs be made manifest throughout his life, throughout eternity."

God's will be done, not man's; God's pattern, not man's pattern, is the command we find running through all the scriptures, and the Bible is a book dealing with the science of the mind. It is a book telling man how to release his soul (or subconscious mind) from bondage.

The battles described are pictures of man waging war against mortal thoughts. "A man's foes shall be they of his own household." Every man is Jehoshaphat, and every man is David, who slays Goliath (mortal thinking) with the little white stone (faith).

So man must be careful that he is not the "wicked and slothful servant" who buried his talent. There is a terrible penalty to be paid for not using one's ability.

Often fear stands between man and his perfect self-expression. Stage-fright has hampered many a genius. This may be overcome by the spoken word, or treatment. The individual then loses all self-consciousness, and feels simply that he is a channel for Infinite Intelligence to express Itself through.

He is under direct inspiration, fearless, and confident; for he feels that it is the "Father within" him who does the work.

A young boy came often to my class with his mother. He asked me to "speak the word" for his coming examinations at school.

I told him to make the statement: "I am one with Infinite Intelligence. I know everything I should know on this subject." He had an excellent knowledge of history, but was not sure of his arithmetic. I saw him afterwards, and he said: "I spoke the word for my arithmetic, and passed with the highest honors; but thought I could depend on myself for history, and got a very poor mark." Man often receives a set-back when he is "too sure of himself," which means he is trusting to his personality and not the "Father within."

Another one of my students gave me an example of this. She took an extended trip abroad one summer, visiting many countries, where she was ignorant of the languages. She was calling for guidance and protection every minute, and her affairs went smoothly and miraculously. Her luggage was never delayed nor lost! Accommodations were always ready for her at the best hotels; and she had perfect service wherever she went. She returned to New York. Knowing the language, she felt God was no longer necessary, so looked after her affairs in an ordinary manner.

Everything went wrong, her trunks delayed, amid inharmony and confusion. The student must form the habit of "practicing the Presence of God" every minute. *"In all thy ways acknowledge him";* nothing is too small or too great.

Sometimes an insignificant incident may be the turning point in a man's life.

Robert Fulton, watching some boiling water, simmering in a tea kettle, saw a steamboat!

I have seen a student, often, keep back his demonstration, through resistance, or pointing the way.

He pins his faith to one channel only, and dictates just the way he desires the manifestation to come, which brings things to a standstill.

"My way, not your way!" is the command of Infinite Intelligence. Like all Power, be it steam or electricity, it must have a nonresistant engine or instrument to work through, and man is that engine or instrument.

Over and over again, man is told to "stand still." "Oh Judah, fear not; but to-morrow go out against them, for the Lord will be with you. You shall not need to fight this battle; set yourselves, stand ye still and see the salvation of the Lord with you."

We see this in the incidents of the two thousand dollars coming to the woman through the landlord when she became *nonresistant* and *undisturbed,* and the woman who won the man's love "after all suffering had ceased."

The student's goal is *Poise! Poise* is *Power,* for it gives God-Power a chance to rush through man, to "will and to do Its good pleasure."

Poised, he thinks clearly, and makes "right decisions quickly." "He never misses a trick."

Anger blurs the visions, poisons the blood, is the root of many diseases, and causes wrong decision leading to failure.

It has been named one of the worst "sins," as its reaction is so harmful. The student learns that in metaphysics sin has a much broader meaning than in the old teaching. "Whatsoever is not of faith is sin."

He finds that fear and worry are deadly sins. They are inverted faith, and through distorted mental pictures, bring to pass the thing he fears. His work is to drive out these enemies (from the subconscious mind). "When Man is *fearless he is finished!*" Maeterlinck says, that "Man is God afraid."

So, as we read in the previous chapters: Man can only vanquish fear by walking up to the thing he is afraid of. When Jehoshaphat and his army prepared to meet the enemy, singing "Praise the Lord, for his mercy endureth forever," they found their enemies had destroyed each other, and there was nothing to fight.

For example: A woman asked a friend to deliver a message to another friend. The woman feared to give the message, as the reasoning mind said, "Don't get mixed-up in this affair, don't give that message."

She was troubled in spirit, for she had given her promise. At last, she determined to "walk up to the lion," and call on the law of divine protection. She met the friend to whom she was to deliver the message. She opened her mouth to speak it, when her friend said, "So-and-So has left town." This made it unnecessary to give the message, as the situation depended upon the person being in town. As she was willing to do it, she was not obliged to; as she did not fear, the situation vanished.

The student often delays his demonstration through a belief in incompletion. He should make this statement:

"In Divine Mind there is only completion, therefore, my demonstration is completed. My perfect work, my perfect home, my perfect health." Whatever he demands are perfect ideas registered in Divine Mind, and must manifest, "under grace in a perfect way." He gives thanks he has already received on the invisible, and makes active preparation for receiving on the visible.

One of my students was in need of a financial demonstration. She came to me and asked why it was not completed.

I replied: "Perhaps, you are in the habit of leaving things unfinished, and the subconscious has gotten into the habit of not completing (as the without, so the within)."

She said, "You are right. I often *begin things* and never finish them.

"I'll go home and finish something I commenced weeks ago, and I know it will be symbolic of my demonstration."

So she sewed assiduously, and the article was soon completed. Shortly after, the money came in a most curious manner.

Her husband was paid his salary twice that month. He told the people of their mistake, and they sent word to keep it.

When man asks, *believing, he must receive, for God creates His own channels!*

I have been sometimes asked, "Suppose one has several talents, how is he to know which one to choose?" Demand to be shown definitely. Say: "Infinite Spirit, give me a definite lead, reveal to me my perfect self-expression, show me which talent I am to make use of now."

I have known people to suddenly enter a new line of work, and be fully equipped, with little or no training. So make the statement: *"I am fully equipped for the Divine Plan of my life,"* and be fearless in grasping opportunities.

Some people are cheerful givers, but bad receivers. They refuse gifts through pride, or some negative reason, thereby blocking their channels, and invariably find themselves eventually with little or nothing. For example: A woman who had given away a great deal of money, had a gift offered her of several thousand dollars. She refused to take it, saying she did not need it. Shortly after that, her finances were "tied up," and she found herself in debt for that amount. Man should receive gracefully the bread returning to him upon the water—freely ye have given, freely ye shall receive.

There is always the perfect balance of giving and receiving, and though man should give without thinking of returns, he violates law if he does not accept the returns which come to him; for all gifts are from God, man being merely the channel.

A thought of lack should never be held over the giver.

For example: When the man gave me the one cent, I did not say: "Poor man, he cannot afford to give me that." I saw him rich and prosperous, with his supply pouring in. It was this thought which brought it. If one has been a bad receiver, he must become a good one, and take even a postage stamp if it is given him, and open up his channels for receiving.

The Lord loveth a cheerful receiver, as well as a cheerful giver.

I have often been asked why one man is born rich and healthy, and another poor and sick.

Where there is an effect there is always a cause; there is no such thing as chance.

This question is answered through the law of reincarnation. Man goes through many births and deaths, until he knows the truth which sets him free.

He is drawn back to the earth plane through unsatisfied desire, to pay his Karmic debts, or to "fulfill his destiny."

The man born rich and healthy has had pictures in his subconscious mind, in his past life, of health and riches; and the poor and sick man, of disease and poverty. Man manifests, on any plane, the sum total of his subconscious beliefs.

However, birth and death are man-made laws, for the "wages of sin is death"; the Adamic fall in consciousness through the belief in *two powers*. The real man, spiritual man, is birthless and deathless! He never was born and has never died—"As he was in the beginning, he is now, and ever shall be!"

So through the truth, man is set free from the law of Karma, sin and death, and manifests the man made in "His image and likeness." Man's freedom comes through fulfilling his destiny, bringing into manifestation the Divine Design of his life.

His lord will say unto him: "Well done thou good and faithful servant, thou hast been faithful over a few things, I will make thee ruler over many things (death itself); enter thou into the joy of thy Lord (eternal life)."

Denials and Affirmations

"Thou shalt also decree a thing, and it shall be established unto thee."

All the good that is to be made manifest in man's life is already an accomplished fact in divine mind, and is released through man's recognition, or spoken word, so he must be careful to decree that only the Divine Idea be made manifest, for often, he decrees, through his "idle words," failure or misfortune.

It is, therefore, of the utmost importance, to word one's demands correctly, as stated in a previous chapter.

If one desires a home, friend, position or any other good thing, make the demand for the "divine selection."

For example: "Infinite Spirit, open the way for my right home, my right friend, my right position. I give thanks *it now manifests under grace in a perfect way.*"

The latter part of the statement is most important. For example: I knew a woman who demanded a thousand dollars. Her daughter was injured and they received a thousand dollars indemnity, so it did not come in a "perfect way." The demand should have been worded in this way: "Infinite Spirit, I give thanks that the one thousand dollars, which is mine by divine right, is now released, and reaches me under grace, in a perfect way."

As one grows in a financial consciousness, he should demand

that the enormous sums of money, which are his by divine right, reach him under grace, in perfect ways.

It is impossible for man to release more than he thinks is possible, for one is bound by the limited expectancies of the subconscious. He must enlarge his expectancies in order to receive in a larger way.

Man so often limits himself in his demands. For example: A student made the demand for six hundred dollars, by a certain date. He did receive it, but heard afterwards, that he came very near receiving a thousand dollars, but he was given just six hundred, as the result of his spoken word.

"They limited the Holy One of Israel." Wealth is a matter of consciousness. The French have a legend giving an example of this. A poor man was walking along a road when he met a traveler, who stopped him and said: "My good friend, I see you are poor. Take this gold nugget, sell it and you will be rich all your days."

The man was overjoyed at his good fortune, and took the nugget home. He immediately found work and became so prosperous that he did not sell the nugget. Years passed, and he became a very rich man. One day he met a poor man on the road. He stopped him and said: "My good friend, I will give you this gold nugget, which, if you sell, will make you rich for life." The mendicant took the nugget, had it valued and found it was only brass. So we see, the first man became rich through feeling rich, thinking the nugget was gold.

Every man has within himself a gold nugget; *it is his consciousness of gold, of opulence, which brings riches into his life*. In making his demands, man begins at his *journey's end*, that is, he declares *he has already received*. "*Before* ye call I shall answer."

Continually affirming establishes the belief in the subconscious.

It would not be necessary to make an affirmation more than once if one had perfect faith! One should not plead or supplicate, but give thanks repeatedly, that he has received.

"The desert shall *rejoice* and blossom as the rose." This rejoicing which is yet in the desert (state of consciousness) opens the way for release. The Lord's Prayer is in the form of command and demand, "Give us this day our daily bread, and forgive us our debts as we forgive our debtors," and ends in praise, "For thine is the Kingdom and the Power and the Glory, forever. Amen." "Concerning the works of my hands, command ye me." So prayer is command and demand, praise and thanksgiving. The student's work is in making himself believe that "with God all things are possible."

This is easy enough to state in the abstract, but a little more difficult when confronted with a problem. For example: It was necessary for a woman to demonstrate a large sum of money within a stated time. She knew she must *do something* to get a realization (for realization is manifestation), and she demanded a "lead."

She was walking through a department store, when she saw a very beautiful pink enamel paper-cutter. She felt the "pull" towards it. The thought came. "I haven't a paper cutter good enough to open letters containing large cheques."

So she bought the papercutter, which the reasoning mind would have called an extravagance. When she held it in her hand, she had a flash of a picture of herself opening an envelope containing a large cheque, and in a few weeks, she received the money. The pink papercutter was her bridge of active faith.

Many stories are told of the power of the subconscious when directed in faith.

For example: A man was spending the night in a farmhouse. The windows of the room had been nailed down, and in the middle of the night he felt suffocated and made his way in the dark to the window. He could not open it, so he smashed the pane with his fist, drew in draughts of fine fresh air, and had a wonderful night's sleep.

The next morning, he found he had smashed the glass of a bookcase and the window had remained closed during the whole night. He had *supplied himself with oxygen, simply by his thought of oxygen.*

When a student starts out to demonstrate, he should never turn back. "Let not that man who wavers think that he shall receive anything of the Lord."

A student once made this wonderful statement, "When I asks the Father for anything, I puts my foot down, and I says: Father, I'll take nothing less than I've asked for, but more!" So man should never compromise: "Having done all—Stand." This is sometimes the most difficult time of demonstrating. The temptation comes to give up, to turn back, to compromise.

"He also serves who only stands and waits."

Demonstrations often come at the eleventh hour because man then lets go, that is, stops reasoning, and Infinite Intelligence has a chance to work.

"Man's dreary desires are answered drearily, and his impatient desires, long delayed or violently fulfilled."

For example: A woman asked me why it was she was constantly losing or breaking her glasses.

We found she often said to herself and others with vexation, "I wish I could get rid of my glasses." So her impatient desire was violently fulfilled. What she should have demanded was perfect eye-sight, but what she registered in the subconscious was simply the impatient desire to be rid of her glasses; so they were continually being broken or lost.

Two attitudes of mind cause loss: depreciation, as in the case of the woman who did not appreciate her husband, *or fear of loss,* which makes a picture of loss in the subconscious.

When a student is able to let go of his problem (cast his burden) he will have instantaneous manifestation.

For example: A woman was out during a very stormy day and her umbrella was blown inside-out. She was about to make a call on some people whom she had never met and she did not wish to make her first appearance with a dilapidated umbrella. She could not throw it away, as it did not belong to her. So in desperation, she exclaimed: "Oh, God, you take charge of this umbrella, I don't know what to do."

A moment later, a voice behind her said: "Lady, do you want your umbrella mended?" There stood an umbrella mender.

She replied, "Indeed, I do."

The man mended the umbrella, while she went into the house to pay her call, and when she returned, she had a good umbrella. So there is always an umbrella mender at hand, on man's pathway, when one puts the umbrella (or situation) in God's Hands.

One should always follow a denial with an affirmation.

For example: I was called on the 'phone late one night to treat a man whom I had never seen. He was apparently very ill. I made the statement: "I deny this appearance of disease. It is unreal, therefore cannot register in his consciousness; this man is a perfect idea in Divine Mind, pure substance expressing perfection."

There is no time or space, in Divine Mind, therefore the word reaches instantly its destination and does not "return void." I have treated patients in Europe and have found that the result was instantaneous.

I am asked so often the difference between visualizing and visioning. Visualizing is a mental process governed by the reasoning or conscious mind; visioning is a spiritual process, governed by intuition, or the superconscious mind. The student should train his mind to receive these flashes of inspiration, and work out the "divine pictures," through definite leads. When a man can say, "I desire only that which God desires for me," his false desires fade from the consciousness, and a new set of blueprints is given him by the Master Architect, the God within. God's plan for each man transcends the limitation of the reasoning mind, and is always the square of life, containing health, wealth, love and perfect self-expression. Many a man is building for himself in imagination a bungalow when he should be building a palace.

If a student tries to force a demonstration (through the reasoning mind) he brings it to a standstill. "I will hasten it," saith the Lord. He should act only through intuition, or definite leads. "Rest in the Lord and wait patiently. Trust also in him, and he will bring it to pass."

I have seen the law work in the most astonishing manner. For example: A student stated that it was necessary for her to have a hundred dollars by the following day. It was a debt of vital importance which had to be met. I "spoke the word," declaring Spirit was "never too late" and that the supply was at hand.

That evening she phoned me of the miracle. She said that the thought came to her to go to her safe-deposit box at the bank to examine some papers. She looked over the papers, and at the bottom of the box, was a new one hundred dollar-bill. She was astounded, and said she knew she had never put it there, for she had gone through the papers many times. It may have been a materialization, as Jesus Christ materialized the loaves and fishes. Man will reach the stage where his "word is made flesh," or materialized, instantly. "The fields, ripe with the harvest," will manifest immediately, as in all of the miracles of Jesus Christ.

There is a tremendous power alone in the name Jesus Christ. It stands for *Truth Made Manifest.* He said, "Whatsoever ye ask the Father, in my name, he will give it to you."

The power of this name raises the student into the fourth dimension, where he is freed from all astral and psychic influences, and he becomes "unconditioned and absolute, as God Himself is unconditioned and absolute."

I have seen many healings accomplished by using the words, "In the name of Jesus Christ."

Christ was both person and principle; and the Christ within each man is his Redeemer and Salvation.

The Christ within, is his own fourth dimensional self, the man made in God's image and likeness. This is the self which has never failed, never known sickness or sorrow, was never born and has never died. It is the "resurrection and the life" of each man! "No man cometh to the Father save by the Son," means, that God, the Universal, working on the place of the particular, becomes the Christ in man; and the Holy Ghost, means God-in-action. So daily, man is manifesting the Trinity of Father, Son and Holy Ghost.

Man should make an art of thinking. The Master Thinker is an artist and is careful to paint only the divine designs upon the canvas of his mind; and he paints these pictures with masterly strokes of power and decision, having perfect faith that there is no power to mar their perfection and that they shall manifest in his life the ideal made real.

All power is given man (through right thinking) to bring *his heaven* upon *his earth,* and this is the *goal of the "Game of Life."*

The simple rules are fearless faith, nonresistance and love!

May each reader be now freed from that thing which has held him in bondage through the ages, standing between him and his own, and "know the Truth which makes him free"—free to fulfill his destiny, to bring into manifestation the *"Divine Design of his life,* Health, Wealth, Love and Perfect Self-Expression." "Be ye transformed by the renewing of your mind."

DENIALS AND AFFIRMATIONS

(For Prosperity)
God is my unfailing supply, and large sums of money come to me quickly, under grace, in perfect ways.

(For Right Conditions)
Every plan my Father in heaven has not planned, shall be dissolved and dissipated, and the Divine Idea now comes to pass.

(For Right Conditions)
Only that which is true of God is true of me, for I and the Father are ONE.

(For Faith)
As I am one with God, I am one with my good, for God is both the Giver *and the* Gift. *I cannot separate the* Giver *from the gift.*

(For Right Conditions)
Divine Love now dissolves and dissipates every wrong condition in my mind, body and affairs. Divine Love is the most powerful chemical in the universe, and dissolves everything which is not of itself!

(For Health)
Divine Love floods my consciousness with health, and every cell in my body is filled with light.

(For the Eyesight)

My eyes are God's eyes, I see with the eyes of spirit. I see clearly the open way; there are no obstacles on my pathway. I see clearly the perfect plan.

(For Guidance)

I am divinely sensitive to my intuitive leads, and give instant obedience to Thy will.

(For the Hearing)

My ears are God's ears, I hear with the ears of spirit. I am nonresistant and am willing to be led. I hear glad tidings of great joy.

(For Right Work)

I have a perfect work
In a perfect way;
I give a perfect service
For perfect pay.

(For Freedom from All Bondage)

I cast this burden on the Christ within, and I go free!

NAPOLEON HILL

Let Ambition Be Your Master

And Other Works

Contents

Introduction

This little volume contains gigantic ideas. If you have dreams, then the ideas contained within can help!

Let's start with a little background information. *Dream Big* is a selection of some of Napoleon Hill's most inspirational and motivational writings on the topic of living your dreams. Hill is most known for his bestselling book *Think and Grow Rich*, which has sold millions of copies since its initial publication in 1937, and continues to inspire millions of readers every year. Hill also helmed several magazines (from which some of the writings in this volume originated), as well as wrote several more books. It has been said that Hill inspired more people to become millionaires and billionaires than any other writer in modern history.

Five of the little chapters in this book are from articles that Hill wrote approximately a hundred years ago. Three of the chapters are adapted from Hill's magnus opus *Think and Grow Rich*, and the final chapter is material taken from his encyclopedic book *The Law of Success*. But all of it is aimed to show the reader—you!—that there are definite steps to take in the attainment of passions and goals. Perhaps it will inspire you to go and read Hill's other writings.

It's important to note that while the ideas Hill writes about are timeless, Hill's writing was very much of his time. His work is easy to read, but at times the examples he uses, or the language he uses, will seem old-fashioned. This is especially true in his use of the masculine pronoun, and using the word "man" to describe "humankind," which was the norm of his time. We've left this intact, in the effort to keep this material as accurate to his original writings as possible.

But *Dream Big* isn't about Napoleon Hill, it's about YOU. The ideas in this volume were chosen to give practical, time-honored advice on such important topics as finding your definite aim in life, turning failure and adversity into blessings, protecting yourself from negative influences, overcoming our own self-defeating attitudes (he calls them "alibis"), and overcoming fear.

There are longer books by Napoleon Hill than *Dream Big,* but there aren't any that have more heart! I invite you to read this book like a short guide to empowerment, with advice by a life coach who wants to help you succeed. Read each little chapter, and then ask yourself which ideas most resonate with you, and perhaps write those down in the margin or in a journal. Next, ask what actions the chapter asks or inspires you to take, and write those down as well. And then . . . take those actions!

Great success is built step by step. Let this book help you find some steps to take toward your success.

One more thing . . .

Enjoy the journey. This book has several reminders that we aren't meant to live small, scared lives. We are meant, Hill would tell us, to have a passion (definite aim) that burns a powerful flame in our hearts. That fire fuels us to wake each day with enthusiasm, and make as many positive choices toward that goal as we can. We can overcome our fears, our alibis, and our procrastination.

How? Turn the page . . .

—*Joel Fotinos*

Adversity—A Blessing in Disguise

Friend, do not become discouraged, disappointed and disheartened, if the seemingly cruel hand of fate knocks you off of your feet. Maybe the blow will prove to be the greatest blessing that ever came your way.

It has happened to many and doubtless it will happen to you, when the dark clouds of despair have darkened the pathway of life's progress, that behind each dark cloud is a silver lining, if we only learn how to see it.

There were two men who established and built up an enormously successful commercial institution. They owned the stock in the company about equally. One of the men, who had lots of initiative, began selling off some of his stock, thus enjoying for personal use a large amount of ready cash from the proceeds.

His associate in the business, who didn't possess quite so much initiative, wanted to sell some of his personal stock that he might also enjoy some ready cash from the proceeds. But not a dollar could he sell. He appealed to his associate who was finding a ready market for his stock, requesting the associate to help him dispose of his stock. But the associate refused, suggesting that "he do his own selling." This refusal resulted in a serious disagreement between the two men, which finally ended in a complete dissolution of their friendly business relations.

Now let us see what happens. The one who could not find a

market for his stock was the fortunate one in the final crisis. The one with the ready initiative, who sold his stock, sold with it by so doing, his voice in the management of the business. When the climax was reached in their disagreement, the one who couldn't sell his stock naturally had, BY FORCE OF CIRCUMSTANCES, the control of the business, so he used his power to his own salvation and to the great detriment of his associate, by voting him out of the Presidency of the corporation and voting himself into that office.

The fact that he couldn't sell his stock was A BLESSING IN DISGUISE.

There was once a young man who was President of a corporation which was making lots of money. He owned automobiles, had servants and all the other luxuries which go with a successful business. He trusted his banker too far by borrowing money for expansion purposes. The banker wanted this young man's interest in the corporation, because he knew the young man was making lots of money and the banker happened to be dishonest. In the 1907 Roosevelt Panic he saw his chance and closed him out. It seemed like a dark day for the young man. All was lost. But watch the roulette wheel of destiny as it spins around by the force of the hand of fate. His loss forced him to go back to the practice of law. This brought him in touch with a million-dollar corporation which employed him at a salary of $5,000.00 a year, a salary which he wouldn't have thought of accepting from an outsider while he was in control of his own business. This brought him to the middle west, and likewise in touch with the "big opportunity" of his life.

So his loss proved a blessing in disguise, for it literally drove him into a greater success.

A young bank clerk was discharged on account of his habit of drawing pictures of automobiles and sketching mechanical parts of automobiles during business hours. The loss of his job was quite a shock to him, for he supported his mother and two sisters from his small earnings as a bank clerk.

The loss of his bank job was the greatest blessing that ever came to him, for six months later he invented an automobile part which made him a fortune. He is now president of the largest automobile accessories companies in America. His clerks are all supplied with desk pads and pencils, with instructions to do all the drawing of automobiles they wish, and to submit to him any new ideas for improvements of automobile parts. Any of their ideas which he uses are paid for extra, at one hundred dollars each.

John D. Rockefeller discharged one of his faithful employees who he thought went too far in the exercise of his authorized duties, in making a financial transaction for Mr. Rockefeller in his absence, even though the deal netted Mr. Rockefeller several thousand dollars in cash.

A blessing in disguise. This office clerk, who had been honest and faithful, but not overly well paid, was immediately employed by one of Mr. Rockefeller's rivals, at a handsome salary. He now holds a high official position with the rival company.

And, while I write, further evidence of the soundness of my theory that "Adversity is usually a blessing in disguise" reaches me. One of the men mentioned in the beginning of this narrative— the one who was successful in selling stock, but who thereby lost the presidency of his company—has been elected president of a ten-million-dollar corporation, with an excellent chance to make $50,000.00 a year from his salary and dividends on his bonus stock in the company.

The ten-million-dollar corporation never would have been organized in all probability, except for the fact that this man's business associate supplanted him in his original position.

A blessing in disguise, for the ten-million-dollar corporation has patents and secret processes for making fuel, heat and light which probably will make this man immensely wealthy.

Every change in one's environment is for a purpose. That which seems like disappointment and ill "luck" usually is a blessing in disguise. If we do not carefully study cause and effect in all that we do and all that comes our way, we may never discover when and where our apparent failures are, in reality, blessings instead.

Stop and take an inventory of your life's record and see if you cannot find evidence in your own case which will support the correctness of this. Take an inventory of the lives of those you know intimately and see if the same is not true.

Then, when you become discouraged; when the hand of fate seems to be against you; when your destiny seems doubtful and life's pathway fraught with many thorns of disappointment; when the rough and rugged hand of time spins the roulette wheel of fate so hard that the little pointer goes past your number just remember, friends, that there is a bigger stake awaiting you, if not in your present environment, then later on in some other "game" in the sphere of human accomplishments.

Hang on!

Let Ambition Be Your Master

LUCKY is the man who is driven by that determined little slave master called AMBITION! Those who have enjoyed the greatest success in life were literally driven to succeed by AMBITION! It made Harriman, Rockefeller, Carnegie, Hill, Roosevelt, and a good many thousands of other successful men of whom we never hear.

Ambition is the mainspring of life, but we must keep it wound up! Self-confidence is the balance wheel which keeps ambition moving at an even momentum. Enthusiasm is the oil with which we keep the human machine greased and in smooth running order. The well-organized, capable, and productive man is AMBITIOUS, EN-THUSIASTIC, and, possesses plenty of SELF-CONFIDENCE. Without these success is uncertain, if not impossible.

One of the greatest men America has ever known divorced his first wife because she was beneath his mental plane, and therefore had a tendency to keep down his ambition. This great man is not with us any more, but the world is testifying to his greatness by quoting his writings and reading his books more than ever before. It is a commonly known fact that his second wife was his chief source of inspiration—that she was responsible for keeping his AMBITION alive and constantly on the alert. That is why he married her. He foresaw the need for a constant attendant who would see to it that his AMBITION let him have no rest.

Lucky is the man who has formed a partnership with such a wife. We all get lazy at times. We need someone to keep our AMBITION alive and spur us on to bigger and better accomplishment. The chief reason that I consent to my wife going back to the farm every summer is that while she is away she constantly writes me letters which fire me with AMBITION. She understands me as few wives understand their husbands. She knows how necessary it is to constantly remind me of my *chief aims in life,* and she has a way of doing it which is pleasing and inspiring.

When I secured my first $5,000 a year position I thought I was fixed for life, and probably I would have been, had it not been for that little master for whom I was slaving—AMBITION! My wife and AMBITION collaborated against me and made me resign that position—FOR A BIGGER ONE! Five thousand a year would have satisfied me had it not been for my master, AMBITION. In my bigger and broader field I serve a hundred of my fellow men where I served one before, which means that I get a hundred times as much enjoyment out of life as well as financial returns which are adequate and in proportion to the service which I perform.

In addition to my regular work I lecture three times a week in one of the local colleges, on the subject of Advertising and Salesmanship. The course is a heavy one, covering a period of ten months. The students are taught everything about Advertising and Selling that I can teach them, both from my own experience and from that of a score or more of able advertising specialists. THE FIRST LECTURE IN THE COURSE IS ON THE SUBJECT OF THE VALUE OF AMBITION! I use every ounce of influence that I possess to fire these young men and young women with an everlasting knowledge of the value of AMBITION, SELF-CONFIDENCE, and ENTHUSIASM! If I succeed no further than to cause my students to cultivate that wonderful power,

AMBITION, my time and theirs will have been well spent in the effort.

AMBITION is what freed America from over-the-sea rulership.

Once in my life, while I was working for a salary, I was discharged from my position—just ONCE! The head of the institution for which I worked told me that I was too "ambitious." That was the greatest compliment anyone ever paid me, even though it cut me off temporarily from my bread and meat.

I have always had my suspicions why this man "fired" me, although he claimed it was because his "help" were unanimously agreed that I ought to go! His "help" who objected to me was one of his brothers who had his eye on the General Managership of the institution. He knew what "AMBITION" might lead me to. I have never blamed the brother, for he has a wife and two babies to support, and "AMBITION" on my part seemed to him a dangerous barrier between him and his coveted goal.

That institution of which I write was organized nearly twenty years ago. It is doing a business of about $600,000 a year. Another institution, engaged in the same line of business, started in just six years ago, on a capital of less than $6,000. I was formerly Advertising Manager of this institution. It does not discourage "AMBITION." It is now doing a business of $1,500,000 a year, and clearing more net profits every month than the other firm is doing in gross business. The older institution, the one which was organized and has been doing business for nearly twenty years, is headed by men who are afraid of the "AMBITIOUS MAN." Those who are working for a salary are afraid he will get their jobs (which said fear is not without some foundation). The head of the firm is afraid of the "AMBITIOUS MAN" because he is afraid he will find in him a competitor in business (which, also, is not without well-grounded foundation).

BUT—AND HERE IS THE CRUX OF MY WHOLE STORY OF THESE TWO FIRMS—THE MAJORITY OF BUSINESS FIRMS ARE LOOKING FOR MEN WHO HAVE PLENTY OF "AMBITION." Do not worry because one firm is afraid of the ambitious man. The very fact that such a firm is afraid of him is, in itself, strong evidence of weakness on the part of those who manage the firm.

While I was Advertising Manager of the younger firm of which I have written, I had three young men in my department. I put them on notice that some day one of them would get my position, and I commenced training them for my job. I told them that the man who "made good" first would get the place, if my recommendations would help any. My Secretary landed the prize. He is still with that firm, making more money than he ever made in his life, and more money than the average man of his age receives. I did not discourage "AMBITION" for fear of losing my job. I encouraged it so that someone would grow to be big enough to push me out of the rut and into a bigger position. That is what happened. I have no patience to speak of, with the man who is so narrow that he is afraid to inspire "AMBITION" in his fellow workers.

Show me a man who believes he has a corner on the details connected with his job and I will show you, in the same person, a man who will never develop beyond petty selfishness. I beseech you not to fall into the habit of neglecting to cultivate your "AMBITION." You will need something more than mere services with which to succeed. You will need that ever alert little master which is the subject of this chapter. But, I must here give you a word of warning—*do not let your ambition become a selfish one*! The greatest object over which to develop ambition is the desire to serve our fellow men. We cannot serve them if we are jealous of them. Remember, also, that AMBITION is a contagious thing. If you give it to the world, the world will give it back to you in increased measure. But keep it unto yourself and you will lose it. It will take wings and fly!

Ambition finds expression in a thousand different forms. It is the foundation which underlies all invention, art, music, industry, commerce—nay, the very foundation upon which the progress of the world has been built. Within the present generation we have seen it expressed in the most wonderful inventions the world has ever known; the automobile, the telephone, the wireless, the submarines, the X-ray, and the airplane. AMBITION was the very warp and woof out of which these things were constructed. Ambition leads us to think, and when we begin to think the nebulous problems in the world's evolution begin to become clarified and simplified. BE AMBITIOUS IF NOTHING MORE. OTHER THINGS WILL TAKE CARE OF THEMSELVES.

What I Have Learned from Analyzing Ten Thousand People

WHEN I was requested to write this article, I was overjoyed at such an opportunity to pass on to thoughtful men and women, who are trying to "find themselves," the benefit of my experience as a personal analyst.

During the past eight years I have analyzed over ten thousand men and women who were earnestly seeking their proper niche in the world's work. Incidentally, through my research I have discovered some of the fundamental qualities without which no human being can hope for success. Five of these are mentioned in this article, in words which a school boy can easily understand.

I have also discovered some of the things which break men's hearts and send them to the scrap-heap of human failures. It is my sincere hope that every person who reads this article may profit by one or more of the points which it covers. I am placing the results of my discoveries in print for the first time, solely out of my deep desire to make life's pathway just a little smoother for my fellow man.

It is my purpose to pass on to you, in as few words as possible, that portion of my discoveries which I believe will aid you in planning and achieving your "chief aim" in life, whatever that may be. I shall not preach to you. Whatever suggestions I make are based upon discoveries which I have made in my work.

I believe it befitting to state that twenty years ago I was working as a laborer, at wages of $1 a day. I had no home and no friends.

I had but little education. My future then looked very unpromis-ing. I was downcast in spirit. I had no ambition. I had no definite purpose in life. All around me I saw men, some young and some old, who were whipped—just as I felt that I was. I absorbed my environment as a sponge absorbs water. I became a part of the daily routine in which I lived.

It had never occurred to me that I could ever amount to any-thing. I believed my lot in life was to be that of a laborer. I was just like a horse which has had the bit slipped into its mouth and the saddle buckled on its back.

Here is the turning point in my career. Note it well!

A chance remark, no doubt made in a half-jocular way, caused me to throw the bit out of my mouth, kick off the saddle, and "run away" as young horses sometimes do. That remark was made by a farmer with whom I lived. I shall never forget it if I live to be a hundred, because it has partly bridged the gap over that awful chasm which nearly all human beings want to cross, "failure"!

The remark was this: "You are a bright boy. What a pity you are not in school instead of at work as a laborer at a dollar a day."

"You are a bright boy!" These were the sweetest words I had ever heard.

That remark aroused in me the first ambition I had ever felt, and, incidentally, it is directly responsible for the personal analysis system which I have worked out. No one had ever hinted to me before that I was "bright." I had always imagined that I was exceed-ingly dull. In fact, I had been told that I was a dunce. As a boy I was defeated in everything I undertook, largely because those with whom I associated ridiculed me and discouraged me from engaging in the things which interested me most. My work was selected for me—my associates were selected for me—my studies were selected for me—and my play, well, I was taught that play was a waste of time.

With this first-hand knowledge of the great handicap under which the average person starts out in life, as a working basis, I began many years ago to work out a system for helping people "find themselves" as early in life as possible. My efforts have yielded splendid returns for I have helped many find the work for which they were most suited, and started them on the road to happiness and success. I have helped not a few to acquire the qualities for success which are mentioned in this article.

THE FIRST TWO SUCCESS REQUISITES

With this prelude I shall tell you first what I believe to be the two most important of the five chief requisites for success. These are SELF-CONFIDENCE and ENTHUSIASM. The other three I will mention later.

What is self-confidence?

I will tell you what it is: It is the little glass window through which you may look and see the real man-power within your body. Self-confidence is self-discovery—finding out who you are and what you can do. It is the banishment of fear. It is the acquirement of mental courage. It is the turning on of the light of human intelligence, through the use of common sense.

It was self-confidence, plus enthusiasm and concentration, that caused the birth of the world's greatest inventions, the incandescent electric light, the automobile, the talking machine, the airplane, the moving picture, and all the other great mechanical creations.

Self-confidence, then, is an essential quality for all worth-while accomplishments. Yet, it is the quality in which most of us are weakest. Not a weakness which many of us acknowledge, but it exists just the same. A man without self-confidence is like a ship without a rudder—he wastes his energy without moving in the right direction.

I wish I might be able to tell you exactly how to acquire full self-confidence. That would be a big undertaking. I will give you this suggestion, however—I made my first step in the direction of self-confidence the day I heard those words, "You are a bright boy." That was the first time I had ever felt ambition tugging at my coat sleeve, and with it, apparently, came self-confidence.

It is remarkable what clothes have to do with building self-confidence. A man came to me for analysis not long ago. He had been earning a good salary, but conditions for which he was in no way responsible caused him to be let out. I asked him how much money he had and he said, "Seventy-five dollars." I told him to invest one-third of it in a new suit of clothes. He demurred on the ground that he "couldn't afford it." But I insisted and went with him to buy the clothes. Then I insisted on his going to the cobbler's and having the heels of his shoes straightened up. Then I persuaded him to have his shoes shined and get a clean shave and a hair cut. I then sent him to see the president of a large corporation who employed him at $3,000 a year.

If I had sent him to interview the president of that corporation without the new suit and the clean-up, he wouldn't have gotten the position, in all probability, because he would not have had the proper self-confidence. Good clothes, clean linen, polished shoes, and a clean shave are not luxuries—they are a necessity to the man who comes in contact with the business public.

THE SECOND SUCCESS REQUISITE

Then comes the second requisite for success, enthusiasm, that great dynamic force which puts self-confidence into action. Enthusiasm may be likened to the steam which runs the locomotive. The most powerful locomotive ever built might stand upon the side-track with coal in the bunker and the engineer in the cab, but if there is no steam, the wheels will not turn—there is no action.

It is exactly the same with the human machine. If there is no enthusiasm, there is little or no action. Lack of these qualities—self-confidence and enthusiasm—stands between the great majority of men and success. This statement is no mere conjecture upon my part. I have proved it in thousands of cases. I am proving it in more than a hundred cases a week right along. Enthusiasm is something which cannot be counterfeited. Only the real article will fill the bill. Enthusiasm usually comes automatically when you find the vocation into which you can pitch your whole heart and soul—the work you love best.

THE THIRD SUCCESS REQUISITE

The third requisite for success is a definite working plan—the habit of working with a "chief aim" in life. From my work as a vocational director, I have learned that most people have no such plan. Men who are working without a well-defined plan—without a pre-determined objective—are going no-where in particular and most of them are getting nowhere. In my personal Analysis Chart, which all whom I examine must fill out, is this question.

"What is your 'chief aim' in life?"

An actual tabulation of answers to this question shows that only one out of every fifty has any "chief aim." But few have any sort of a real aim, "chief" or otherwise. Yet, nearly all whom I have analyzed expect to succeed. Just when or how or in what work the majority of them do not undertake to say.

Nearly every man wants a "big position," yet not one out of a hundred, even though he may be competent, knows how to get it. A "big position" is not something that we find hanging on a bush ready to be plucked off by "pull" by the first person who comes along. It is the sum total of a number of smaller positions or tasks which we have efficiently filled; not necessarily with different firms, but, as often as otherwise, in the employment of one firm. A big position is built just as we build a big skyscraper—by first formulating a definite plan and then building according to that plan, step by step.

The possible exception to this rule is the man who gets into a "big position" through "pull." There are exceptions to most rules, but the question to ask yourself is this: "Am I willing to go through life and take a chance on getting ahead on 'pull'?" Look about you and I dare say you will find that for every man who is succeeding by "pull" you may find a hundred who are succeeding by "push"!

There are varying degrees of success, just as there are different ideas as to what success is, but whether your idea of success is the accumulation of wealth or the rendering of some great service to mankind, or both, you will not likely achieve it unless you have a "chief aim"—a definite goal with a definite plan mapped out for reaching it.

No architect ever started a building until he had first created a perfect picture of it in his mind, and then carefully transferred the detail of the picture to a blueprint. And no human being may hope to build a worthwhile success until he has planned the building and decided what it shall be.

SELECTING A VOCATION

A very large proportion of the people whom I have analyzed are in positions which they hold, not by **selection,** but by **chance.** Even those who are following vocations which they deliberately chose, in the majority of cases, have not observed even the most elementary rules of self-analysis. They have never stopped to find out whether or not the work in which they are engaged is the work for which they are best fitted by nature and education.

For example, a young man whom I recently analyzed, had prepared himself for the practice of law, but had made an utter failure of that profession. He failed, first, because he did not like the profession after he got into it; secondly, because he had absolutely no native ability for that profession. He was badly deformed physically and, as a consequence, made a very poor impression before courts and juries. He lacked enthusiasm and that dynamic force which we call "personality," without which he could not hope to succeed as a lawyer. Such a person might succeed to some extent as advisory counsel or "office lawyer," but not as a trial lawyer where a strong personality and the ability to speak with force and conviction count for so much.

The surprising part of this particular case was the fact that this man had never understood just why he did not succeed in the practice of law. It seemed simple enough to him after I had pointed out the negative qualities which I believed had stood between him and success. When I asked him how he came to take up law, he replied, "Well, I just had a hunch that I would like it!"

"I just had a hunch that I would like it!"

Selecting a life work on a "hunch" is a dangerous thing. You wouldn't purchase a race-horse on a "hunch"; you would want to see him perform on the track. You wouldn't purchase a bird-dog on a "hunch"; you would want to see him in action or know something of his pedigree. If you selected a bird-dog in this haphazard way, you might find yourself trying to set birds with a bull-pup!

A court reporter, whom I analyzed, said to me: "My fifteen years of experience have proved to me that a jury seldom tries the defendant, but instead, they try the lawyers in the case. The lawyer who makes the best impression generally wins." Everyone who is familiar with court actions knows that this is too often true. You can see, therefore, what an important part "personality" plays in the practice of law.

Mr. Carnegie says that his success is due largely to his ability to pick men. Mr. Frank A. Vanderlip and Mr. Rockefeller say the same. If you will stop and analyze all the successful men you know, you will probably find that they either possess all the requisites for success in the business in which they are engaged, or, they know how to select men who will supply what they lack—men who are their opposites in nearly every particular.

Probably 50% of those who call themselves salesmen are of poor personal appearance, have weak faces, and speak without force. A salesman conveys to his prospective buyer a positive or negative influence, according to his own personality and manner of approach in presenting his case. A man who is badly deformed, or the man who suffers from impediment of speech and otherwise makes a negative appearance had better not take up oral salesmanship. If he can hide behind the written page, he may succeed, but in person never!

THE FOURTH SUCCESS REQUISITE

The fourth success requisite is the habit of performing more service than you are actually paid for. It is the practice of the majority of men to perform no more service than they feel they are being paid to perform. Fully 80% of all whom I have analyzed were suffering on account of this great mistake.

You need have no fear of competition from the man who says, "I'm not paid to do that, therefore I'll not do it." He will never be a dangerous competitor for your job, but watch out for the fellow who does not let his pick hang in the air when the whistle blows, or the man who stays at his desk or work bench until his work is finished—watch out that such a fellow does not "Challenge you at the post and pass you at the grandstand," as Andrew Carnegie said.

Before mentioning the fifth and last requisite for success I shall ask your indulgence while I digress for just a few moments. After I had commenced work on this article I decided to have the five points which I have covered put to the acid test to see whether or not they would square up with the experience of other vocational directors. I took the manuscript to Dr. J. M. Fitzgerald, Chicago, who is, without doubt, the most able vocational director in the world.

Dr. Fitzgerald went over the manuscript with me word for word and I have his permission to quote him as saying that he fully endorses the five chief points covered by this article. He says that they square up with his own experience, exactly. But, before we went over the manuscript, I asked Dr. Fitzgerald to state the chief negative qualities which he had discovered to be standing as barriers between those whom he had analyzed and success. His reply was quick and concise, as follows:

1. Lack of self-discernment; the lack of ability upon part of most men to analyze themselves and find the work for which they are best prepared.
2. Lack of intensified concentration and the disposition not to put more into their work than they expect to get out of it.
3. Lack of moral self-control.

Dr. Fitzgerald has analyzed, in person, more than 15,000 men and women. Many of the largest corporations of the middle West will not employ a man for any important position until he has been analyzed by Dr. Fitzgerald. He has taken men from the bookkeeper's desk and enabled them to become successful executives. He has converted clerks into managers in much less time than is ordinarily required, merely by having started them in the right direction, through accurate personal analysis.

I mention these details concerning Dr. Fitzgerald's work because I want you to feel that my own experience, as stated in this article, is not mere conjecture on my part—that it is authentic and that it has the endorsement of the world's greatest personal analyst. Bear in mind that the five chief points covered by this article have been discovered, classified, and charted from the personal analysis of 25,000 people, 10,000 of whom I have analyzed and 15,000 of whom were analyzed by Dr. Fitzgerald.

THE FIFTH SUCCESS REQUISITE

This article ought to be of benefit to those who are about to select a vocation and those who are in the wrong vocation but wish to make a change. However, there is another class to be taken into consideration. It is represented by those who have selected the right vocation but who, nevertheless, are not succeeding. I have found the Key to Success for this class. In this Great Magic Key you will find the fifth and last of the success rules which I have discovered in my vocational work.

In presenting to you this key let me first explain that it is no invention of mine.

This Great Magic Key is a most wonderful power, yet perfectly simple of operation. So simple that most people have failed to make use of it. We human beings are too prone to look askance at so simple a formula for success—a formula which will open the door to health and wealth; yet, such a formula is the Great Magic Key.

Through the Great Magic Key we have unlocked the secret

doors to all of the world's great inventions. Through its magic powers all of our great geniuses have been produced. We will suppose that you desire a better position. The Great Magic Key will help you attain it! Through its use Carnegie, Rockefeller, Hill, Harriman, Morgan, and Guggenheim have accumulated millions of dollars in material wealth.

You ask—"What is this Great Magic Key?"

And I answer with one word: CONCENTRATION!

To stop here would be insufficient. You must know how to use this Great Magic Key! First, let me tell you that AMBITION and DESIRE are the great dynamic powers which you must summon to the aid of CONCENTRATION. They form the lock which this great key fits. Without ambition and desire the Great Magic Key is useless. The reason that so few people use the key is that most people lack ambition!

Desire whatever you may, and if your desire is strong enough the Great Magic Key of CONCENTRATION will help you attain it, if the object of your desire is something which it is humanly possible for you to attain.

There are learned men of science who tell us that the wonderful powers of prayer itself operate through the principle of CONCENTRATION, plus faith and strong DESIRE!

I am making no attempt to associate the Great Magic Key with occultism or religion. I am treating it from the ordinary layman's viewpoint. I am dealing with it from actual knowledge that I have gained in carefully analyzing and charting over ten thousand people.

We will assume that you are skeptical of the powers of CONCENTRATION and DESIRE. Let's put these powers to the test, through a concrete example, for unless we do this it would be just like telling you to be honest without telling you how to be honest.

HOW TO CONCENTRATE

First, you must do away with skepticism and doubt! No unbeliever ever enjoyed the benefits of these great powers. You must believe in the test which I am going to ask you to make. You must let no feeling of unbelief creep in.

Now we will suppose that you have thought of becoming a great writer, or a great public speaker, or a great business executive, or a great advertising manager. Suppose we take the latter as the subject of this test. But remember that if you expect results you must follow instructions to the letter.

Take a plain piece of paper, ordinary letter size, and write on it in large letters—the largest it will carry—these words:

I AM GOING TO BECOME A SUCCESSFUL ADVERTISING MANAGER BECAUSE THIS WILL ENABLE ME TO RENDER THE WORLD A USEFUL SERVICE—AND BECAUSE IT WILL PROVIDE ME WITH THE NECESSARY MATERIAL THINGS OF LIFE!

I WILL CONCENTRATE ON THIS DESIRE FOR TEN MINUTES DAILY, JUST BEFORE RETIRING AND JUST AFTER RISING.

. . . .

(Sign your name.)

If you are not good at lettering just clip out the foregoing, sign it, and place where you will read it just before retiring and just after getting up each day. Do exactly as you have pledged yourself to do, for at least ten days.

Now when you come to do your "CONCENTRATING" this

is the way to go about it: Look ahead three, five, ten, or even fifteen years from now and see yourself in a position as advertising manager paying a big salary. See the happy faces of your loved ones—maybe a wife and babies—maybe a mother with silvery hair. Be a dreamer if you choose to call it that, but be also a "doer"! The world needs this combination of "dreamer-doers." They are the Lincolns, Grants, Edisons, Hills, Carnegies, Vanderlips, and Schwabs.

See yourself laying aside a "nest-egg" for a rainy day. See yourself in your motor car which you will be able to afford. See yourself in your own cozy little home that you will own. See yourself a person of influence in the business world.

See yourself INCREASING IN VALUE AND EARNING STILL MORE MONEY as you grow older. See yourself engaged in a line of work where you will not fear the loss of a job when the gray hairs begin to put in their appearance.

Paint this picture through the powers of your imagination, and lo! it will turn into Desire. Use this Desire as the chief object of your CONCENTRATION, and see what happens!

It may take longer than ten days for you to master this lesson in CONCENTRATION. Again it may take only one day. That will depend upon how well you perform the task.

You now have the secret of the Great Magic Key!

It will unlock the door to whatever position in life you want, if that position is one that you are prepared by nature and education to fill. It will make of you a better citizen and show you the road to true happiness if the object of your CONCENTRATION is a worthy one.

Use this Great Key with intelligence! Use it only for the attainment of worthy purposes, and it will give you the things of life for which your heart may crave. So simple, so easy of application, yet so MARVELOUS IN RESULTS! Try it! Begin right now. Forget the mistakes you have made in the past. Start all over again, and make the next five or ten years tell a story of human accomplishment in whatever line of work your calling may have placed you, that you will not be ashamed of—that the future generations of your family will be PROUD OF!

MAKE A NAME FOR YOURSELF THROUGH AMBITION, DESIRE, AND CONCENTRATION!

Vocational guidance has not yet become a universally accepted science. It may never be accepted as a science by everyone, but this does not preclude a person from using common sense in selecting a vocation. The trouble is, too many people act on a "hunch." If you are engaged in work in which you are not succeeding, take inventory of yourself and see if you cannot locate the trouble. The chances are that you can. Just apply common sense in selecting a life work. You may not be able to analyze yourself as well as a man who has many years of experience could do, therefore, if you have any doubts place yourself in the hands of a man who is experienced in analyzing men. He will undoubtedly see your weak spots more quickly than you could. Few of us can be our own best critics because we are inclined to overlook our weaknesses or place too little importance on them.

There are but few, if any, ironclad rules to follow in the selection of a vocation that would apply in every case. Probably these come as near being applicable in all cases as is possible: **Be sure you love the vocation you adopt.** Be sure you are enthusiastic over it and that you intend to stick to it. Be sure you are prepared, educationally, for the work you select. Be sure the vocation is one in which you can render a service that is beneficial to humanity. Be sure the work is permanent. Be sure that it is work that will not impair your health.

Let me summarize the five chief requisites for success, so you will not forget them. They are—first, Self-confidence; second,

Enthusiasm; third, Working with a "chief aim"; fourth, Performing more work than you are paid for; fifth, Concentration, backed by desire and unwavering faith. By a reasonably intelligent application of these qualities you can become master of your own career.

Finally, I wish to leave this thought with you. It has been my constant companion through life. It has supported my tired legs when they would otherwise have allowed me to fall by the wayside. It is this:

"EVERY ADVERSITY IS, IN REALITY, A BLESSING IN DISGUISE. THE UNIVERSITY OF HARD KNOCKS SENDS FORTH ITS GRADUATES TO FIGHT LIFE'S BATTLES, WITH PLENTY OF STRENGTH TO OVERCOME EVERY OBSTACLE THAT MAY CONFRONT THEM. FROM EVERY FAILURE WE MAY LEARN A GREAT LESSON IF WE WILL. SOMEWHERE IN THE WORLD **YOUR** PLACE IS WAITING FOR YOU. THROUGH PERSISTENCE AND INTELLIGENT EFFORT YOU WILL EVENTUALLY FIND IT. YOU WILL NEVER BE DEFEATED IN YOUR LIFE'S PURPOSE IF YOU KEEP FAITH IN THE ONLY PERSON IN THE WORLD WHO CONTROLS YOUR DESTINY— **YOURSELF!**"

How to Outwit the Six Ghosts of Fear

Excerpted from Think and Grow Rich

Before you can put any portion of this philosophy into successful use, your mind must be prepared to receive it. The preparation is not difficult. It begins with study, analysis, and understanding of three enemies which you shall have to clear out. These are **indecision, doubt, and fear**! The members of this unholy trio are closely related; where one is found, the other two are close at hand.

Indecision is the seedling of fear! Remember this, as you read. Indecision crystallizes into **doubt**; the two blend and become **fear**! The "blending" process often is slow. This is one reason why these three enemies are so dangerous. They germinate and grow *without their presence being observed.*

The purpose of this chapter is to turn the spotlight of attention upon the cause and the cure of the six basic fears. Before we can master an enemy, we must know its name, its habits, and its place of abode. As you read, analyze yourself carefully, and determine which, if any, of the six common fears have attached themselves to you.

Do not be deceived by the habits of these subtle enemies. Sometimes they remain hidden in the subconscious mind, where they are difficult to locate, and still more difficult to eliminate.

THE SIX BASIC FEARS

There are six basic fears, with some combination of which every human suffers at one time or another. Most people are fortunate if they do not suffer from the entire six. Named in the order of their most common appearance, they are:

The fear of **POVERTY**
The fear of **CRITICISM**
The fear of **ILL HEALTH**
(the above three are at the bottom of most of one's worries)
The fear of **LOSS OF LOVE OF SOMEONE**
The fear of **OLD AGE**
The fear of **DEATH**

All other fears are of minor importance; they can be grouped under these six headings.

The prevalence of these fears, as a curse to the world, runs in cycles. For almost six years, while the depression was on, we floundered in the cycle of fear of poverty. During the world war, we were in the cycle of fear of death. Just following the war, we were in the cycle of fear of ill health, as evidenced by the epidemic of disease which spread itself all over the world.

Fears are nothing more than states of mind. One's state of mind is subject to control and direction. Physicians, as everyone knows, are less subject to attack by disease than ordinary laymen, for the reason that physicians do not fear disease. Physicians, without fear or hesitation, have been known to physically contact hundreds of people, daily, who were suffering from such contagious diseases as small-pox, without becoming infected. Their immunity against the disease consisted, largely, if not solely, in their absolute lack of fear.

Man can create nothing which he does not first conceive in the form of an impulse of thought. Following this statement, comes another of still greater importance, namely man's thought impulses begin immediately to translate themselves into their physical equivalent, whether those thoughts are voluntary or involuntary. Thought impulses which are picked up through the ether, by mere chance (thoughts which have been released by other minds) may determine one's financial, business, professional, or social destiny just as surely as do the thought impulses which one creates by intent and design.

We are here laying the foundation for the presentation of a fact of great importance to the person who does not understand why some people appear to be "lucky" while others of equal or greater ability, training, experience, and brain capacity, seem destined to ride with misfortune. This fact may be explained by the statement that *every human being has the ability to completely control his own mind,* and with this control, obviously, every person may open his mind to the tramp thought impulses which are being released by other brains, or close the doors tightly and admit only thought impulses of his own choice.

Nature has endowed man with absolute control over but one thing, and that is thought. This fact, coupled with the additional fact that everything which man creates begins in the form of a thought, leads one very near to the principle by which fear may be mastered.

If it is true that all thought has a tendency to clothe itself in its physical equivalent (and this is true, beyond any reasonable room for doubt), it is equally true that thought impulses of fear and poverty cannot be translated into terms of courage and financial gain.

The people of America began to think of poverty, following the Wall Street crash of 1929. Slowly, but surely that mass thought was crystallized into its physical equivalent, which was known as a "depression." This had to happen; it is in conformity with the laws of Nature.

THE FEAR OF POVERTY

There can be no compromise between poverty and riches! The two roads that lead to poverty and riches travel in opposite directions. If you want riches, you must refuse to accept any circumstance that leads toward poverty. (The word "riches" is here used in its broadest sense, meaning financial, spiritual, mental, and material estates.) The starting point of the path that leads to riches is desire. In chapter two, you received full instructions for the proper use of desire. In this chapter, on fear, you have complete instructions for preparing your mind to make practical use of desire.

Here, then, is the place to give yourself a challenge which will definitely determine how much of this philosophy you have absorbed. Here is the point at which you can turn prophet and foretell, accurately, what the future holds in store for you. If, after reading this chapter, you are willing to accept poverty, you may as well make up your mind to receive poverty. This is one decision you cannot avoid.

If you demand riches, determine what form, and how much will be required to satisfy you. You know the road that leads to riches. You have been given a road map which, if followed, will keep you on that road. If you neglect to make the start, or stop before you arrive, no one will be to blame but you. This responsibility is yours. No alibi will save you from accepting the responsibility if you now fail or refuse to demand riches of Life, because the acceptance calls for but one thing—incidentally, the only thing you can control—and that is a state of mind. A state of mind is something that one assumes. It cannot be purchased; it must be created.

Fear of poverty is a state of mind, nothing else! But it is sufficient to destroy one's chances of achievement in any undertaking, a truth which became painfully evident during the depression.

This fear paralyzes the faculty of reason, destroys the faculty of imagination, kills off self-reliance, undermines enthusiasm, discourages initiative, leads to uncertainty of purpose, encourages procrastination, wipes out enthusiasm, and makes self-control an impossibility. It takes the charm from one's personality, destroys the possibility of accurate thinking, diverts concentration of effort; it masters persistence, turns the will-power into nothingness, destroys ambition, beclouds the memory, and invites failure in every conceivable form; it kills love and assassinates the finer emotions of the heart, discourages friendship, and invites disaster in a hundred forms, leads to sleeplessness, misery, and unhappiness—and all this despite the obvious truth that we live in a world of over-abundance of everything the heart could desire, with nothing standing between us and our desires, excepting lack of a definite purpose.

The Fear of Poverty is, without doubt, the most destructive of the six basic fears. It has been placed at the head of the list, because it is the most difficult to master. Considerable courage is required to state the truth about the origin of this fear, and still greater courage to accept the truth after it has been stated. The fear of poverty grew out of man's inherited tendency to prey upon his fellow man economically. Nearly all animals lower than man are motivated by instinct, but their capacity to "think" is limited, therefore, they prey upon one another physically. Man, with his superior sense of intuition, with the capacity to think and to reason, does not eat his fellow man bodily, he gets more satisfaction out of "eating" him financially. Man is so avaricious that every conceivable law has been passed to safeguard him from his fellow man.

Of all the ages of the world, of which we know anything, the age in which we live seems to be one that is outstanding because of man's money-madness. A man is considered less than the dust of the earth, unless he can display a fat bank account; but if he has money—never mind how he acquired it—he is a "king" or a "big shot"; he is above the law, he rules in politics, he dominates in business, and the whole world about him bows in respect when he passes.

Nothing brings man so much suffering and humility as poverty! Only those who have experienced poverty understand the full meaning of this.

It is no wonder that man *fears* poverty. Through a long line of inherited experiences man has learned, for sure, that some men cannot be trusted, where matters of money and earthly possessions are concerned. This is a rather stinging indictment, the worst part of it being that it is true.

The majority of people, if asked what they fear most, would reply, "I fear nothing." The reply would be inaccurate, because few people realize that they are bound, handicapped, whipped spiritually and physically through some form of fear. So subtle and deeply seated is the emotion of fear that one may go through life burdened with it, never recognizing its presence. Only a courageous analysis will disclose the presence of this universal enemy. When you begin such an analysis, search deeply into your character. Here is a list of the symptoms for which you should look:

Symptoms of the Fear of Poverty

INDIFFERENCE: Commonly expressed through lack of ambition; willingness to tolerate poverty; acceptance of whatever compensation life may offer without protest; mental and physical laziness; lack of initiative, imagination, enthusiasm, and self-control.

INDECISION: The habit of permitting others to do one's thinking. Staying "on the fence."

DOUBT: Generally expressed through alibis and excuses designed to cover up, explain away, or apologize for one's failures, sometimes expressed in the form of envy of those who are successful, or by criticising them.

WORRY: Usually expressed by finding fault with others, a tendency to spend beyond one's income, neglect of personal appearance, scowling and frowning; intemperance in the use of alcoholic drink, sometimes through the use of narcotics; nervousness, lack of poise, self-consciousness, and lack of self-reliance.

OVER-CAUTION: The habit of looking for the negative side of every circumstance, thinking and talking of possible failure instead of concentrating upon the means of succeeding. Knowing all the roads to disaster, but never searching for the plans to avoid failure. Waiting for "the right time" to begin putting ideas and plans into action, until the waiting becomes a permanent habit. Remembering those who have failed, and forgetting those who have succeeded. Seeing the hole in the doughnut, but overlooking the doughnut. Pessimism, leading to indigestion, poor elimination, auto-intoxication, bad breath, and bad disposition.

PROCRASTINATION: The habit of putting off until tomorrow that which should have been done last year. Spending enough time in creating alibis and excuses to have done the job. This symptom is closely related to over-caution, doubt, and worry. Refusal to accept responsibility when it can be avoided. Willingness to compromise rather than put up a stiff fight. Compromising with difficulties instead of harnessing and using them as stepping stones to advancement. Bargaining with Life for a penny, instead of demanding prosperity, opulence, riches, contentment, and happiness. Planning what to do if and when overtaken by failure, instead of burning all bridges and making retreat impossible. Weakness of, and often total lack of self-confidence, definiteness of purpose, self-control, initiative, enthusiasm, ambition, thrift, and sound reasoning ability. Expecting poverty instead of demanding riches. Association with those who accept poverty instead of seeking the company of those who demand and receive riches.

MONEY TALKS!

Some will ask, "Why did you write a book about money? Why measure riches in dollars, alone?" Some will believe, and rightly so, that there are other forms of riches more desirable than money. Yes, there are riches which cannot be measured in terms of dollars, but there are millions of people who will say, "Give me all the money I need, and I will find everything else I want."

The major reason why I wrote on how to get money is the fact that the world has but lately passed through an experience that left millions of men and women paralyzed with the fear of poverty.

THE FEAR OF CRITICISM

Just how man originally came by this fear, no one can state definitely, but one thing is certain—he has it in a highly developed form. Some believe that this fear made its appearance about the time that politics became a "profession." Others believe it can be traced to the age when women first began to concern themselves with "styles" in wearing apparel.

This author, being neither a humorist nor a prophet, is inclined to attribute the basic fear of criticism to that part of man's inherited nature which prompts him not only to take away his fellow man's goods and wares, but to justify his action by criticism of his fellow man's character. It is a well-known fact that a thief will criticise the man from whom he steals—that politicians seek office, not by displaying their own virtues and qualifications, but by attempting to besmirch their opponents.

The astute manufacturers of clothing have not been slow to capitalize on this basic fear of criticism, with which all mankind has been cursed. Every season the styles in many articles of wearing apparel change. Who establishes the styles? Certainly not the purchaser of clothing, but the manufacturer. Why does he change the styles so often? The answer is obvious. He changes the styles so he can sell more clothes.

For the same reason the manufacturers of automobiles (with a few rare and very sensible exceptions) change styles of models every season. No man wants to drive an automobile which is not of the latest style, although the older model may actually be the better car.

We have been describing the manner in which people behave under the influence of fear of criticism as applied to the small and petty things of life. Let us now examine human behavior when this fear affects people in connection with the more important events of human relationship. Take for example practically any person who has reached the age of "mental maturity" (from thirty-five to forty years of age, as a general average), and if you could read the secret thoughts of his mind, you would find a very decided disbelief in most of the fables taught by the majority of the dogmatists and theologians a few decades back.

Not often, however, will you find a person who has the courage to openly state his belief on this subject. Most people will, if pressed far enough, tell a lie rather than admit that they do not believe the stories associated with that form of religion which held people in bondage prior to the age of scientific discovery and education.

Why does the average person, even in this day of enlightenment, shy away from denying his belief in the fables which were the basis of most of the religions a few decades ago? The answer is, "because of the fear of criticism." Men and women have been burned at the stake for daring to express disbelief in ghosts. It is no wonder we have inherited a consciousness which makes us fear criticism. The time was, and not so far in the past, when criticism carried severe punishments—it still does in some countries.

The fear of criticism robs man of his initiative, destroys his power of imagination, limits his individuality, takes away his self-reliance, and does him damage in a hundred other ways.

Criticism is the one form of service, of which everyone has too much. Everyone has a stock of it which is handed out, gratis, whether called for or not. One's nearest relatives often are the worst offenders. It should be recognized as a crime (in reality it is a crime of the worst nature) for any parent to build inferiority complexes in the mind of a child, through unnecessary criticism. Employers who understand human nature get the best there is not by criticism, but by constructive suggestion. Parents may accomplish the same results with their children. Criticism will plant fear in the human heart, or resentment, but it will not build love or affection.

Symptoms of the Fear of Criticism

This fear is almost as universal as the fear of poverty, and its effects are just as fatal to personal achievement, mainly because this fear destroys initiative, and discourages the use of imagination.

The major symptoms of the fear are:

SELF-CONSCIOUSNESS: Generally expressed through nervousness, timidity in conversation and in meeting strangers, awkward movement of the hands and limbs, shifting of the eyes.

LACK OF POISE: Expressed through lack of voice control, nervousness in the presence of others, poor posture of body, poor memory.

PERSONALITY: Lacking in firmness of decision, personal charm, and ability to express opinions definitely. The habit of sidestepping issues instead of meeting them squarely. Agreeing with others without careful examination of their opinions.

INFERIORITY COMPLEX: The habit of expressing self-approval by word of mouth and by actions, as a means of covering up a feeling of inferiority. Using "big words" to impress others (often without knowing the real meaning of the words). Imitating others in dress, speech, and manners. Boasting of imaginary achievements. This sometimes gives a surface appearance of a feeling of superiority.

EXTRAVAGANCE: The habit of trying to "keep up with the Joneses," spending beyond one's income.

LACK OF INITIATIVE: Failure to embrace opportunities for self-advancement, fear to express opinions, lack of confidence in one's own ideas, giving evasive answers to questions asked by superiors, hesitancy of manner and speech, deceit in both words and deeds.

LACK OF AMBITION: Mental and physical laziness, lack of self-assertion, slowness in reaching decisions, easily influenced by others, the habit of criticising others behind their backs and flattering them to their faces, the habit of accepting defeat without protest, quitting an undertaking when opposed by others, suspicious of other people without cause, lacking in tactfulness of manner and speech, unwillingness to accept the blame for mistakes.

THE FEAR OF ILL HEALTH

This fear may be traced to both physical and social heredity. It is closely associated, as to its origin, with the causes of fear of Old Age and the fear of Death, because it leads one closely to the border of "terrible worlds" of which man knows not, but concerning which he has been taught some discomforting stories. The opinion is somewhat general, also, that certain unethical people engaged in the business of "selling health" have had not a little to do with keeping alive the fear of ill health.

In the main, man fears ill health because of the terrible pictures which have been planted in his mind of what may happen if death should overtake him. He also fears it because of the economic toll which it may claim.

A reputable physician estimated that 75% of all people who visit physicians for professional service are suffering with hypochondria (imaginary illness). It has been shown most convincingly that the fear of disease, even where there is not the slightest cause for fear, often produces the physical symptoms of the disease feared.

Powerful and mighty is the human mind! It builds or it destroys.

Playing upon this common weakness of fear of ill health, dispensers of patent medicines have reaped fortunes. This form of imposition upon credulous humanity became so prevalent some twenty years ago that *Colliers' Weekly Magazine* conducted a bitter campaign against some of the worst offenders in the patent medicine business.

During the "flu" epidemic which broke out during the world war, the mayor of New York City took drastic steps to check the damage which people were doing themselves through their inherent fear of ill health. He called in the newspaper men and said to them, "Gentlemen, I feel it necessary to ask you not to publish any *scare headlines* concerning the 'flu' epidemic. Unless you cooperate with me, we will have a situation which we cannot control." The newspapers quit publishing stories about the "flu," and within one month the epidemic had been successfully checked.

Through a series of experiments conducted some years ago, it was proved that people may be made ill by suggestion. We conducted this experiment by causing three acquaintances to visit the "victims," each of whom asked the question, "What ails you? You look terribly ill." The first questioner usually provoked a grin, and a nonchalant "Oh, nothing, I'm all right," from the victim. The second questioner usually was answered with the statement, "I don't know exactly, but I do feel badly." The third questioner was usually met with the frank admission that the victim was actually feeling ill.

There is overwhelming evidence that disease sometimes begins in the form of negative thought impulse. Such an impulse may be passed from one mind to another, by suggestion, or created by an individual in his own mind.

Doctors send patients into new climates for their health, because a change of "mental attitude" is necessary. The seed of fear of ill health lives in every human mind. Worry, fear, discouragement, disappointment in love and business affairs, cause this seed to germinate and grow. The recent business depression kept the doctors on the run, because every form of negative thinking may cause ill health.

Symptoms of the Fear of Ill Health

The symptoms of this almost universal fear are:

AUTO-SUGGESTION: The habit of negative use of self-suggestion by looking for, and expecting to find the symptoms of all kinds of disease. "Enjoying" imaginary illness and speaking of it as being real. The habit of trying all "fads" and "isms" recommended by others as having therapeutic value. Talking to others of operations, accidents, and other forms of illness. Experimenting with diets, physical exercises, reducing systems, without professional guidance. Trying home remedies, patent medicines, and "quack" remedies.

HYPOCHONDRIA: The habit of talking of illness, concentrating the mind upon disease, and expecting its appearance until a nervous break occurs. Nothing that comes in bottles can cure this condition. It is brought on by negative thinking and nothing but positive thought can effect a cure. Hypochondria (a medical term for imaginary disease) is said to do as much damage on occasion, as the disease one fears might do. Most so-called cases of "nerves" come from imaginary illness.

EXERCISE: Fear of ill health often interferes with proper physical exercise, and results in over-weight, by causing one to avoid outdoor life.

SUSCEPTIBILITY: Fear of ill health breaks down Nature's body resistance, and creates a favorable condition for any form of disease one may contact. The fear of ill health often is related to the fear of Poverty, especially in the case of the hypochondriac, who constantly worries about the possibility of having to pay doctor's bills, hospital bills, etc. This type of person spends much time preparing for sickness, talking about death, saving money for cemetery lots, and burial expenses, etc.

SELF-CODDLING: The habit of making a bid for sympathy, using imaginary illness as the lure. (People often resort to this trick to avoid work.) The habit of feigning illness to cover plain laziness, or to serve as an alibi for lack of ambition.

INTEMPERANCE: The habit of using alcohol or narcotics to destroy pains such as headaches, neuralgia, etc., instead of eliminating the cause.

THE FEAR OF LOSS OF LOVE

The original source of this inherent fear needs but little description, because it obviously grew out of man's polygamous habit of stealing his fellow man's mate, and his habit of taking liberties with her whenever he could.

Jealousy, and other similar forms of dementia praecox grow out of man's inherited fear of the loss of love of someone. This fear is the most painful of all the six basic fears. It probably plays more havoc with the body and mind than any of the other basic fears, as it often leads to permanent insanity.

Symptoms of the Fear of Loss of Love

The distinguishing symptoms of this fear are:

JEALOUSY: The habit of being suspicious of friends and loved ones without any reasonable evidence of sufficient grounds. (Jealousy is a form of dementia praecox which sometimes becomes violent without the slightest cause.) The habit of accusing wife or husband of infidelity without grounds. General suspicion of everyone, absolute faith in no one.

FAULT FINDING: The habit of finding fault with friends, relatives, business associates, and loved ones upon the slightest provocation, or without any cause whatsoever.

GAMBLING: The habit of gambling, stealing, cheating, and otherwise taking hazardous chances to provide money for loved ones, with the belief that love can be bought. The habit of spending beyond one's means, or incurring debts, to provide gifts for loved ones, with the object of making a favorable showing. Insomnia, nervousness, lack of persistence, weakness of will, lack of self-control, lack of self-reliance, bad temper.

THE FEAR OF OLD AGE

In the main, this fear grows out of two sources. First, the thought that old age may bring with it poverty. Secondly, and by far the most common source of origin, from false and cruel teachings of the past which have been too well mixed with "fire and brimstone," and other bogies cunningly designed to enslave man through fear.

In the basic fear of old age, man has two very sound reasons for his apprehension—one growing out of his distrust of his fellow man, who may seize whatever worldly goods he may possess, and the other arising from the terrible pictures of the world beyond, which were planted in his mind, through social heredity before he came into full possession of his mind.

The possibility of ill health, which is more common as people grow older, is also a contributing cause of this common fear of old age. Eroticism also enters into the cause of the fear of old age, as no man cherishes the thought of diminishing sex attraction.

The most common cause of fear of old age is associated with the possibility of poverty. "Poorhouse" is not a pretty word. It throws a chill into the mind of every person who faces the possibility of having to spend his declining years on a poor farm.

Another contributing cause of the fear of old age is the possibility of loss of freedom and independence, as old age may bring with it the loss of both physical and economic freedom.

Symptoms of the Fear of Old Age

The commonest symptoms of this fear are:

The tendency to slow down and develop an inferiority complex at the age of mental maturity, around the age of forty, falsely believing oneself to be "slipping" because of age. (The truth is that man's most useful years, mentally and spiritually, are those between forty and sixty.)

The habit of speaking apologetically of one's self as "being old" merely because one has reached the age of forty, or fifty, instead of reversing the rule and expressing gratitude for having reached the age of wisdom and understanding.

The habit of killing off initiative, imagination, and self-reliance by falsely believing one's self too old to exercise these qualities. The habit of the man or woman of forty dressing with the aim of trying to appear much younger, and affecting mannerisms of youth; thereby inspiring ridicule by both friends and strangers.

THE FEAR OF DEATH

To some this is the cruelest of all the basic fears. The reason is obvious. The terrible pangs of fear associated with the thought of death, in the majority of cases, may be charged directly to religious fanaticism. So-called "heathen" are less afraid of death than the more "civilized." For hundreds of millions of years man has been asking the still-unanswered questions, "whence" and "whither." Where did I come from, and where am I going?

During the darker ages of the past, the more cunning and crafty were not slow to offer the answer to these questions, for a price. Witness, now, the major source of origin of the fear of death.

"Come into my tent, embrace my faith, accept my dogmas, and I will give you a ticket that will admit you straightaway into heaven when you die," cries a leader of sectarianism. "Remain out of my tent," says the same leader, "and may the devil take you and burn you throughout eternity."

Eternity is a long time. Fire is a terrible thing. The thought of eternal punishment, with fire, not only causes man to fear death, it often causes him to lose his reason. It destroys interest in life and makes happiness impossible.

During my research, I reviewed a book entitled *A Catalogue of the Gods,* in which were listed the *30,000 gods* which man has worshiped. Think of it! Thirty thousand of them, represented by everything from a crawfish to a man. It is little wonder that men have become frightened at the approach of death.

While the religious leader may not be able to provide safe conduct into heaven, nor, by lack of such provision, allow the unfortunate to descend into hell, the possibility of the latter seems so terrible that the very thought of it lays hold of the imagination in such a realistic way that it paralyzes reason, and sets up the fear of death.

In truth, no man knows, and no man has ever known, what heaven or hell is like, nor does any man know if either place actually exists. This very lack of positive knowledge opens the door of the human mind to the charlatan so he may enter and control that mind with his stock of legerdemain and various brands of pious fraud and trickery.

The fear of death is not as common now as it was during the age when there were no great colleges and universities. Men of science have turned the spotlight of truth upon the world, and this truth is rapidly freeing men and women from this terrible fear of death. The young men and young women who attend the colleges and universities are not easily impressed by "fire" and "brimstone." Through the aid of biology, astronomy, geology, and other related sciences, the fears of the dark ages which gripped the minds of men and destroyed their reason have been dispelled.

Insane asylums are filled with men and women who have gone mad, because of the fear of death.

This fear is useless. Death will come, no matter what anyone may think about it. Accept it as a necessity, and pass the thought out of your mind. It must be a necessity, or it would not come to all. Perhaps it is not as bad as it has been pictured.

The entire world is made up of only two things, energy and matter. In elementary physics we learn that neither matter nor energy (the only two realities known to man) can be created or destroyed. Both matter and energy can be transformed, but neither can be destroyed.

Life is energy, if it is anything. If neither energy nor matter can be destroyed, of course life cannot be destroyed. Life, like other forms of energy, may be passed through various processes of transition, or change, but it cannot be destroyed. Death is mere transition.

If death is not mere change, or transition, then nothing comes after death except a long, eternal, peaceful sleep, and sleep is nothing to be feared. Thus you may wipe out, forever, the fear of Death.

Symptoms of the Fear of Death

The general symptoms of this fear are:

The habit of thinking about dying instead of making the most of life, due, generally, to lack of purpose, or lack of a suitable occupation. This fear is more prevalent among the aged, but sometimes the more youthful are victims of it. The greatest of all remedies for the fear of death is a burning desire for achievement, backed by useful service to others. A busy person seldom has time to think about dying. He finds life too thrilling to worry about death. Sometimes the fear of death is closely associated with the Fear of Poverty, where one's death would leave loved ones poverty-stricken. In other cases, the fear of death is caused by illness and the consequent breaking down of physical body resistance. The commonest causes of the fear of death are: ill health, poverty, lack of appropriate occupation, disappointment over love, insanity, religious fanaticism.

OLD MAN WORRY

Worry is a state of mind based upon fear. It works slowly, but persistently. It is insidious and subtle. Step by step it "digs itself in" until it paralyzes one's reasoning faculty, destroys self-confidence and initiative. Worry is a form of sustained fear caused by indecision, therefore it is a state of mind which can be controlled.

An unsettled mind is helpless. Indecision makes an unsettled mind. Most individuals lack the will-power to reach decisions promptly, and to stand by them after they have been made, even during normal business conditions. During periods of economic unrest (such as the world recently experienced), the individual is handicapped, not alone by his inherent nature to be slow at reaching decisions, but he is influenced by the indecision of others around him who have created a state of "mass indecision."

During the depression the whole atmosphere, all over the world, was filled with "Fearenza" and "Worryitis," the two mental disease germs which began to spread themselves after the Wall Street frenzy in 1929. There is only one known antidote for these germs; it is the habit of prompt and firm decision. Moreover, it is an antidote which every individual must apply for himself.

The six basic fears become translated into a state of worry, through indecision. Relieve yourself, forever of the fear of death, by reaching a decision to accept death as an inescapable event. Whip the fear of poverty by reaching a decision to get along with whatever wealth you can accumulate without worry. Put your foot upon the neck of the fear of criticism by reaching a decision not to worry about what other people think, do, or say. Eliminate the fear of old age by reaching a decision to accept it, not as a hand-icap, but as a great blessing which carries with it wisdom, self-control, and understanding not known to youth. Acquit yourself of the fear of ill health by the decision to forget symptoms. Master the fear of loss of love by reaching a decision to get along without love, if that is necessary.

Kill the habit of worry, in all its forms, by reaching a general, blanket decision that nothing which life has to offer is worth the price of worry. With this decision will come poise, peace of mind, and calmness of thought which will bring happiness.

A man whose mind is filled with fear not only destroys his own chances of intelligent action, but, he transmits these destructive vibrations to the minds of all who come into contact with him, and destroys, also, their chances.

Even a dog or a horse knows when its master lacks courage; moreover, a dog or a horse will pick up the vibrations of fear thrown off by its master, and behave accordingly. Lower down the line of intelligence in the animal kingdom, one finds this same capacity to pick up the vibrations of fear. A honey-bee immediately senses fear in the mind of a person—for reasons unknown, a bee will sting the person whose mind is releasing vibrations of fear, much more readily than it will molest the person whose mind registers no fear.

The vibrations of fear pass from one mind to another just as quickly and as surely as the sound of the human voice passes from the broadcasting station to the receiving set of a radio—and by the self-same medium.

Mental telepathy is a reality. Thoughts pass from one mind to another, voluntarily, whether or not this fact is recognized by either the person releasing the thoughts, or the persons who pick up those thoughts.

The person who gives expression, by word of mouth, to negative or destructive thoughts is practically certain to experience the results of those words in the form of a destructive "kick-back." The release of destructive thought impulses, alone, without the aid of words, produces also a "kick-back" in more ways than one. First of all, and perhaps most important to be remembered, the person who releases thoughts of a destructive nature must suffer damage through the breaking down of the faculty of creative imagination. Secondly, the presence in the mind of any destructive emotion develops a negative personality which repels people, and often converts them into antagonists. The third source of damage to the person who entertains or releases negative thoughts, lies in this significant fact—these thought-impulses are not only damaging to others, but they imbed themselves in the subconscious mind of the person releasing them, and there become a part of his character.

One is never through with a thought, merely by releasing it.

When a thought is released, it spreads in every direction, through the medium of the ether, but it also plants itself *permanently* in the subconscious mind of *the person releasing it.*

Your business in life is presumably to achieve success. To be successful, you must find peace of mind, acquire the material needs of life, and above all, attain happiness. All of these evidences of success begin in the form of thought impulses.

You may control your own mind; you have the power to feed it whatever thought impulses you choose. With this privilege goes also the responsibility of using it constructively. You are the master of your own earthly destiny just as surely as you have the power to control your own thoughts. You may influence, direct, and eventually control your own environment, making your life what you want it to be—or, you may neglect to exercise the privilege which is yours, to make your life to order, thus casting yourself upon the broad sea of "Circumstance" where you will be tossed hither and yon, like a chip on the waves of the ocean.

How to Protect Yourself Against Negative Influences

Excerpted from Think and Grow Rich

To protect yourself against negative influences, whether of your own making, or the result of the activities of negative people around you, recognize that you have a will-power, and put it into constant use, until it builds a wall of immunity against negative influences in your own mind.

Recognize the fact that you, and every other human being, are, by nature, lazy, indifferent, and susceptible to all suggestions which harmonize with your weaknesses.

Recognize that you are, by nature, susceptible to all the six basic fears, and set up habits for the purpose of counteracting all these fears.

Recognize that negative influences often work on you through your subconscious mind, therefore they are difficult to detect, and keep your mind closed against all people who depress or discourage you in any way.

Deliberately seek the company of people who influence you to think and act for yourself.

Do not expect troubles as they have a tendency not to disappoint.

Without doubt, the most common weakness of all human beings is the habit of leaving their minds open to the negative influence of other people. This weakness is all the more damaging, because most people do not recognize that they are cursed by it, and many who acknowledge it, neglect or refuse to correct the evil until it becomes an uncontrollable part of their daily habits.

To aid those who wish to see themselves as they really are, the following list of questions has been prepared. Read the questions and state your answers aloud, so you can hear your own voice. This will make it easier for you to be truthful with yourself.

If you answer all these questions truthfully, you know more about yourself than the majority of people. Study the questions carefully, come back to them once each week for several months, and be astounded at the amount of additional knowledge of great value to yourself, you will have gained by the simple method of answering the questions truthfully. If you are not certain concerning the answers to some of the questions, seek the counsel of those who know you well, especially those who have no motive in flattering you, and see yourself through their eyes. The experience will be astonishing.

Self-Analysis Test Questions

- Do you complain often of "feeling bad," and if so, what is the cause?
- Do you find fault with other people at the slightest provocation?
- Do you frequently make mistakes in your work, and if so, why?
- Are you sarcastic and offensive in your conversation?
- Do you deliberately avoid the association of anyone, and if so, why?
- Do you suffer frequently with indigestion? If so, what is the cause?
- Does life seem futile and the future hopeless to you? If so, why?
- Do you like your occupation? If not, why?

- Do you often feel self-pity, and if so why?
- Are you envious of those who excel you?
- To which do you devote most time, thinking of success, or of failure?
- Are you gaining or losing self-confidence as you grow older?
- Do you learn something of value from all mistakes? Are you permitting some relative or acquaintance to worry you? If so, why?
- Are you sometimes "in the clouds" and at other times in the depths of despondency?
- Who has the most inspiring influence upon you? What is the cause?
- Do you tolerate negative or discouraging influences which you can avoid?
- Are you careless of your personal appearance? If so, when and why?
- Have you learned how to "drown your troubles" by being too busy to be annoyed by them?
- Would you call yourself a "spineless weakling" if you permitted others to do your thinking for you?
- Do you neglect internal bathing until auto-intoxication makes you ill-tempered and irritable?
- How many preventable disturbances annoy you, and why do you tolerate them?
- Do you resort to liquor, narcotics, or cigarettes to "quiet your nerves"? If so, why do you not try will-power instead?
- Does anyone "nag" you, and if so, for what reason?
- Do you have a definite major purpose, and if so, what is it, and what plan have you for achieving it?
- Do you suffer from any of the Six Basic Fears? If so, which ones?

- Have you a method by which you can shield yourself against the negative influence of others?
- Do you make deliberate use of auto-suggestion to make your mind positive?
- Which do you value most, your material possessions, or your privilege of controlling your own thoughts?
- Are you easily influenced by others, against your own judgment?
- Has today added anything of value to your stock of knowledge or state of mind?
- Do you face squarely the circumstances which make you unhappy, or sidestep the responsibility?
- Do you analyze all mistakes and failures and try to profit by them or, do you take the attitude that this is not your duty?
- Can you name three of your most damaging weaknesses? What are you doing to correct them?
- Do you encourage other people to bring their worries to you for sympathy?
- Do you choose, from your daily experiences, lessons or influences which aid in your personal advancement?
- Does your presence have a negative influence on other people as a rule?
- What habits of other people annoy you most?
- Do you form your own opinions or permit yourself to be influenced by other people?
- Have you learned how to create a mental state of mind with which you can shield yourself against all discouraging influences?
- Does your occupation inspire you with faith and hope?
- Are you conscious of possessing spiritual forces of sufficient

power to enable you to keep your mind free from all forms of fear?

- Does your religion help you to keep your own mind positive?
- Do you feel it your duty to share other people's worries? If so, why?
- If you believe that "birds of a feather flock together" what have you learned about yourself by studying the friends whom you attract?
- What connection, if any, do you see between the people with whom you associate most closely, and any unhappiness you may experience?
- Could it be possible that some person whom you consider to be a friend is, in reality, your worst enemy, because of his negative influence on your mind?
- By what rules do you judge who is helpful and who is damaging to you?
- Are your intimate associates mentally superior or inferior to you?

How much time out of every twenty-four hours do you devote to:

a. your occupation
b. sleep
c. play and relaxation
d. acquiring useful knowledge
e. plain waste

Who among your acquaintances,

a. encourages you most
b. cautions you most

c. discourages you most

d. helps you most in other ways

- What is your greatest worry? Why do you tolerate it?
- When others offer you free, unsolicited advice, do you accept it without question, or analyze their motive?
- What, above all else, do you most desire? Do you intend to acquire it? Are you willing to subordinate all other desires for this one? How much time daily do you devote to acquiring it?
- Do you change your mind often? If so, why?
- Do you usually finish everything you begin?
- Are you easily impressed by other people's business or professional titles, college degrees, or wealth? Are you easily influenced by what other people think or say of you?
- Do you cater to people because of their social or financial status?
- Whom do you believe to be the greatest person living? In what respect is this person superior to yourself?
- How much time have you devoted to studying and answering these questions? (At least one day is necessary for the analysis and the answering of the entire list.)

You have absolute control over but one thing, and that is your thoughts. This is the most significant and inspiring of all facts known to man! It reflects man's Divine nature. This Divine prerogative is the sole means by which you may control your own destiny. If you fail to control your own mind, you may be sure you will control nothing else.

If you must be careless with your possessions, let it be in connection with material things. *Your mind is your spiritual estate!* Protect and use it with the care to which Divine Royalty is entitled. You were given a will-power for this purpose.

Unfortunately, there is no legal protection against those who, either by design or ignorance, poison the minds of others by negative suggestion. This form of destruction should be punishable by heavy legal penalties, because it may and often does destroy one's chances of acquiring material things which are protected by law.

Men with negative minds tried to convince Thomas A. Edison that he could not build a machine that would record and reproduce the human voice, "because" they said, "no one else had ever produced such a machine." Edison did not believe them. He knew that the mind could produce anything the mind could conceive and believe, and that knowledge was the thing that lifted the great Edison above the common herd.

Men with negative minds told F. W. Woolworth he would go "broke" trying to run a store on five and ten cent sales. He did not believe them. He knew that he could do anything, within reason, if he backed his plans with faith. Exercising his right to keep other men's negative suggestions out of his mind, he piled up a fortune of more than a hundred million dollars.

Men with negative minds told George Washington he could not hope to win against the vastly superior forces of the British, but he exercised his Divine right to believe, therefore this book was published under the protection of the Stars and Stripes, while the name of Lord Cornwallis has been all but forgotten.

Doubting Thomases scoffed scornfully when Henry Ford tried out his first crudely built automobile on the streets of Detroit. Some said the thing never would become practical. Others said no one would pay money for such a contraption. Ford said, "I'll belt the earth with dependable motor cars," and he did! His decision to trust his own judgment has already piled up a fortune far greater than the next five generations of his descendants can squander.

Mind control is the result of self-discipline and habit. You either control your mind or it controls you. There is no half-way compromise. The most practical of all methods for controlling the mind is the habit of keeping it busy with a definite purpose, backed by a definite plan. Study the record of any man who achieves noteworthy success, and you will observe that he has control over his own mind, moreover, that he exercises that control and directs it toward the attainment of definite objectives. Without this control, success is not possible.

Fifty-Seven Famous Alibis

Excerpted from Think and Grow Rich

BY OLD MAN "IF"

People who do not succeed have one distinguishing trait in common. They know *all the reasons for failure,* and have what they believe to be airtight alibis to explain away their own lack of achievement.

Some of these alibis are clever, and a few of them are justifiable by the facts. But alibis cannot be used for money. The world wants to know only one thing—have you achieved success?

A character analyst compiled a list of the most commonly used alibis. As you read the list, examine yourself carefully, and determine how many of these alibis, if any, are your own property. Remember, too, the philosophy presented in this book makes every one of these alibis obsolete.

IF I didn't have a wife and family . . .
IF I had enough "pull" . . .
IF I had money . . .
IF I had a good education . . .
IF I could get a job . . .
IF I had good health . . .
IF I only had time . . .
IF times were better . . .

IF other people understood me . . .

IF conditions around me were only different . . .

IF I could live my life over again . . .

IF I did not fear what "they" would say . . .

IF I had been given a chance . . .

IF I now had a chance . . .

IF other people didn't "have it in for me" . . .

IF nothing happens to stop me . . .

IF I were only younger . . .

IF I could only do what I want . . .

IF I had been born rich . . .

IF I could meet "the right people" . . .

IF I had the talent that some people have . . .

IF I dared assert myself . . .

IF I only had embraced past opportunities . . .

IF people didn't get on my nerves . . .

IF I didn't have to keep house and look after the children . . .

IF I could save some money . . .

IF the boss only appreciated me . . .

IF I only had somebody to help me . . .

IF my family understood me . . .

IF I lived in a big city . . .

IF I could just get started . . .

IF I were only free . . .

IF I had the personality of some people . . .

IF I were not so fat . . .

IF my talents were known . . .

IF I could just get a "break" . . .

IF I could only get out of debt . . .

IF I hadn't failed . . .

IF I only knew how . . .

IF everybody didn't oppose me . . .

IF I didn't have so many worries . . .

IF I could marry the right person . . .

IF people weren't so dumb . . .

IF my family were not so extravagant . . .

IF I were sure of myself . . .

IF luck were not against me . . .

IF I had not been born under the wrong star . . .

IF it were not true that "what is to be will be" . . .

IF I did not have to work so hard . . .

IF I hadn't lost my money . . .

IF I lived in a different neighborhood . . .

IF I didn't have a "past" . . .

IF I only had a business of my own . . .

IF other people would only listen to me . . .

IF * * * and this is the greatest of them all * * *

I had the courage to see myself as I really am, I would *find out what is wrong with me, and correct it,* then I might have a chance to profit by my mistakes and learn something from the experience of others, for I know that there is something wrong with me, or I would now be where *I would have been if* I had spent more time analyzing my weaknesses, and less time building alibis to cover them.

Building alibis with which to explain away failure is a national pastime. The habit is as old as the human race, and *is fatal to success!* Why do people cling to their pet alibis? The answer is obvious. They defend their alibis because they create them! A man's alibi is the child of his own imagination. It is human nature to defend one's own brainchild.

Building alibis is a deeply rooted habit. Habits are difficult to break, especially when they provide justification for something we do. Plato had this truth in mind when he said, "The first and best victory is to conquer self. To be conquered by self is, of all things, the most shameful and vile."

Another philosopher had the same thought in mind when he said, "It was a great surprise to me when I discovered that most of the ugliness I saw in others, was but a reflection of my own nature."

"It has always been a mystery to me," said Elbert Hubbard, "why people spend so much time deliberately fooling themselves by creating alibis to cover their weaknesses. If used differently, this same time would be sufficient to cure the weakness, then no alibis would be needed."

In parting, I would remind you that "Life is a checkerboard, and the player opposite you is time. If you hesitate before moving, or neglect to move promptly, your men will be wiped off the board by time. You are playing against a partner who will not tolerate indecision!"

Previously you may have had a logical excuse for not having forced Life to come through with whatever you asked, but that alibi is now obsolete, because you are in possession of the Master Key that unlocks the door to Life's bountiful riches.

The Master Key is intangible, but it is powerful! It is the privilege of creating, *in your own mind,* a burning desire for a definite form of riches. There is no penalty for the use of the Key, but there is a price you must pay if you do not use it. The price is failure. There is a reward of stupendous proportions if you put the Key to use. It is the satisfaction that comes to all who *conquer self and force Life to pay whatever is asked.*

The reward is worthy of your effort. Will you make the start and be convinced?

Self-Control

You can never become a great leader nor a person of influence in the cause of justice until you have developed great self-control.

Before you can be of great service to your fellow men in any capacity you must master the common human tendency of anger, intolerance and cynicism.

When you permit another person to make you angry you are allowing that person to dominate you and drag you down to his level.

To develop self-control you must make liberal and systematic use of the Golden Rule philosophy; you must acquire the habit of forgiving those who annoy and arouse you to anger.

Intolerance and selfishness make very poor bed-fellows for self-control. These qualities always clash when you try to house them together. One or the other must get out.

The first thing the shrewd lawyer usually does when he starts to cross-examine a witness is to make the witness angry and thereby cause him to lose his self-control.

Anger is a state of insanity!

The well-balanced person is a person who is slow at anger and who always remains cool and calculating in his procedure. He remains calm and deliberate under all conditions.

Such a person can succeed in all legitimate undertakings! To master conditions you must first master self! A person who exercises great self-control never slanders his neighbor. His tendency is to build up and not to tear down. Are you a person of self-control? If not, why do you not develop this great virtue?

A Definite Aim in Life

Careful analysis of more than 10,000 people disclosed a remarkable weakness which 95 percent of them had in common—they had no definite aim in life!

Another notable fact disclosed by these ten thousand analyses was that those who were financially successful had a definite aim and a well formulated plan for achieving it.

As far as this writer has ever been able to ascertain, there are two steps which every successful person must take: first, he must formulate a very definite aim as an objective for which to strive, and secondly, he must reduce that aim to a concrete plan.

If you wish to witness a miracle which will equal anything that happened during biblical days, write out on paper a clear, concise statement of your aim in life, then memorize that which you have written.

Each night, just before you go to sleep; repeat your definite aim aloud several times, then, during the day, do everything within your power to further the achievement of that aim. In a short time the forces of the whole universe will seem to conspire to the end that you may realize your aim. Try it, doubting brother, try it.

MORE ON A DEFINITE AIM FROM
THINK AND GROW RICH

Every human being who reaches the age of understanding of the purpose of money wishes for it. *Wishing* **will not bring riches. But** *desiring* **riches with a state of mind that becomes an obsession, then planning definite ways and means to acquire riches, and backing those plans with persistence which** *does not recognize failure,* **will bring riches.**

The method by which desire for riches can be transmuted into its financial equivalent consists of six definite, practical steps, viz:

FIRST: **Fix in your mind the exact amount of money you desire**. It is not sufficient merely to say, "I want plenty of money." Be definite as to the amount. (There is a psychological reason for definiteness which will be described in a subsequent chapter.)

SECOND: **Determine exactly what you intend to give in return for the money you desire.** (There is no such reality as "something for nothing.")

THIRD: **Establish a definite date when you intend to** *possess* **the money you desire.**

FOURTH: **Create a definite plan for carrying out your desire,** and begin *at once,* whether you are ready or not, to put this plan into *action.*

FIFTH: **Write out a clear, concise statement** of the amount of money you intend to acquire, name the time limit for its acquisition, state what you intend to give in return for the money, and describe clearly the plan through which you intend to accumulate it.

SIXTH: **Read your written statement aloud, twice daily,** once just before retiring at night, and once after arising in the morning. As you read—see and feel and believe yourself already in possession of the money.

It is important that you follow the instructions described in these six steps. It is especially important that you observe and follow the instructions in the sixth paragraph. You may complain that it is impossible for you to "see yourself in possession of money" before you actually have it. Here is where a burning desire will come to your aid. If you truly desire money so keenly that your desire is an obsession, you will have no difficulty in convincing yourself that you will acquire it. The object is to want money, and to become so determined to have it that you convince yourself you will have it.

Only those who become "money conscious" ever accumulate great riches. "Money consciousness" means that the mind has become so thoroughly saturated with the desire for money, that one can see one's self already in possession of it.

Enthusiasm and the Golden Rule

Excerpted from The Law of Success

ENTHUSIASM

"You Can Do It If You Believe You Can!"

Enthusiasm is a state of mind that inspires and arouses one to put action into the task at hand. It does more than this—it is contagious, and vitally affects not only the enthusiast, but all with whom he comes in contact.

Enthusiasm bears the same relationship to a human being that steam does to the locomotive—it is the vital moving force that impels action. The greatest leaders of men are those who know how to inspire enthusiasm in their followers. Enthusiasm is the most important factor entering into salesmanship. It is, by far, the most vital factor that enters into public speaking. The finest sermon ever delivered would fall upon deaf ears if it were not backed with enthusiasm by the speaker.

How Enthusiasm Will Affect You

Mix enthusiasm with your work and it will not seem hard or monotonous. Enthusiasm will so energize your entire body that you can get along with less than half the usual amount of sleep and at the same time it will enable you to perform from two to three times as much work as you usually perform in a given period, without fatigue.

For many years I have done most of my writing at night. One night, while I was enthusiastically at work over my typewriter, I looked out of the window of my study, just across the square from the Metropolitan tower, in New York City, and saw what seemed to be the most peculiar reflection of the moon on the tower. It was of a silvery gray shade, such as I had never seen before. Upon closer inspection I found that the reflection was that of the early morning sun and not that of the moon. It was daylight! I had been at work all night, but I was so engrossed in my work that the night had passed as though it were but an hour. I worked at my task all that day and all the following night without stopping, except for a small amount of light food.

Two nights and one day without sleep, and with but little food, without the slightest evidence of fatigue, would not have been possible had I not kept my body energized with enthusiasm over the work at hand.

Enthusiasm is not merely a figure of speech; it is a vital force that you can harness and use with profit. Without it you would resemble an electric battery without electricity.

Enthusiasm is the vital force with which you recharge your body and develop a dynamic personality. Some people are blessed with natural enthusiasm, while others must acquire it. The procedure through which it may be developed is simple. It begins by the doing of the work or rendering of the service which one likes best. If you should be so situated that you cannot conveniently engage in the work which you like best, for the time being, then you can proceed along another line very effectively by adopting a definite chief aim that contemplates your engaging in that particular work at some future time.

Lack of capital and many other circumstances over which you have no immediate control may force you to engage in work which you do not like, but no one can stop you from determining in your own mind what your definite chief aim in life shall be, nor can anyone stop you from planning ways and means for translating this aim into reality, nor can anyone stop you from mixing enthusiasm with your plans.

Happiness, the final object of all human effort, is a state of mind that can be maintained only through the hope of future achievement. Happiness lies always in the future and never in the past. The happy person is the one who dreams of heights of achievement that are yet unattained. The home you intend to own, the money you intend to earn and place in the bank, the trip you intend to take when you can afford it, the position in life you intend to fill when you have prepared yourself, and the preparation, itself—these are the things that produce happiness. Likewise, these are the materials out of which your definite chief aim is formed; these are the things over which you may become enthusiastic, no matter what your present station in life may be.

More than twenty years ago I became enthusiastic over an idea. When the idea first took form in my mind I was unprepared to take even the first step toward its transformation into reality. But I nursed it in my mind—I became enthusiastic over it as I looked ahead, in my imagination, and saw the time when I would be prepared to make it a reality.

The idea was this: I wanted to become the editor of a magazine, based upon the Golden Rule, through which I could inspire people to keep up courage and deal with one another squarely.

Finally my chance came! and, on armistice day, 1918, I wrote the first editorial for what was to become the material realization of a hope that had lain dormant in my mind for nearly a score of years.

With enthusiasm I poured into that editorial the emotions which I had been developing in my heart over a period of more than twenty years. My dream had come true. My editorship of a national magazine had become a reality.

As I have stated, this editorial was written with enthusiasm. I took it to a man of my acquaintance and with enthusiasm I read it to him. The editorial ended in these words: "At last my twenty-year-old dream is about to come true. It takes money, and a lot of it, to publish a national magazine, and I haven't the slightest idea where I am going to get this essential factor, but this is worrying me not at all because I know I am going to get it somewhere!" As I wrote those lines, I mixed enthusiasm and faith with them.

I had hardly finished reading this editorial when the man to whom I read it—the first and only person to whom I had shown it—said:

"I can tell you where you are going to get the money, for I am going to supply it."

And he did!

Yes, enthusiasm is a vital force; so vital, in fact, that no man who has it highly developed can begin even to approximate his power of achievement.

I wish to repeat and to emphasize the fact that you may develop enthusiasm over your definite chief aim in life, no matter whether you are in position to achieve that purpose at this time or not. You may be a long way from realization of your definite chief aim, but if you will kindle the fire of enthusiasm in your heart, and keep it burning, before very long the obstacles that now stand in the way of your attainment of that purpose will melt away as if by the force of magic, and you will find yourself in possession of power that you did not know you possessed.

How Your Enthusiasm Will Affect Others

We come, now, to the discussion of one of the most important subjects, namely, suggestion.

Suggestion is the principle through which your words and

your acts and even your state of mind influence others. If you now understand and accept the principle of telepathy (the communication of thought from one mind to another without the aid of signs, symbols, or sounds) as a reality, you of course understand why enthusiasm is contagious, and why it influences all within its radius.

When your own mind is vibrating at a high rate, because it has been stimulated with enthusiasm, that vibration registers in the minds of all within its radius, and especially in the minds of those with whom you come in close contact. When a public speaker "senses" the feeling that his audience is "*en rapport*" with him he merely recognizes the fact that his own enthusiasm has influenced the minds of his listeners until their minds are vibrating in harmony with his own.

When the salesman "senses" the fact that the "psychological" moment for closing a sale has arrived, he merely feels the effect of his own enthusiasm as it influences the mind of his prospective buyer and places that mind "*en rapport*" (in harmony) with his own.

The subject of suggestion constitutes so vitally an important part of this lesson, and of this entire course, that I will now proceed to describe the three mediums through which it usually operates; namely, what you say, what you do and what you think!

When you are enthusiastic over the goods you are selling or the services you are offering, or the speech you are delivering, your state of mind becomes obvious to all who hear you, by the tone of your voice. Whether you have ever thought of it in this way or not, it is the tone in which you make a statement, more than it is the statement itself, that carries conviction or fails to convince. No mere combination of words can ever take the place of a deep belief in a statement that is expressed with burning enthusiasm. Words are but devitalized sounds unless colored with feeling that is born of enthusiasm.

Here the printed word fails me, for I can never express with mere type and paper the difference between words that fall from unemotional lips, without the fire of enthusiasm back of them, and those which seem to pour forth from a heart that is bursting with eagerness for expression. The difference is there, however.

Thus, what you say, and the way in which you say it, conveys a meaning that may be just the opposite to what is intended. This accounts for many a failure by the salesman who presents his arguments in words which seem logical enough, but lack the coloring that can come only from enthusiasm that is born of sincerity and belief in the goods he is trying to sell. His words said one thing, but the tone of his voice suggested something entirely different; therefore, no sale was made.

That which you say is an important factor in the operation of the principle of suggestion, but not nearly so important as that which you do. Your acts will count for more than your words, and woe unto you if the two fail to harmonize.

Your thoughts constitute the most important of the three ways in which you apply the principle of suggestion, for the reason that they control the tone of your words and, to some extent at least, your actions. If your thoughts and your actions and your words harmonize, you are bound to influence those with whom you come in contact, more or less toward your way of thinking.

The Golden Rule

Do unto others as you would have them do unto you!

We have heard that injunction expressed thousands of times, yet how many of us understand the law upon which it is based? To make this injunction somewhat clearer it might be well to state it more in detail, about as follows:

Do unto others as you would have them do unto you, bearing in mind the fact that human nature has a tendency to retaliate in kind.

Confucius must have had in mind the law of retaliation when he stated the Golden Rule philosophy in about this way:

Do not unto others that which you would not have them do unto you.

And he might well have added an explanation to the effect that the reason for his injunction was based upon the common tendency of man to retaliate in kind.

Those who do not understand the law upon which the Golden Rule is based are inclined to argue that it will not work, for the reason that men are inclined toward the principle of exacting "an eye for an eye and a tooth for a tooth," which is nothing more nor less than the law of retaliation. If they would go a step further in their reasoning they would understand that they are looking at the negative effects of this law, and that the selfsame law is capable of producing positive effects as well.

In other words, if you would not have your own eye plucked out, then insure against this misfortune by refraining from plucking out the other fellow's eye. Go a step further and render the other fellow an act of kindly, helpful service, and through the operation of this same law of retaliation he will render you a similar service.

And, if he should fail to reciprocate your kindness—what then?

You have profited, nevertheless, because of the effect of your act on your own sub-conscious mind!

Thus by indulging in acts of kindness and applying, always, the Golden Rule philosophy, you are sure of benefit from one source and at the same time you have a pretty fair chance of profiting from another source.

It might happen that you would base all of your acts toward others on the Golden Rule without enjoying any direct reciprocation for a long period of time, and it might so happen that those to whom you rendered those acts of kindness would never reciprocate, but meantime you have been adding vitality to your own character and sooner or later this positive character which you have been building will begin to assert itself and you will discover that you have been receiving compound interest on compound interest in return for those acts of kindness which appeared to have been wasted on those who neither appreciated nor reciprocated them.

Remember that your reputation is made by others, but your character is made by you!

You want your reputation to be a favorable one, but you cannot be sure that it will be for the reason that it is something that exists outside of your own control, in the minds of others. It is what others believe you to be. With your character it is different. Your character is that which you are, as the results of your thoughts and deeds. You control it. You can make it weak, good, or bad. When you are satisfied and know in your mind that your character is above reproach you need not worry about your reputation, for it is as impossible for your character to be destroyed or damaged by anyone except yourself as it is to destroy matter or energy.

It was this truth that Emerson had in mind when he said: "A political victory, a rise of rents, the recovery of your sick or the return of your absent friend, or some other quite external event raises your spirits, and you think your days are prepared for you. Do not believe it. It can never be so. Nothing can bring you peace but yourself. Nothing can bring you peace but the triumph of principles."

One reason for being just toward others is the fact that such action may cause them to reciprocate, in kind, but a better reason is the fact that kindness and justice toward others develop positive character in all who indulge in these acts.

You may withhold from me the reward to which I am entitled for rendering you helpful service, but no one can deprive me of the benefit I will derive from the rendering of that service in so far as it adds to my own character.

EMMET FOX

The Golden Key

Contents

Introduction

Each of the chapters in this book is short, and yet this small publication contains huge ideas that have gone on to change millions of lives.

Emmet Fox, the author of this volume, was a hugely popular and influential leader of what is called the New Thought philosophy, a transcendental-based thought system that was created in the late nineteenth century, and gained steam in the early twentieth. Born in 1886 in County Cork, Ireland, Fox discovered New Thought in England and eventually was ordained as a minister through Divine Science, one of the early New Thought organizations, along with Unity and Religious Science (now Centers for Spiritual Living). All three of those organizations are still around today.

Fox eventually moved to the United States and became the minister of a Divine Science spiritual center in New York City. His charisma, brilliance, and common sense quickly won him large crowds, and soon his talks moved to famed Carnegie Hall, with weekly attendance in the thousands.

His teachings struck a nerve, and his books became top sellers; his work became a key influence in New Thought, as well as the burgeoning Alcoholics Anonymous movement. Fox was able to synthesize ideas into practical application. He was also able to take traditional teachings, most often from the Christian Bible, and explain them in a way that made them accessible, helpful, and inspiring. Not only have his books never gone out of print, they've gone on to become spiritual classics that continue to reach new readers in every generation.

Fox's most widespread work is undoubtedly *The Golden Key*. *The Golden Key* began its life as a series of dozens of short pamphlets. These were originally on sale at his standing-room-only lectures, as well as through mail order. For spiritual seekers, these little pamphlets were like powerful mental vitamins that could reframe and expand the reader's thinking and perspective in just a couple of minutes. Some were only a few paragraphs long, others a bit longer—but all contained Fox's take on time-honored principles in his trademark style: to-the-point, friendly, comforting, challenging, motivational. Fox knew that simple ideas were the ones that could bring the biggest and longest-lasting changes.

But it was specifically this one pamphlet—*The Golden Key*—that captured the imagination of millions. It is referenced in countless books, taught in countless churches and spiritual organizations, and has helped countless people overcome challenges and experience a greater, deeper, richer life.

What is the Golden Key? As you'll see in the following pages, the Golden Key is essentially focusing one's thoughts on God rather than on one's problems. We all can choose *what* we think about and *how* we direct our thoughts, and Fox explains that what we focus on directly influences our reality. Focus on the negative, and you'll no doubt experience more negativity. However, Fox shows, when we focus on the good, we tend to see more good, experience more good, and attract more good. He expands on this idea, and shows how life-changing this concept can be. In approximately a thousand words, Fox teaches a life-changing principle that can—and has for millions—change literally everything in your life. That's how potent a teacher Fox is: he can tell you more in a thousand perfectly chosen words than many authors can over the course of hundreds of pages.

Also included in this volume are several other powerful and popular pamphlets by Fox. Many of these have also reached millions of people and continue to inspire readers of all walks of life and all ages around the world.

You can read the included pamphlets in any order you want. However, my recommendation is to start with *The Golden Key*. Read it over and over again, perhaps when you wake up and right before bed, every day for a week (or a month, or a year). Memorize it, embody it, use it, apply it. When anything happens in your life, apply the Golden Key to it as best you can. Since, as Fox notes, you are responsible for your own life, use and adapt these ideas to infuse it with as much positivity as possible. After you experience the Golden Key, move on to the next one, and then the next.

Even though this volume is small, it has the potential to bring unlimited inspiration to you. It's small enough to remember, but big enough to move mountains.

What mountains do you need moved in your life? Turn the page, and start the process . . .

—*Joel Fotinos*

Foreword

I have compressed this booklet into six pages. Had it been possible I would have reduced it to six lines. It is not intended to be an instructional treatise, but a practical recipe for getting out of trouble. Study and research are well in their own time and place, but no amount of either will get you out of a concrete difficulty. Nothing but practical work in your own consciousness will do that. The mistake made by many people, when things go wrong, is to skim through book after book, without getting anywhere.

Read the Golden Key several times. DO exactly what it says, and if you are persistent enough, you will overcome any difficulty.

—Emmet Fox

The Golden Key

Scientific prayer will enable you, sooner or later, to get yourself, or anyone else, out of any difficulty on the face of the earth. It is the Golden Key to harmony and happiness.

To those who have no acquaintance with the mightiest power in existence, this may appear to be a rash claim, but it needs only a fair trial to prove that, without a shadow of doubt, it is a just one. You need take no one's word for it, and you should not. Simply try it for yourself and see.

God is omnipotent, and man is His image and likeness and has dominion over all things. This is the inspired teaching, and it is intended to be taken literally, at its face value. Man means every man, and so the ability to draw on this power is not the special prerogative of the Mystic or the Saint, as is so often supposed, or even of the highly-trained practitioner. Whoever you are, wherever you may be, the Golden Key to harmony is in your hand now. This is because in scientific prayer it is God who works, and not you, and so your particular limitations or weaknesses are of no account in the process. You are only the channel through which the Divine action takes place, and your treatment will really be just the getting of yourself out of the way. Beginners often get startling results at the first time of trying, for all that is absolutely essential is to have an open mind and sufficient faith to try the experiment. Apart from that, you may hold any views on religion, or none.

As for the actual method of working, like all fundamental things, it is simplicity itself.

All that you have to do is this: **Stop thinking about the difficulty, whatever it is, and think about God instead.** This is the complete rule, and if only you will do this, the trouble, whatever it is, will presently disappear. It makes no difference what kind of trouble it is. It may be a big thing or a little thing; it may concern health, finance, a lawsuit, a quarrel, an accident, or anything else conceivable; but whatever it is, just stop thinking about it, and think of God instead—that is all you have to do.

The thing could not be simpler, could it? God Himself could scarcely have made it simpler, and yet it never fails to work when given a fair trial.

Do not try to form a picture of God, which is, of course, impossible. Work by rehearsing anything or everything that you know about God. God is Wisdom, Truth, inconceivable Love. God is present everywhere; has infinite power; knows everything; and so on. It matters not how well you may think you understand these things; go over them repeatedly.

But you must stop thinking of the trouble, whatever it is. The rule is to think about God, and if you are thinking about your difficulty you are not thinking about God. To be continually glancing over your shoulder, as it were, in order to see how matters are progressing, is fatal, because that is thinking of the trouble, and you must think of God, and of nothing else.

Your object is to drive the thought of the difficulty right out of your consciousness, for a few moments at least, substituting for it the thought of God. This is the crux of the whole thing. If you can become so absorbed in this consideration of the spiritual world that you really forget for a while all about the trouble concerning which you began to pray, you will presently find that you are safely and comfortably out of your difficulty—that your demonstration is made.

In order to "Golden Key" a troublesome person or a difficult situation, think, "Now I am going to 'Golden Key' John, or Mary, or that threatened danger"; then proceed to drive all thought of John, or Mary, or the danger right out of your mind, replacing it by the thought of God.

By working in this way about a person, you are not seeking to influence his conduct in any way, except that you prevent him from injuring or annoying you and you do him nothing but good. Thereafter he is certain to be in some degree a better, wiser, and more spiritual person, just because you have "Golden Keyed" him. A pending lawsuit or other difficulty would probably fade out harmlessly without coming to a crisis, justice being done to all parties concerned.

If you find that you can do this very quickly, you may repeat the operation several times a day with intervals between. Be sure, however, each time you have done it, that you drop all thought of the matter until the next time. This is important.

We have said that the Golden Key is simple, and so it is, but, of course, it is not always easy to turn. If you are very frightened or worried it may be difficult, at first, to get your thoughts away from material things. But by constantly repeating some statement of absolute Truth that appeals to you, such as *There is no power but God*, or *I am the child of God, filled and surrounded by the perfect peace of God*, or *God is Love*, or *God is guiding me now*, or, perhaps best and simplest of all, just *God is with me*—however mechanical or dead it may seem at first—you will soon find that the treatment has begun to "take" and that your mind is clearing. Do not struggle violently; be quiet but insistent. Each time that you find your attention wandering, just switch it straight back to God.

Do not try to think out in advance what the solution of your difficulty will probably turn out to be. This is technically called "outlining" and will only delay the demonstration. Leave the question of ways and means strictly to God. You want to get out of your difficulty—that is sufficient. You do your half, and God will never fail to do His.

Whosoever shall call upon the name of the Lord shall be saved.

The Mental Equivalent

This booklet is the substance of two lectures delivered by Emmet Fox at Unity School of Christianity.

We are all supremely interested in one subject. There is one thing that means more to us than all the other things in the world put together, and that is our search for God and the understanding of His nature. The aim of the metaphysical movement is to teach the practice of the presence of God.

We practice the presence of God by seeing Him everywhere, in all things and in all people, despite any appearances to the contrary. As we look about the world with the eyes of the flesh, we see inharmony, fear, and all sorts of difficulties; but our leader Jesus Christ taught us, saying, "Judge not according to appearance, but judge righteous judgment." So when we see the appearance of evil we look through it to the truth that lies back of it. As soon as we see this truth, and see it spiritually, the appearance changes, because this is a mental world. Now most people do not know this: they think it is a material world, and that is why humanity has so many problems. After nineteen centuries of formal Christianity the world is passing through desperate difficulties. But we know the Truth; we do not judge by appearances. We know that we live in a mental world, and to know that is the key to life.

If a child could be taught only one thing, it should be taught that this is a mental world. I would let all the other things go and teach him that.

Whatever enters into your life is but the material expression of some belief in your own mind. The kind of body you have, the kind of home you have, the kind of work you do, the kind of people you meet, are all conditioned by and correspond to the mental concepts you are holding. The Bible teaches that from beginning to end. I am putting it in the language of metaphysics; the Bible gives it in the language of religion, but it is the same Truth.

About twenty years ago I coined the phrase "mental equivalent." And now I want to say that for anything that you want in your life—a healthy body, a satisfactory vocation, friends, opportunities, and above all the understanding of God—you must furnish a mental equivalent. Supply yourself with a mental equivalent, and the thing must come to you. Without a mental equivalent it cannot come. Now as to the things in your life that you would like to be rid of (everyone has such things in his life). Perhaps bodily difficulties or faults of character are the most important. We all have habits of thought and action, and we all have business, family, and personal conditions we would like to be rid of. If we rid our minds of the mental equivalent of them, they must go.

Everything that you see or feel on the material plane, whether it is your body, your home, your business, or your city, is but the expression in the concrete of a mental equivalent held by you. Everything in your city is the embodiment of mental equivalents held by the citizens. Everything in your country is the embodiment of mental equivalents held by the people of the country; and the state of the world embodies the mental equivalent of the two thousand million people who make up the world.

What about war? That is the physical expression of a mental equivalent held by the human race. The human race has believed in the old bogey of fear. It has believed that you can enrich yourself by taking something belonging to someone else. It has believed in death. It has believed in lack. It has believed that aggression pays and that helping yourself to other people's things is a good policy. We have all believed this in some degree. The natural result of this has been to precipitate in the outer a picture of war, death, suffering, and so on. Because humanity had the mental equivalent of war the war came.

Today the world is beginning to get the mental equivalent of peace, and that is why peace will come. A new world will come. The new world will be worth living in. In the great new world that is going to come a little later on—and it will come sooner than some people think—there will be peace, harmony, and understanding between man and man and between nation and nation; but *always the thing you see in the outer is the precipitation on the physical plane of a mental equivalent held by one or more people.*

Now of course I borrowed this expression "mental equivalent" from physics and chemistry. We speak of the mechanical equivalent of heat, for example, and engineers constantly have to work out the equivalent of one kind of energy in another kind of energy. They have to discover how much electricity they will need to do certain mechanical work, such as driving a compressor. They have to find out how much coal will be needed to produce so much electricity, and so on. In like manner *there is a mental equivalent of every object or occurrence on the physical plane.*

The secret of successful living is to build up the mental equivalent that you want; and to get rid of, to expunge, the mental equivalent that you do not want.

Suppose you have rheumatism. I have friends in London who have it all the time; in fact, rheumatism used to be called the national British disease. Some people there have it beginning in October and lasting until March; others only have it until Christmas;

others do not get it before Christmas and then have it until February. Of two men living in the same town, doing the same work, eating the same food, drinking the same water, why does one have to have rheumatism from October until February and the other does not have it at all or has it at a different time? Why? Because they have furnished the mental equivalent for what they get. Why is a quarrelsome person always in trouble? He makes New York too hot to hold him, so he goes to Chicago. He thinks he will like it in Chicago; but pretty soon he has enemies in Chicago, so he goes down to Kansas City. He has heard there are nice people there. But soon he is in trouble again. Why? He has what we call a quarrelsome disposition. He has the mental equivalent of strife.

There is another man, and wherever he goes there is peace. If there is a quarrelsome family and he visits them, there is peace while he is there. He has the mental equivalent of peace and true divine love.

So the key to life is to build in the mental equivalents of what you want and to expunge the equivalents of what you do not want. How do you do it? You build in the mental equivalents by thinking quietly, constantly, and persistently of the kind of thing you want, and by thinking that has two qualities: *clearness* or definiteness, and *interest*. If you want to build anything into your life—if you want to bring health, right activity, your true place, inspiration; if you want to bring right companionship, and above all if you want understanding of God—form a mental equivalent of the thing which you want by thinking about it a great deal, by thinking clearly and with interest. Remember *clarity* and *interest;* those are the two poles.

Universal Polarity

The law of polarity is of course a cosmic law. Everything is produced by two other things. Anything that is ever produced anywhere in the universe is produced by two other things. That is the law of polarity. In the organic world we see it as parenthood. In the inorganic world, the world of physics and chemistry, we see it as the protons and electrons. That is how the material universe is built up; it always takes two things to produce a third. And that is the real ultimate meaning back of the Trinity.

There were Trinitarian doctrines before the time of Christ. Thy had trinities in ancient Egypt and India and in Chaldea and Babylonia—always there is the trinity: father, mother, child; activity, material, production. Go where you like, seek where you will, you find the Trinity.

In the building up of thought the two poles are clarity of thought and warmth of feeling; the knowledge and the feeling. Ninety-nine times in a hundred the reason why metaphysical students do not demonstrate is that they lack the feeling in their treatments. They speak the Truth, oh, yes! "I am divine Spirit. I am one with God." But they do not feel it. The second pole is missing. When they talk about their troubles they are full of feeling, but when they speak of Truth they are about as cold as a dead fish; and I cannot think of anything chillier than a cold fish unless it is a metaphysician who has lost his contact with God. They say, "I am divine Spirit," and they say it with no feeling; but when they say, "I have a terrible pain!" it is loaded with feeling, and so the pain they get and the pain they keep.

A man is out of work and he says: "God is my infinite supply. Man is always in his true place." It is said perfunctorily, with no feeling. But if someone asks him whether he has found work, he says: "I have been out of work two years. I wrote letters. I went after that job, but they were prejudiced against me. They wouldn't give me a chance." As soon as he gets on the negative side, the feeling comes in, and he demonstrates that—he remains unemployed. To think clearly and with feeling leads to demonstration, because you have then built a *mental equivalent*.

Think of the conditions you want to produce. If you want to be healthy, happy, prosperous, doing a constructive work, having a continuous understanding of God, you do not picture it necessarily, but you think it, feel it, and get interested in it. What we call "feeling" in connection with thought is really interest. Feeling is not excitement. Did you ever hear of anything coming from excitement except apoplexy? True "feeling" in thought is *interest*.

You cannot show me any man or woman who is successful in his field, from president down to shoeblack, who is not interested in his work; nor can you show me any man who has his heart in his work who is not successful. The most successful shoeblack you have in town here is vitally interested in his work. He has his heart in it. He did such good work that I gave him an extra tip when he finished polishing my shoes, but no money could really pay him for his work. He was so tickled as he did his work, he loved it so much, that I did not really pay him. He paid himself. He enjoyed it. And he had a line of people waiting for him.

You build a mental equivalent for what you want by getting interested in it. That is the way you create feeling. If you want health, get interested in health. If you want the right place, get interested in service, doing something that is really serving your fellow man.

The reason people do not get ahead in business is that they try to think up schemes to get their fellow men's money instead of thinking up opportunities for service. The successful man gets interested in what he wants to do, and gets rid of things he is not interested in.

How are you going to expunge the wrong mental equivalents? Suppose you have a mental equivalent of resentment, or unemployment, or criticism, or not understanding God. When somebody talks about God, it does not interest you much, you get sleepy or bored. Perhaps you do not get along with people—not that you quarrel with them, but they quarrel with you—the quarrel happens! What is to be done?

The only way to expunge a wrong mental equivalent is to supply the opposite. Think the right thing. The right thought automatically expunges the wrong thought. If you say: "I am not going to think resentment any more. I don't believe in it. There is nothing to it. I am not going to think of it any more," what are you thinking about except resentment? You are still thinking resentment all the time and strengthening the mental equivalent of resentment. Forget it! Think of health and bodily ease and peace and harmony and speak the word for it. Then you are building up a mental equivalent of health. If you want your true place—if your problem is unemployment, no job, the wrong job, or a job you do not like—if you say, "I am not going to think unemployment any more," you are wrong. That is thinking "unemployment," is it not? Think "true place."

If I say to you, "Don't think of the Statue of Liberty in New York," you know what you are thinking about. You are not thinking of anything except the Statue of Liberty. There she is, complete with torch in her hand! I said, "Don't think of her," but you do.

Now I am going to say that some time ago I visited, near Springfield, Illinois, a perfect reproduction of the village of New Salem as it was in the days of Abraham Lincoln. Even the log cabin is furnished as it was in his day. The National Park Commission has done it all.

Now you have forgotten the Statue of Liberty for a few seconds, haven't you? You have been thinking of New Salem. I gave you a different idea. That is the key to the management of your mind, the management of your thinking, and therefore the key to the management of your destiny.

Do not dwell on negative things but replace them, supplant them, with the right, constructive things. The law of mind is that you can only get rid of one thought by substituting another. If a carpenter drives a nail into a wooden wall or into a beam, there it is. Now if he takes a second nail and drives it against the first, the first is driven out and falls on the floor and the second one takes the place of the first one. That is what happens in the mind when you substitute one image for another. For everything in life there has to be a mental equivalent.

If you will start in this very day and refuse to think of your mistakes—and of course that includes the mistakes of other people—if you will cease to think of mistakes and hold the right concepts instead, cease to think fear and think of divine love instead, cease to think lack and think prosperity and the presence of God's abundance instead—and then if you will think as clearly as possible and get *interested;* you will be building a mental equivalent of happiness and prosperity.

If your thought is very vague, you do not build a mental equivalent. If your thought is lacking in interest, you do not build a mental equivalent. So make your thoughts as clear and definite as possible. Never strain. As soon as you start straining, taking the clenching-the-fist attitude, saying, "I am going to get what I want; I am going to get it if it kills me," all mental building stops.

We have all been told to relax. I have seen people tense up as soon as they were told to relax. They were going to relax if it killed them; and of course they missed the whole point.

Get the thought of what you want as clear as you can. Be definite but not too specific.

If you live in an apartment and say, "I want a house in the country or in the suburbs, and I want it to have a porch and a large yard with trees and flowers," that is all right. But do not say, "I must have a certain house—the one at 257 Ninth Street or 21 Fifth Avenue."

Suppose you go shopping. Well, you should know what you are shopping for. You should have some definite idea. If you say, "I want something, I don't know what—I will leave it to God"; if you say, "I want a business, it may be a farm or a shop I want—I will leave it to Divine Mind," you are foolish. What are you here for? You must have some desires and wishes, because you represent God here. So you must say, "Yes, I want a shop; and I know the kind of shop I want."

I know a woman who demonstrated a hat shop. She had no capital, but she wanted to go into business. She wanted a hat shop. She loves to make hats. She has a natural flair for it. She can make hats that look well on the homeliest people; and this is the art of millinery, isn't it? She was a good businesswoman, so she built the mental equivalent of a hat shop. She did not say, "I must be in a certain block on a certain street." She did not say, "I am going to get a hat shop if it kills me" or "I am going to get a hat shop, and I want Jane Smith's hat shop." She built a definite mental equivalent, and that is the right way. If you say, "I want a strong, healthy body," and build up a mental equivalent for it by constantly thinking of your body as perfect, that is fine. Do not think of details very much. Do not say, "First of all I'm going to get my teeth fixed up with right thought, and I'll let my bald head wait" or "Maybe I should get my bald head fixed up first, because my teeth can wait." It is the details that are wrong. The evil of outlining lies in going into small details and in saying, "I want it in my time, in my way, whether God wants it or not." Apart from that (going too much into small details) you must have definite ideas.

Do not strain to get your ideas clear. They will be clearer the second day or the fifty-second day. If you have a pair of field glasses and you look at something and want the focus clearer, you slowly turn the wheel until the focus is clear.

Getting your mental equivalent may take you a week or a month or a year. *Charge it with interest,* like an electric charge, or it is dead. Love is the only way. You cannot be interested in a thing unless you love it. If you love it, it is filled with interest, it is filled with energy and life, and it comes true.

There is an interesting story about Napoleon. He thought a big nose was a sign of strong character. He said, "Give me a man with plenty of nose." If someone came to him and said that a certain officer ought to be promoted, he would say: "Has he got plenty of nose? Give me a man with a big nose." If an officer was killed, he replaced him with someone with a big nose. You know what happened. The law sent him Wellington, and Wellington destroyed him. Wellington had the largest nose in English history. He said himself it was more of a handle than a nose. Take that as a joke if you like, but it does carry an important lesson.

The doctrine of the mental equivalent is the essence of the metaphysical teaching; the doctrine that you will get whatever you provide the mental equivalent for.

I have known some very, very remarkable cases where people furnished the mental equivalent and out of the blue came things they never could have hoped for in the ordinary way. I know many men and women in London and New York and other places who seemingly had no human chance to attain success; but they got hold of this knowledge of mental equivalents, they quietly and faithfully applied this knowledge; and sometime sooner or later the thing they wanted came to them, without any help from anything outside; and it stayed with them and brought a blessing.

Building a New Mental Equivalent

It is your bounden duty to demonstrate, and in order to do so successfully you need to know why you should do so. Why should you demonstrate at all? Some people say, "Since God is all, and everything is perfect, why should I seek to demonstrate His law?" Because you have to prove the harmony of being in your own life. That is why. If there were no need to demonstrate, one might just as well go to bed and stay there or, more simply still, stroll around to the nearest undertaker.

Of course we are here on earth to express God, and true expression is what we call demonstration, because it demonstrates the law of Being. It is your duty to be healthy, prosperous, and free. It is your duty to express God to the utmost of your power; and you have no right to relinquish your efforts until you have accomplished this. Until you have excellent health and are visibly regenerating, until you have found your true place and right activity, until you are free from conscious fear, anxiety, and criticism, you are not demonstrating, and you must find out why and correct the error, whatever it is.

Jesus has told us that we always demonstrate our consciousness, and Unity is teaching the same truth today. You always demonstrate what you habitually have in your mind. What sort of mind have you? I am not going to tell you—and do not let anyone else tell you either, because they do not know. People who like you will think your mentality is better than it is; those who do not like you will think it is worse. So do not ask anybody about your mentality; but examine your conditions and see what you are demonstrating. This method is scientific and infallible.

If an automobile engineer is working out a new design for an engine, if he is going to do something different about the valves, for instance, he doesn't say: "I wonder what Smith thinks about this. I like Smith. If Smith is against this I won't try it." Nor does he say, "I won't try this idea because it comes from France, and I don't like those people." He is impersonal and perfectly unemotional about it. He says, "I will test it out, and decide by the results I obtain."

Then he tries it out, measuring the results carefully, and decides accordingly. He does not laugh, or cry, or get excited, or bang the table; but he tests out the idea scientifically and judges only by results.

That is how you should handle your mentality. That is how you should practice the metaphysical teaching. You demonstrate the state of your mind at any given time. You experience in the outer what you really think in the inner. This is the meaning of the old saying "As within so without." Note carefully that in the Bible the word "within" always means thought and the word "without" means manifestation or experience. That is why Jesus said that the kingdom of heaven (health, harmony, and freedom) is within. Harmonious thought means harmonious experience. Fear thought or anger thought means suffering or frustration.

This brings me to the most important thing I want to say, namely that if you want to change your life; if you want to be healthier, happier, younger, more prosperous; above all, if you want to get nearer to God—and I know that you do—*you must change your thought and keep it changed.* That is the secret of controlling your life, and there is no other way. Jesus Himself could not have done it in any other way, because this is a cosmic law. Change your thought and keep it changed. We have all been taught this very thing since the metaphysical movement began. I heard it stated in those very words many times nearly forty years ago in London; but most of us are slow to realize the importance of it. If you want to change some condition in your life, you must change your thought about it and keep it changed. Then the condition will change accordingly. All that anyone else can do for you is to help you change your thought. That is what a metaphysician can do for you, but you yourself must keep it changed. No one else can think for you. "No man can save his brother's soul or pay his brother's debt."

To change your thought and keep it changed is the way to build a new mental equivalent; it is the secret of accomplishment. You already have a mental equivalent for everything that is in your life today; and you must destroy the patterns for the things you do not want, and then they will disappear. You must build a new pattern or mental equivalent for the things you want, and then they will come into your life.

Of course changing your thought for a short time is the easiest thing in the world. Everyone does this when he goes to a metaphysical meeting. The beautiful atmosphere and the positive instruction make people feel optimistic. The teacher reminds the audience of the Truth of Being, and they think, "I believe that, and I am going to practice it." But five minutes after they have left the meeting they forget about it, perhaps for hours. The trouble with most students is not that they do not change their thought but that they do not keep it changed.

If you want health you must cease to think sickness and fear, and you must get the habit of thinking health and harmony. There can be no sickness without fear. You cannot be adversely affected by anything if you really have no fear concerning it. Everyone has many fears in the subconscious mind that he is not consciously aware of, but they are operating just the same.

A man said: "I entered a town in a foreign country in the east of Europe during a typhoid epidemic. I did not know there was any typhoid. I never thought about it. I didn't know the language and couldn't read the papers. They were printed in Greek. Yet I got typhoid and had quite a siege. How do you account for that?"

The explanation is that he believed in typhoid fever. He believed one can catch it from others, and that it makes one very ill, for so many days, and therefore he had a subconscious fear of it. He subconsciously knew there was typhoid around, and as it always does, the subconscious enacted or dramatized his real beliefs and fears, and presented him with a good hearty case of typhoid.

If he had really believed that he was a child of God who could not be hurt by anything, he would not have had typhoid.

Change your thought and keep it changed, not for ten seconds or even ten days but steadily and permanently. Then you will build a new mental equivalent, and *a mental equivalent is always demonstrated*.

The secret of harmony and success is to concentrate your thought upon harmony and success. That is why I teach that attention is the key to life. What you attend to or concentrate upon you bring into your life, because you are building a mental equivalent.

Many people fail to concentrate successfully because they think that concentration means will power. They actually try to concentrate with their muscles and blood vessels. They frown. They clench their hands. Unwittingly they are thinking of an engineer's drill or a carpenter's bit and brace. They suppose that the harder you press the faster you get through. But all this is quite wrong.

Forget the drill and think of a photographic camera. In a camera there is of course no question of pressure. There the secret lies in *focus*. If you want to photograph something you focus your camera lens quietly, steadily, and persistently on it for the necessary length of time. Suppose I want to photograph a vase of flowers. What do

I do? Well, I do not press it violently against the lens of the camera. That would be silly. I place the vase in front of the camera and keep it there. But suppose that after a few moments I snatch away the vase and hold a book in front of the camera, and then snatch that away, and hold up a chair, and then put the flowers back for a few moments, and so forth. You know what will happen to my photograph. It will be a crazy blur. Is not that what people do to their minds when they cannot keep their thoughts concentrated for any length of time? They think health for a few minutes and then they think sickness or fear. They think prosperity and then they think depression. They think about bodily perfection and then they think about old age and their pains and aches. Is it any wonder that man is so apt to demonstrate the "marred image"?

Note carefully that I did not advocate taking one thought and trying to hold it by will power. That is bad. You must allow a train of *relevant* thoughts to have free play in your mind, one leading naturally to the next, but they must all be positive, constructive, and harmonious, and appertaining to your desire; and you must think quietly and without effort. Then you will get the mental equivalent of all-round success, and then success itself will follow; success in health, in social relationships, in your work, in your spiritual development.

Maintaining the New Equivalent

It is always good to make a practical experiment, so I advise you to take a single problem in your life—something you want to get rid of or something you want to obtain—and change your thought about this thing, and keep it changed. Do not be in a hurry to select your problem; take your time.

Do not tell anyone you are doing this. If you tell a friend about it you are thereby strongly affirming the existence of the problem, which is the very thing you are trying to get rid of. If you tell your friend that you are going to work on your rheumatism or on lack, you are making these things very real to your subconscious mind. Also your spiritual energy is leaking away, as electricity does in what we call a "ground."

Take your problem and change your mind concerning it, and keep it changed for a month, and you will be astonished at the results you will get. If you really do keep your thought changed you will not have to wait a month. If you really change your thought and keep it changed, the demonstration may come in a few hours. But to keep tensely looking for the demonstration is really affirming the existence of the problem, is it not? The secret is to keep your thought changed into the new condition. So keep your thought carefully, quietly expressive of the new condition that you want to produce. Believe what you are thinking, and to prove that you believe it you must act the part.

By changing your mind about your problem in this way and keeping it changed, you are building a new mental equivalent, a mental equivalent of harmony and success, and that mental equivalent, as we know, must be outpictured in your experience.

For a while you will find that your thought will keep slipping back into the old rut. Such is the force of habit. But if you are quietly persistent you will gain the victory. It is always a little difficult to change a habit, but it can be done, and then the new right habit becomes easier than the old wrong habit, and that is how a new mental equivalent is built.

Change your mind and keep it changed.

Do not talk about the negative thing or act as if it were there. Act your part as though the new condition were already in being in the outer. If you will do this, the new condition will presently appear in the outer, because the outer is always but the projection or outpicturing of the inner.

We project our own belief and call it experience, and this gives us the clue to the difference between a true action and a false or unreal action.

What is true action? A true action is one that really changes things, that gets you somewhere. A false action does not. For example, if your car has traction it is moving. That is a true action, and you will presently reach your destination; but if it does not have traction there will be movement, vibration, but you will not get anywhere. You are wearing out the engine and perhaps the tires, but you do not get anywhere. The same thing happens when a soldier is "marking time" as we say. He is tiring himself and wearing out his shoes but not getting anywhere. These are examples of false action.

Suppose you have a difficult letter to write or a sermon or a lecture to prepare. Suppose you sit in front of a sheet of paper and draw curlicues or cut the pencil to pieces or tear your hair. These would be false actions, and many people do just that. Such actions get you nowhere. To decide what you are going to say, to start a current of thought and then write it down, is true action. You will note that the difference is that in the false action you begin from the outside. You had not prepared your thoughts. You tried to begin by writing. With the true action you got your thoughts in order first and then the writing or outer activity followed. A false action means deadlock; a true action is always fruitful.

True activity is always from within outward. False activity tries to work from without inward. One is centrifugal and the other centripetal, if you want to be technical. If you are working from within out, your work is alive and will be productive. If you are working from outside inward, your work is dead, and it will have a bad effect on you.

Artists and literary people speak of "potboilers." You know what a potboiler is. It is a picture that you paint or a story that you write, not because you are interested but just to keep the monetary returns coming in. It is never good, because it is not the result of inspiration. It is done from the outside and is a false action. It is a common saying among writers that three potboilers will kill any talent; and that is true. The proper way to paint a picture is to see beauty somewhere, in a landscape or in a beautiful face, or wherever you please. You thrill to that beauty, and then you go to the canvas and express your inspiration there. That is art, and that is true action. It inspires other people and it helps and develops you yourself.

If you write a story or a novel because you have observed life, because you have seen certain things happen and studied certain people, and write it all down because you are alive with it, that is a true action and you write a great book. Dickens, George Eliot, Balzac, and all the great authors wrote in that way. But if you say, "I will do fifteen hundred words a day and give my publishers the 'mixture as before' and that will secure my income," your work will be dead. And this policy will kill any talent that you may have.

If you are in business and you are interested in your job and love it, your work is a positive action and must ultimately bring you success. Even if the work is uncongenial but nevertheless you say, "This is my job for the moment; I am going to do it as well as I can, and then something better will open up," you are working from within outward. Your work is a positive action, and before long something really congenial will come to you.

Most people know that these things are true. They know that they are true for pictures and stories and business life, but they do not realize that they are equally true for the things of the soul. Yet such is the case. If you pray and meditate from the outside just because you think it is a duty or because you will feel guilty if you do not, your prayers will be dead. You will get no demonstration and make no spiritual progress, and you will get no joy. But if you feel that when you are praying and meditating you are visiting with God, and that these moments are the happiest in the twenty-four hours, then you are working from within outward. Your spiritual growth will be fruitful, and you will grow very rapidly in spiritual understanding. When you pray in this way there is no strain and your soul is filled with peace.

The great enemy of prayer is a sense of tension. When you are tense you are always working from the outside inward. Tension in prayer is probably the greatest cause of failure to demonstrate. Remember that the mind always works inefficiently when you are tense. When you think, "I must demonstrate this" or "I must get that in three days," you are tense; you are using your will power, and you will do more harm than good.

Remember this: The door of the soul opens inward. If you will remember this it will save you years and years of waiting for demonstrations. Write in your notebook, the one you carry in your pocket—not the notebook you keep locked in your desk, because that is a mausoleum—or better still, write it on a card, and place it on your dresser: "The door of the soul opens inward." And pray to God that you may remember that truth every time you turn to Him in prayer. You know what it means when a door opens inward: the harder you push against it the tighter you close it. When you press or force or hurl yourself against it you only close it on yourself. When you relax and draw back, you give it a chance to open. In all theaters and other public buildings the doors open outward. The law insists upon this because crowds are apt to become panic-stricken and then they push, and if the doors opened inward the people would imprison themselves and be killed. *The door of the soul opens inward!* That is the law. Relax mentally, draw away from your problem spiritually, and the action of God will open the door for you and you will be free.

There is an old legend of the Middle Ages that is very instructive. It seems that a citizen was arrested by one of the Barons and shut up in a dungeon in his castle. He was taken down dark stairs, down, down, down, by a ferocious-looking jailer who carried a great key a foot long. The door of a cell was opened, and he was thrust into a dark hole. The door shut with a bang, and there he was.

He lay in that dark dungeon for twenty years. Each day the jailer would come, the big door would be opened with a great creaking and groaning, a pitcher of water and a loaf of bread would be thrust in and the door closed again.

Well, after twenty years the prisoner decided that he could not stand it any longer. He wanted to die but he did not want to commit suicide, so he decided that the next day when the jailer came he would attack him. The jailer would then kill him in self-defense, and thus his misery would be at an end. He thought he would examine the door carefully so as to be ready for tomorrow and, going over, he caught the handle and turned it. To his amazement the door opened, and upon investigation he found that there was no lock upon it and never had been, and that for all those twenty years he had not been locked in, except in belief.

At any time in that period he could have opened the door if only he had known it. He thought it was locked, but it was not. He groped along the corridor and felt his way upstairs. At the top of the stairs two soldiers were chatting, and they made no attempt to stop him. He crossed the great yard without attracting attention. There was an armed guard on the drawbridge at the great gate, but they paid no attention to him, and he walked out a free man.

He went home unmolested and lived happily ever after. He could have done this any time through those long years since his arrest if he had known enough, but he did not. He was a captive, not of stone and iron but of false belief. He was not locked in; he only thought he was. Of course this is only a legend, but it is an extremely instructive one.

We are all living in some kind of prison, some of us in one kind, some in another; some in a prison of lack, some in a prison of remorse and resentment, some in a prison of blind, unintelligent fear, some in a prison of sickness. But always the prison is in our thought and not in the nature of things.

There is no truth in our seeming troubles. There is no reality in lack. There is no power in time or conditions to make us old or tired or sick.

The Jesus Christ teaching, and the Unity movement in particular, comes to us and says: "You are not locked in a prison of circumstances. You are not chained in any dungeon. In the name of God, turn the handle, walk out, and be free."

Build a mental equivalent of freedom, of vibrant physical health, of true prosperity, of increasing understanding and achievement for God. Build it by thinking of it, having faith in it and acting the part, and the old limitation equivalent will gradually fade out, for the door is unlocked and the voice of God in your heart says, "Be free."

Life Is Consciousness

I feel it to be a great honor to have this opportunity of speaking at the Unity headquarters. As Charles Fillmore has said, I am very familiar with the Unity message, for I have read it for over thirty years.

Of course that is giving myself away quite a bit, but people on the platform always give themselves away sooner or later, so it may as well be sooner.

I have lived all my life in London until recently, and we were there, I suppose, about forty-five hundred miles from Kansas City. So this gives me the opportunity to realize how far-flung this work has been. I doubt if you people here at Unity realize how great and how big a work the Unity work is.

The Truth movement, as we call it, is the most important thing in the world today. The Truth movement, which centers in the belief in the omnipresence and availability of God, is the most important thing in the world, because it is the only thing that can save the world. Nothing else can. Everything else has been tried.

People have tried building up might and power, and have used it to wreck themselves. Man has built up intellectual power; and especially since four centuries ago, since the Renaissance, education has been intellectual. People are surprised when you tell them that there is any other kind of education.

Those of us who have had the advantages of a higher education know that so-called intellectual study gives very, very little help in the practical business of living. This Truth movement comes along, takes hold of people and changes them. It restores health if that has been lost, restores estate if that has been lost, restores self-respect if that has been lost. It puts people on their feet, and shows them that there is something in life worth living for.

Among the various sections of the present-day Truth movement Unity is probably the most important. Your work is practical. It has the character and quality of Jesus Christ, because it is kindly and friendly. You do not put fear into people. When they come, you tell them that God is the only power; you tell them to relax, and become quiet, and turn to that power; and that is the highest message that you can teach.

I am one of Mr. Fillmore's spiritual children, so I just thought I would say that before getting on to the thing that I actually came to say.

I am not speaking to the general public now but to the people who are devoting their lives to the study and expression of this Truth.

I think it is well for us to remind ourselves what it is that we really believe and have. The answer is that we really have the key to life. We do not just approach life from a particular angle as other schools of healing do, but we have the key to life; and that key is the knowledge that *life is a state of consciousness*.

The explanation of all your problems, the explanation of your difficulties, and the explanation of your triumphs in life boil down to this: *Life is a state of consciousness*. That is the beginning and the end. That is the final step in metaphysics. All the other steps but lead up to that.

Isaac Pennington, the Quaker, said, "All truth is a shadow, but the last truth." And the last truth is that life is consciousness. You are and you have and you do in accordance with your consciousness.

That is the beginning and the end. There are other ways of looking at life that are superficially correct, but ultimately the truth is that your life is a state of consciousness. Your so-called physical body is the embodiment of a part of your consciousness. Your home is the embodiment of another part of your consciousness. The kind of work you are doing—whether you are in work that you love, or whether you are doing drudgery that you hate—is the expression of your consciousness at that point. The kind of people you meet, the people you attract into your life, are the expression of your consciousness about your fellow men.

If you came to me and told me that you can't get along with people, I should tell you to get a card about the size of a post card, and write this on it, *"Like attracts like,"* and then put it inside your closet—not where other members of your family will see it, because that would sometimes be embarrassing. When you are grumbling and finding fault they could point their finger at it, and that would be very embarrassing; so put your card inside the closet.

People come to me and say, "If you only knew the kind of family I have, if you only knew the kind of people I have to be with and work with!" I say, "The law of Being says, 'Like attracts like.'"

The ultimate explanation of all things is that life is a state of consciousness.

Take this table. You say this is solid wood, and that is true as far as it goes. But the next step, going deeper, is that we find it is really made up of molecules with great distances, relatively between them. So it is not solid at all. It is made up of molecules, and that is true as far as it goes. But these again are made up of atoms, and these of electrons and protons, and so on. We hear talk of vibrations, of rays, of all these things, and they are good descriptions as far as they go; but in the ultimate, beyond all these things, we come back to a state of consciousness.

Before you change your state of consciousness nothing else can change.

All trouble, all disappointment, all depression, all limitation is a state of consciousness that must be changed. People are trying to change outer conditions but leaving their consciousness unchanged, and it cannot be done.

The only fundamental way to change things is to change your consciousness because you always must and always will get the conditions that belong to your consciousness. You cannot cheat nature. You can drag to you, through will power, certain things that do not belong to you, but you can only keep them for a short time. The moment you take your hands off they fly away. That was the real cause of the financial collapse of 1929. Then Wall Street made its famous nose dive. The prosperity that had been built up was not true prosperity. People had been gambling on the stock market and elsewhere and had attracted or dragged to themselves prosperity that they were not entitled to by right of consciousness, and of course they could not keep it.

The same thing applies to health. You can compel a certain part of the body to picture health for a short time, but if you do not have the consciousness of health you cannot keep it. You "heal" a person of rheumatism and he has sciatica, you "heal" him of that and he has trouble with his sight, you "heal" his sight and his right lung weakens, and so on. These are not healings. They are temporary cures, because they are attempts to put into the body something that doesn't belong there by right of consciousness.

When you want to solve your problems you can see at once that the only scientific way is to start in to change your consciousness. Likewise you must change the consciousness of a patient if you want to heal him. Nothing can come to you securely, nothing can stay with you permanently, except what you are entitled to by your consciousness.

Emerson said, "No man and no institution was ever ridden down or talked down by anything but itself." People may slander you, but nobody can hurt you except yourself. Nobody can wreck a church or a center or a movement or a country except itself.

A woman said, "I started a center and everything went beautifully until some horrible person spoiled everything." I replied, "You are the horrible person who spoiled your center, because if you started a center and it didn't go, then you did not have a right consciousness for that work. You should have changed your consciousness until you did have a good center, and then nobody else could spoil it for you."

Your body, your home, your city, your country, the universe are pictures of consciousness. Your private life out-pictures your own consciousness. The national life is the outpicturing of the national consciousness. So you see how foolish it is to try to change the outer picture without changing the inner consciousness.

People come to me and say, "I am broke. I need a thousand dollars. I need the money." Or, "I have had a quarrel with somebody," which usually means that they expect the other person to bend to their will and come crawling on his knees for forgiveness. They say, "Put these things right." I say, "Change your consciousness. I do not treat for money. I do not patch up quarrels like that. But I do help you to change your consciousness." Some of them smile and say, "Oh, no, my consciousness is really quite good. Other people are to blame—my mother or my sister." I answer, "No; the real trouble is in your consciousness; and all the time you are trying to work on outer things and leaving your consciousness unchanged no permanent good can come to you."

The movies came to the big cities first, and finally arrived in a remote mining camp in the Rockies. The picture was announced and the tent was put up. The residents had never been to a movie before. The tent was packed with cowboys and miners, and at a given moment during the showing of a blood-curdling melodrama the villain began to choke the heroine. An old cowboy in the front row pulled out his gun and fired six shots into the villain. Everybody laughed, because in those days a gunshot didn't mean much. There were only a few bullet holes in the wall, and of course the picture went on as scheduled.

Why do we laugh at the cowboy? You all laughed, you know. What should he have done? Instead of firing at the screen, he should have turned around and fired into the projector. That would have stopped the picture.

Too often you try to change outer things instead of changing the inner. Then you are firing at the screen instead of the projector. So nothing happens. But when you start to change your consciousness you are firing at the projector, and then things happen. If you don't like the picture on the screen, change the reel. If you didn't like the picture you were seeing, and would like to see some other, you wouldn't get a cloth and try to rub it off as if from a blackboard. You would take out that reel and put in the reel you wanted.

The scientific way to approach life, if you do not like the picture you are getting, is to change the reel.

How do we change the reel? By rising in consciousness. *The only real healers are practical ones.* I have met a few theoretical so-called healers. I have met people who told me just how healing should be done. They understood the theory. They knew how it should be done but couldn't do it. They were purely theoretical.

The way to meet a problem is to raise your consciousness. If you do this, the problem disappears. In the Bible a valley always stands for trouble, sin, limitation; and the mount for uplifted thought, and prayer for understanding. We must go up the mount; raise our consciousness.

Most people who have a problem concentrate on that problem.

They take it to bed with them and stay awake all night thinking it over. Let go of the problem. Rise above it in consciousness. How can you do this? Go up quickly, in a flash if you can; but you can't always do it that way. You will find that by reading the Bible, or some available spiritual book, or a Unity publication, or by repeating some favorite inspirational hymn, your consciousness is rising. If a diver goes down to the bottom of the sea he wears lead shoes, but if he wants to come up to the surface of the water quickly he kicks off the lead shoes. Then he rises rapidly. When we rise in consciousness we kick off our lead shoes, and then we begin to be healed, or the patient begins to be healed; but it is the consciousness that you have to heal.

There is no other way. The great key to consciousness lies in the "Word," which Unity has been teaching for more than fifty years. "In the beginning was the Word, and the Word was with God, and the Word was God. All things are made by it, and without it is not anything made that is made."

The 1st chapter of John is a reflection of the 1st chapter of Genesis; both deal with creation: "God *said.*" John explains the Logos. The Greek word *Logos* means the great creative Word. The great creative word is I AM. It is the secret of life. We are given it in Deuteronomy, and Jesus identified Himself with it. Jesus was a great reader of the Psalms and Isaiah and Deuteronomy. The key to life is not somewhere outside of life. You can't go up to it. No great seer or saint will go up and bring it down for you. It is not thousands of miles across the sea. It is very nigh unto you. It is with you all the time. I AM is the great secret. I AM is the famous Lost Word.

All through history mankind has felt intuitively that there is a way out, if only it can find it. All the old fairy tales tell the story again and again. Aladdin had a wonderful lamp. He rubbed it and received the things he wanted. The lamp was the creative word. You know about Cinderella. She was in the kitchen, miserable and unhappy like so many others, and then something happened. A pumpkin turned into a carriage, and a pair of white rats turned into white horses, and so on. But there must have been a change in Cinderella's consciousness first.

Always men and women have felt intuitively that there is a way out; that it is not necessary to be angry and mean and resentful and bitter; that it is not necessary to grow old and die; that it is not necessary that man should fight and grab for prosperity and food. What is life worth if living is to be a constant struggle for necessities? Men and women have always known intuitively that there is a way out if only they can find it. They have always known that God means all life to be noble and creative and joyous. And this is true.

The way out lies in the spoken word. In the Bible the "word" means any definitely formulated thought—not just the drifting thought that floats through your mind. The word is creative, and the strongest and most creative word is "I am." Whenever you say "I am," you are calling upon the universe to do something for you and it will do it. Whenever you say "I am," you are drawing a check on the universe. It will be honored and cashed sooner or later and the proceeds will go to you. If you say, "I am tired, sick, poor, fed up, disappointed, getting old," then you are drawing checks for future trouble and limitation. When you say, "I am divine life," "I am divine Truth," "I am divine freedom," "I am substance," "I am eternal substance," you are drawing a check on the bank of heaven, *and surely that check will be honored with health and plenty for you.*

Remember you don't have to use the actual grammatical form "I am." Every time you associate yourself in thought with anything, or think of yourself as having anything, you are using a form of "I am." The verb "to have" is a part of the verb "to be." In the very ancient languages, there is no verb "to have." It is a modern improvement like the radio and the automobile. "I have" means "I am," because you always have what you are, and you always do what you are.

That is the significance of "I am," and today more people have come to know about it than ever before, and this is a wonderful thing. Unity has taught it. In the Truth movement in London we taught it. But few people realize what it means. Whatever you associate yourself with, that you are bringing into your consciousness. What is the first thing we do when we talk at all? We say, "I am this," "I am that." Perhaps my father was Mr. Jones. Therefore I am a Jones. The neighbors across the way are Robinsons. They are strangers to me, because I am a Jones. Immediately the baby picks up all the prejudices of old man Jones. Or we say, "I am a Frenchman," or "I am a German," or "I am an Englishman." The Frenchman gets a great many prejudices concerning the German and the Englishman, the German gets prejudices concerning the Frenchman and the Englishman, and the Englishman gets them concerning the Frenchman and the German. Why pick up any prejudices?

Then the child grows older, and of course his family is interested in politics. Again he sets up in his mind a whole army of prejudices. He belongs to a certain party because his father does. He goes to a particular school or college and collects more prejudice. He should use the "I am" to say "I am for freedom." He should use it to throw down the walls of resentment.

It is your "I am" whatever way you use it, and there is one thing that nobody can do for you, and that is save your soul, because nobody can speak the "I am" for you. Nobody can say "I am" for you or another; he would have to say "You are" or "He is," and that would not be "I am."

In Revelation we read, "To him that overcometh . . . I will give him a white stone, and upon the stone a new name written, which no one knoweth but he that receiveth it." The white stone means the ascension of the divine nature, because of its understanding. The new name is the new character and the new life. You speak for yourself and you save your own soul, and it is said to be secret because only you can use it.

Teachers can write books for you, they can talk to you, but they cannot save your soul, because they cannot think for you. When anyone uses "I am" for you, it becomes "You are." It is *your* "I am" that must save you, and nobody on earth can use it but you. The "I am" is God in action. God is not a man. God is working through you. You are not separated from God. God does not sit far up in the sky and send you a good idea. God is the I AM giving you a new embodiment, a new creation. Whatever you believe, that you create. You are the I AM. God knows Himself in your consciousness, and that is knowing God. God is I AM THAT I AM, but you are I AM.

I want to emphasize this point. You build your consciousness with your "I am." Nobody else can do it for you, and you can't cheat. Sometimes you can cheat in business, sometimes you can cheat in gambling, but you cannot cheat with the "I am." Appearances count for nothing. Your consciousness is built with the "I am." According to your "I am" so are your conditions. You are not using the "I am" only when you think and speak affirmations. Perhaps this has been a weakness in our movement, that we have tended to overrate affirmations. We have to use them because they are a memorandum of what we are to think. The class thoughts in *Unity* magazine are a memorandum. But you are using the "I am" in every action all day long. Every action that you do all day long you are building into your consciousness. You will never build anything into your consciousness until you do it in practice. Meditating an hour in the morning before breakfast helps very little unless you carry the realization with you into your everyday living.

If you lie or cheat or are selfish, then that is what you are building into consciousness. We have dwelt much on thought (what we call words), but we haven't always insisted that it is the practical conduct all day long that builds up consciousness. People tell me that they spend an hour every morning building up their consciousness, but often as soon as the hour is up they have forgotten it.

You build your consciousness by the things you do all day long. It is by such things that we are judged. God does not judge us. We judge ourselves by the consciousness we build, because life is a state of consciousness. Let us build true consciousness and hasten the day of freedom.

Getting Results by Prayer

A great deal of confusion seems to exist in many minds concerning the precise avenue through which the Divine Power is to be approached, and realization and harmony attained. So many schools of thought seem to be competing for the attention of the student; so busy is the printing press; so many new books and pamphlets are written; so many magazines come and go; that people have told me that they have felt quite in despair of ever discovering what it really is that they must do to be saved.

Sometimes it seems as though the story of Babel were repeating itself in the metaphysical movement—and yet we all know in our hearts that the true Gate is narrow and the real Way strait. One well known Eastern teacher of great spiritual power has actually published a pamphlet from which it appears that the genuine criterion of authenticity is to have no Path at all. This is the *reductio ad absurdum* which pulls us up short and restores the light.

The truth, of course, is this, that the only solution of the problem is definitely to contact the Divine Power which dwells within your own soul; and, having consciously done that, to bring it to bear upon the various difficulties in your life, taking them in due order, that is, attacking the most urgent first. This is the right way of working, and it is the only way that can possibly help you, or your affairs, in the long run. The real remedy for every one of your difficulties is, as we are told on every page of the Bible, to find and *know* the Indwelling Presence. *Acquaint now thyself with Him and be at peace. In His Presence is fulness of joy. Behold, I am with you alway.*

This, then, is the task, and the only one—to find, and consciously know, your own Indwelling Lord.

You see now how the confusion disappears, melts away, and the perfect simplicity of the whole thing emerges once you realize this fact. From this it necessarily follows that all schools and churches; all teachers, under whatever name they may be called; all the textbooks, magazines, pamphlets, and what-not; are but temporary expedients for enabling you to make this contact. In themselves they are of no importance except as a means to an end. The best mode of approach to Divine things for you is the one that happens to make it easiest for you to locate the Inner Light within yourself.

Such things as temperament, education, family tradition, and so on, will make one book, or one teacher, or one school, more useful than another; but never as anything more than the means to a certain end. That end is effective self discovery. "Man know *thyself*"—thy true self which is the Divine I Am. And so we see that the best "movement," the finest textbook, the greatest teacher, is just the one that happens best to fit the individual need. It is entirely a practical matter, and the only test that ever could, or ever will, be of any use, is the practical one of *judgment by results.* Of course, Jesus anticipated this difficulty, and met it, as he has met all our difficulties. He gave us the simple and perfect standard: *By their fruits ye shall know them.*

The great peril to true religion has always been the building up of vested interests in wealthy organizations, or in the exploitation by individuals of their own personalities. An organized church is always in danger of developing into an "industry" which has to provide a living for numerous officials. When this happens the rank and file are sure to be severely discouraged from seeking spiritual things for themselves at first hand. A tradition of "loyalty" to the organization is built up as a means of self protection. Not loyalty to Truth, or to your own soul, be it remarked, but to the ecclesiastical machine. Thus the means becomes an end in itself and spiritual power then fades out. Rash promises and vague claims take the place of real verifiable demonstrations.

In the case of leaders who exploit their own personalities, the student is discouraged from going elsewhere for enlightenment or help; and here again "loyalty" to something other than God is allowed to block the avenue of Truth, and therefore becomes antichrist. What is this but the jealousy of the petty tradesman who warns a doubtful customer of the danger he runs in going to the "shop next door."

Remember that you absolutely owe no loyalty whatever to anything or anyone but your own soul and to the furtherance of its spiritual development. Your most solemn duty is to make everything secondary to that. "To thine own self be true; and it must follow, as the night the day, thou canst not then be false to any man."—*Shakespeare*.

The first step that the earnest student must take is to settle on a definite method of working, selecting whichever one seems to suit him best, and then giving it a fair trial. That means that you must acquire a definite method or system of spiritual treatment or scientific prayer. Merely reading books, making good resolutions, or talking plausibly about the thing will get you nowhere. *Get a definite method of working,* practise it conscientiously every day; and stick to one method long enough to give it a fair chance. You would not expect to play the violin after two or three attempts, or to drive a car without a little preliminary practice.

Having got your method, set to work definitely on some concrete problem in your own life, choosing preferably whichever is causing you the most trouble at the moment, or, better still, *whatever it is that you are most afraid of.* Work at it steadily; and if nothing has happened, if no improvement at all shows itself within, say, a couple of weeks at the outside, then try it on another problem. If you still get no result, then scrap that method and adopt a new one. Remember, *there is a way out;* that is as certain as the rising of the sun. The problem really is, not the getting rid of your difficulties, but the finding of your own best method for doing it.

If ill health is your difficulty, do not rest until you have brought about at least one bodily healing. There is no malady that has not been healed by someone at some time, and what others have done you can do, for God is Principle, and Principle changes not.

If poverty is the trouble, go to work on that, and clear it up once and for all. It can be done. It has been done. Others have done it, and you can.

If you are unhappy, dissatisfied with your lot, or your surroundings, above all, with yourself, set to work on that; refuse to take no for an answer; and insist upon the happiness and satisfaction that are yours by Divine right.

If your need is self-expression—artistic, literary, or otherwise—if your heart's desire is to attain to eminence in a profession, or some kind of public career, that, too, approached in the right spirit, is a legitimate and worthy object, and the right method of scientific prayer will bring you the prize.

Keep a record of your results, and on no account be satisfied with anything less than success. Above all things, avoid the deadly error of making excuses. There are no excuses for failing to demonstrate. When you do not demonstrate, it never by any chance means anything except that you have not worked in the right way. Excuses are the true and veritable devil, who comes to tempt you to remain outside the Kingdom of Heaven, while the Gate stands open. Excuses, in fact, are the only enemy that you really need to fear.

Find the method that suits you; cultivate simplicity—simplicity and spontaneity are the secret of effective prayer—work away steadily; *keep your own counsel;* and *whatsoever ye shall ask in My name, that will I do.*

You Must Be Born Again

We are told concerning the teaching of Jesus that the common people heard him gladly. This could easily have been inferred from the most superficial study of the Gospels. The "man in the street," unsophisticated by theology or philosophy, has an intuitive perception of fundamental Truth when he meets it, that is often lacking in highly trained minds. Intellectual attainments may easily beget spiritual pride, and this is the only sin upon which Our Lord was severe. Yet among the learned, too, there were those, the more spiritually minded, who felt themselves attracted to the new Teacher. He was unconventional, hopelessly out of favor with the ecclesiastical authorities, a flouter of hallowed traditions; and yet, deep calleth unto deep, and so he had his friends and followers in high places also. One of these who felt irresistibly drawn to seek for further light was Nicodemus. He had the thirst for Divine things that will not be denied, but moral courage was not his strong point, and so he sought out the Teacher by night. That he should have gone at all was proof of the compelling power of the urge. Clearly the unfoldment of his spiritual nature was, in spite of defects in character, the principal thing in his life, and clearly he was dissatisfied with the progress he was making. Jesus, he believed, had something to give that was vital, and that gift might be just the secret that had hitherto eluded him, just the key he needed to unlock the spiritual treasure-house of his soul. Jesus might be able to show him why he had so far failed to attain; why, as we should say in modern phraseology, he had failed to demonstrate. And the Master's explanation was simple, concise, almost overwhelming in its directness. He said: *"You must be born again."*

This statement sums up the whole science of demonstration as it is practised on the spiritual basis. It is verily a textbook on metaphysics compressed into five words. It tells the whole story. You stand where you do today, wherever that is, because you are the man that you are. There is only one way under heaven by which you can be brought to stand anywhere else, and that is by becoming another man. The man you are cannot stand anywhere else; a different man cannot stand where you are now. If you wish to go up higher you can do so, and there is no limit to the height which you can attain upon that flight; but *you must be born again!*

Why is it that we make so little progress, compared, that is to say, with what we might and should make in view of the knowledge that we all, in this movement, possess—at least in theory? Why do we not change day by day and week by week from glory to glory, until our friends can scarcely recognize us for the same man or woman? Why should we not march about the world looking like gods, and feeling it; healing instantaneously all who come to us; reforming the sinner; setting the captives free; and generally "doing the works"? "Who did hinder you?"

And the reply is that demonstration, like all other things, has its price; that the price is that we be *born again,* and that in our secret hearts, too often, that is a price that we are not prepared to pay. We are in love with the present man, and all the things that constitute him, and we are not prepared to slay him that the other may be born.

We come into Truth with our little finger, and the great things will not come to us until we come in with the entire body; and there's the rub.

To come into Truth with your whole body is to bring every conscious thought and belief to the touchstone of Divine Intelligence and Divine Love. It is to reject every single thing, mental or physical, that does not square with that standard. It is to revise every opinion, every habit of thought, every policy, every branch of practical conduct, without any exception whatever.

This, of course, is something absolutely tremendous. It is no mere spring cleaning of the soul. It is nothing less than a wholesale tearing down and rebuilding of the entire house. Is it any wonder that all but the very strongest spirits shirk it. And yet, is it any wonder that without it one never really does get anywhere.

It means, as St. Paul said, "dying daily." It means parting with all the prejudices that you have inherited and acquired during all your life long. It means taking the knife to all the little faults of character, petty vanities, minor deceits, and all those lesser forms of selfishness and pride that crystallize your spiritual joints, and are so dear to you. It may mean giving up the biggest thing in your present life, but if it does—well, that is the price that must be paid, and that is all about it.

If you are not prepared to pay this price, well and good; but you must not expect to receive from the Law more than you pay for. A little finger in Truth is well, but it can only produce a little finger result. For a full-length demonstration the whole body must be full of light. *You must be born again.*

The Great Adventure

Many people seem to have the impression that the sole object of Divine Science is the overcoming of difficulties; but to suppose that, is to lose all sense of proportion. The Truth is to be sought for its own sake. The knowledge of Truth is its own reward, and that reward is health, harmony, and prosperity, to begin with; but this is only the beginning. The real object of the seeker should be the development of his own higher faculties and powers; in a word, his Spiritual Evolution.

Now it so happens that as fast as one acquires spiritual understanding, his circumstances improve in every respect—his health, his temper, his happiness, and his material surroundings rapidly and automatically change for the better. *Per contra,* a want of true understanding automatically and necessarily expresses itself in some sort of difficulty on the physical plane, culminating in sin, sickness, and death.

When people find themselves in any difficulty, should they have some glimmerings of spiritual truth, they realize, however dimly, that a way out is to be found along the path of spiritual enlightenment, and consequently they study books, consult friends in the movement, ask for treatment or guidance, or take whatever step appears to be appropriate at the moment. This is the natural and proper course to pursue, and, provided they understand what it is that they are doing, it is only a matter of time before their difficulties—their ill-health, their poverty, their trouble, whatever it is—must disappear. They are, in fact, seeking spiritual enlightenment; they are working for a change in consciousness; and one cannot seek for an improved consciousness without getting it, nor get it without making a demonstration. To know this is to have "come into Truth," to use the common phrase.

Misunderstanding and disappointment arise when people mistake the teaching for some kind of elaborate conjuring trick. When a man supposes that by a wave of the hand, or the repetition of an incantation, his circumstances can be changed for the better without any corresponding change in his own mentality, he is doomed to disappointment. He has not come into Truth, and the Truth movement has nothing for him.

During the past few years a large number of people of all sorts have consulted me about their difficulties, and they easily divide themselves into those two groups. Some people, for instance, are in trouble owing to some very obvious defect in character, but are quite unwilling to overcome this defect, or even, in many cases, to acknowledge it; they wish to continue in their mistake and to have prosperity or happiness as well. Needless to say, for them there is no relief until they have suffered a little more, and have been punished sufficiently to make them do what is necessary. The man who drinks, for example, is certain to ruin his business, and you cannot help him as long as he prefers whiskey to prosperity. Of course, if he is trying to give up whiskey, you can help him to do so, and then all will be well, but otherwise he will just have to go on suffering until his lesson is learned. Other people complain that they have no friends, cannot keep servants, and that they live unhappy, isolated lives; and a few minutes' conversation makes it obvious that there is an atrociously bad temper there which has driven everyone away. If such people are prepared to work to change themselves, the road is clear; but until they are, there is very little to be done for them.

Most of you who read this, however, will be seeking the Truth in the right way, and to seek the Truth in that spirit is really to have come into Truth. "You would not have sought Me had you not already found Me." That being so, you should not allow yourself to be worried or depressed merely because the demonstration is delayed. If you have sufficient understanding to believe in treatment, you have sufficient understanding to know that it must be only a matter of time before you are out of the wood—and what does it really matter whether it is a little sooner or a little later. Any delay in getting results can only be due to one of two things: Either the mental cause of your difficulty is very deeply seated in your consciousness and is requiring a good deal of work; or else you are not yet working in the best way, and if this is so, again it will be only a matter of time before you find what is the best way for you. In other words, once you are on the Path there is no hurry. "Oh, but," says someone, "in my case there is the most urgent hurry, because unless I make my demonstration by Saturday the verdict of the Court will be given against me," or "my creditors will foreclose," or "I shall lose the boat," or what not. But the answer in Truth is still—*There is no hurry,* for the gates of hell shall never prevail. Let evil do its worst on Saturday; let the Court give its verdict; let the creditors strike their blow; let the boat sail. When Monday comes, prayer will still put everything right, if you can get your realization, and if not on Monday, then Wednesday, or Friday, or the week after next. Time does not really matter, for prayer is creative, and will build the New Jerusalem for you anywhere, at any time, irrespective of what may have happened, just as soon as you can get your realization of Truth, Omnipresent Good—Emanuel, which is God with you. This is the New Jerusalem which comes down out of heaven like a bride adorned for her husband, and is independent of any conditions on the physical plane.

When you are in difficulties, look upon the overcoming of them as a great adventure. Resist the temptation to be tragic, to give way to self-pity or discouragement; and approach the problems as though you were an explorer seeking a path through Darkest Africa, or an Edison working to overcome difficulties in connection with a new invention. You know that there is a way out of any difficulty whatever, no matter what it may be, through the changing of your own consciousness by prayer. You know that by thus raising your consciousness any conceivable form of good that you can desire will be yours; and you know that nobody else can by any means hinder you from doing this when you really want to do it—relatives, customers, employers, the government, bad times, so-called—nothing can hinder you from the rebuilding of your own consciousness—and this rebuilding is the Great Adventure.

JOSEPH MURPHY

How to Attract Money

Contents

Introduction

Most people discover this little gem of a book after reading the author Joseph Murphy's most famous and enduring book, *The Power of Your Subconscious Mind*. Once readers encounter that particular book, they often seek out all of Murphy's other titles. Why? Because Joseph Murphy had the gift of taking complicated ideas and making them not just easy to understand, but also easy to practice.

My first introduction to the motivational works of Joseph Murphy wasn't with *The Power of Your Subconscious Mind*. Years ago, when I was living in Denver, Colorado, I was browsing in a large bookstore, walking up and down the aisles to see which books caught my attention. It was then that I saw a slim little book with a bright pink cover, with the title in large white type—*How to Attract Money*. The book itself was fewer than one hundred pages, and was a small trim size. It had an attractively old-fashioned look to it, like a book from the era depicted in the television show *Mad Men*. Could such a little book still have information that would be useful to me?

I didn't buy the book on that visit, or the next, or the next. But every time I went to the bookstore, I would see that book, and think *Someday I'll get that book and see what it has to say*. Eventually I bought the book, and it sat on my shelf for a few months before I picked it up. I read a lot of self-help books at that time, and this one—which called to me—always seemed too slight, and therefore didn't seem like an urgent read.

Eventually I picked up the book, settled in, and began to read. It speaks to how powerful the book is that I can remember where I was when I first read it! Murphy wrote things like *Wealth is a state of consciousness; it is a mind conditioned to Divine supply forever flowing,* which spoke directly to what I most needed to learn at that moment.

In my experience, the right book will arrive when you most need to read it—and this was no exception. I devoured the book quickly, and then started back on page 1 and reread it. On virtually every page I found little gems of information and inspiration, and I found myself highlighting and underlining whole sections.

After reading it a second time, I decided to read other Murphy books. I picked up *Your Power to Be Rich, Believe in Yourself, How to Use the Laws of Mind, The Amazing Laws of Cosmic Mind Power, The Cosmic Power Within You, The Miracle of Mind Dynamics,* and several more. And yes, I eventually did get a copy of his magnum opus, *The Power of Your Subconscious Mind,* and I loved it. Over the years I learned that Murphy had been born in Ireland (which might explain all of the stories he fills his books with!) in 1898, moved to the United States, became a noted New Thought minister, and wrote more than thirty books, which were translated all around the world. He died in 1981, but his tremendous legacy continues through his books.

You can tell from the titles that many of his books were about the same core principles in which he believed, each coming from a slightly different angle. Pick up any one of them, including this one, and you'll get Murphy's no-nonsense approach to the great laws of the Universe, and how to use them. Don't let the size fool you. This is vintage Murphy wisdom, distilled and full octane, free of fluff and filler, and straight to the point.

All these years later, I still pick up this book from time to time. My old copy is tattered and falling apart, so I'm glad to have this beautiful new edition available. If this is your first Murphy book—or your thirtieth—I believe it holds some good information that can help to improve your life. Read it with an open mind and an open heart, and see what positive ideas speak to you most. And then try to implement those positive ideas in your life. One final suggestion: keep this book close by. Whenever you feel down, or like life isn't quite working the way you think it should, or just need a quick jolt of positivity, pick up this book, start flipping through it, and let Murphy's writings inspire you to live the life you have always dreamed of.

—Joel Fotinos

Your Right to Be Rich

It is your right to be rich. You are here to lead the abundant life, and be happy, radiant, and free. You should, therefore, have all the money you need to lead a full, happy, prosperous life.

There is no virtue in poverty; the latter is a mental disease, and it should be abolished from the face of the earth. You are here to grow, expand, and unfold, spiritually, mentally, and materially. You have the inalienable right to fully develop and express yourself along all lines. You should surround yourself with beauty and luxury.

Why be satisfied with just enough to go around when you can enjoy the riches of the Infinite? In this book you will learn to make friends with money, and you will always have a surplus. Your desire to be rich is a desire for a fuller, happier, more wonderful life. It is a cosmic urge. It is good and very good.

Begin to see money in its true significance—as a symbol of exchange. It means to you freedom from want, and beauty, luxury, abundance, and refinement.

As you read this chapter, you are probably saying, "I want more money." "I am worthy of a higher salary than I am receiving."

I believe most people are inadequately compensated. One of the causes many people do not have more money is that they are silently or openly condemning it. They refer to money as "filthy lucre," or "Love of money is the root of all evil," etc. Another reason they do not prosper is that they have a sneaky, subconscious feeling there is some virtue in poverty; this subconscious pattern may be due to early childhood training, superstition, or it could be based on a false interpretation of the Scriptures.

There is no virtue in poverty; it is a disease like any other mental disease. If you were physically ill, you would think there was something wrong with you; you would seek help, or do something about the condition at once. Likewise if you do not have money constantly circulating in your life, there is something radically wrong with you.

Money is only a symbol; it has taken many forms as a medium of exchange down through the centuries, such as salt, beads, and trinkets of various kinds. In early times man's wealth was determined by the number of sheep or oxen he had. It is much more convenient to write a check than to carry some sheep around with you to pay your bills.

God does not want you to live in a hovel or go hungry. God *wants* you to be happy, prosperous, and successful. God is always successful in all His undertakings, whether He makes a star or a cosmos!

You may wish to make a trip around the world, study art in foreign countries, go to college, or send your children to a superior school. You certainly wish to bring your children up in lovely surroundings, so that they might learn to appreciate beauty, order, symmetry, and proportion.

You were born to succeed, to win, to conquer all difficulties, and have all your faculties fully developed. If there is financial lack in your life, do something about it.

Get away immediately from all superstitious beliefs about money. Do not ever regard money as evil or filthy. If you do, you cause it to take wings and fly away from you. Remember that you lose what you condemn.

Suppose, for example, you found gold, silver, lead, copper, or iron in the ground. Would you pronounce these things evil? God pronounced all things good. The evil comes from man's darkened understanding, from his unillumined mind, from his false interpretation of life, and his misuse of Divine Power. Uranium, lead, or some other metal could have been used as a medium of exchange. We use paper bills, checks, etc.; surely the piece of paper is not evil; neither is the check. Physicists and scientists know today that the only difference between one metal and another is the number and rate of motion of the electrons revolving around a central nucleus. They are now changing one metal into another through a bombardment of the atoms in the powerful cyclotron. Gold under certain conditions becomes mercury. It will only be a little while until gold, silver, and other metals will be made synthetically in the chemical laboratory. I cannot imagine seeing anything evil in electrons, neutrons, protons, and isotopes.

The piece of paper in your pocket is composed of electrons and protons arranged differently; their number and rate of motion is different; that is the only way the paper differs from the silver in your pocket.

Some people will say, "Oh, people kill for money. They steal for money!" It has been associated with countless crimes, but that does not make it evil.

A man may give another $50 to kill someone; he has misused money in using it for a destructive purpose. You can use electricity to kill someone or light the house. You can use water to quench the baby's thirst, or use it to drown the child. You can use fire to warm the child, or burn it to death.

Another illustration would be if you brought some earth from your garden, put it in your coffee cup for breakfast, that would be your evil; yet the earth is not evil; neither is the coffee. The earth is displaced; it belongs in your garden.

Similarly if a needle were stuck in your thumb, it would be

your evil; the needle or pin belongs in the pin cushion, not in your thumb.

We know the forces or the elements of nature are not evil; it depends on our use of them whether they bless or hurt us.

A man said to me one time, "I am broke. I do not like money; it is the root of all evil."

Love of money to the exclusion of everything else will cause you to become lopsided and unbalanced. You are here to use your power or authority wisely. Some men crave power; others crave money. If you set your heart on money, and say, "That is all I want. I am going to give all my attention to amassing money; nothing else matters," you can get money and attain a fortune, but you have forgotten that you are here to lead a balanced life. "Man does not live by bread alone."

For example, if you belong to some cult or religious group, and become fanatical about it, excluding yourself from your friends, society, and social activities, you will become unbalanced, inhibited, and frustrated. Nature insists on a balance. If all your time is devoted to external things and possessions, you will find yourself hungry for peace of mind, harmony, love, joy, or perfect health. You will find you cannot buy anything that is real. You can amass a fortune, or have millions of dollars; this is not evil or bad. Love of money to the exclusion of everything else results in frustration, disappointment, and disillusionment; in that sense it is the root of your evil.

By making money your sole aim, you simply made a wrong choice. You thought that was all you wanted, but you found after all your efforts that it was not only the money you needed. What you really desired was true place, peace of mind, and abundance. You could have the million or many millions, if you wanted them, and still have peace of mind, harmony, perfect health, and Divine expression.

Everyone wants enough money, and not just enough to go around. He wants abundance and to spare; he should have it. The urges, desires, and impulses we have for food, clothing, homes, better means of transportation, expression, procreation, and abundance are all God-given, Divine, and good, but we may misdirect these impulses, desires, and urges resulting in evil or negative experiences in our lives.

Man does not have an evil nature; there is no evil nature in you; it is God, the Universal Wisdom, or Life seeking expression through you.

For example, a boy wants to go to college, but he does not have enough money. He sees other boys in the neighborhood going off to college and the university; his desire increases. He says to himself, "I want an education, too." Such a youth may steal and embezzle money for the purpose of going to college. The desire to go to college was basically and fundamentally good; he misdirected that desire or urge by violating the laws of society, the cosmic law of harmony, or the golden rule; then he finds himself in trouble.

However if this boy knew the laws of mind, and his unqualified capacity through the use of the Spiritual Power to go to college, he would be free and not in jail. Who put him in jail? He placed himself there. The policeman who locked him up in prison was an instrument of the man-made laws which he violated. He first imprisoned himself in his mind by stealing and hurting others. Fear and a guilt consciousness followed; this is the prison of the mind followed by the prison walls made of bricks and stones.

Money is a symbol of God's opulence, beauty, refinement, and abundance, and it should be used wisely, judiciously, and constructively to bless humanity in countless ways. It is merely a symbol of the economic health of the nation. When your blood is circulating freely, you are healthy. When money is circulating freely in your life, you are economically healthy. When people begin to hoard money, to put it away in tin boxes, and become charged with fear, there is economic illness.

The crash of 1929 was a psychological panic; it was fear seizing the minds of people everywhere. It was a sort of negative, hypnotic spell.

You are living in a subjective and objective world. You must not neglect the spiritual food, such as peace of mind, love, beauty, harmony, joy, and laughter.

Knowledge of the spiritual power is the means to the Royal Road to Riches of all kinds, whether your desire is spiritual, mental, or material. The student of the laws of mind, or the student of the spiritual principle, believes and knows absolutely that regardless of the economic situation, stock market fluctuation, depression, strikes, war, other conditions, or circumstances, he will always be amply supplied regardless of what form money may take. The reason for this is he abides in the consciousness of wealth. The student has convinced himself in his mind that wealth is forever flowing freely in his life, and that there is always a Divine surplus. Should there be a war tomorrow, and all the student's present holdings become valueless, as the German marks did after the First World War, he would still attract wealth, and be cared for regardless of the form the new currency took.

Wealth is a state of consciousness; it is a mind conditioned to Divine supply forever flowing. The scientific thinker looks at money or wealth like the tide; i.e., it goes out, but it always comes back. The tides never fail; neither will man's supply when he trusts a tireless, changeless, immortal Presence which is Omnipresent, and flows ceaselessly. The man who knows the workings of the subconscious mind is never, therefore, worried about the economic situation, stock market panics, devaluation, or inflation of currency, since he abides in the consciousness of God's eternal supply. Such a man is always supplied and watched over by an overshadowing Presence. *Behold the fowls of the air: for they sow not, neither do they reap, nor gather into barns; yet your heavenly Father feedeth them. Are ye not much better than they?* MATTHEW 6:26.

As you consciously commune with the Divine-Presence claiming and knowing that It leads and guides you in all your ways, that It is a Lamp unto your feet, and a Light on your path, you will be Divinely prospered and sustained beyond your wildest dreams.

Here is a simple way for you to impress your subconscious mind with the idea of constant supply or wealth: Quiet the wheels of your mind. Relax! Let go! Immobilize the attention. Get into a sleepy, drowsy, meditative state of mind; this reduces effort to the minimum; then in a quiet, relaxed, passive way reflect on the following simple truths: Ask yourself where do ideas come from? Where does wealth come from? Where did you come from? Where did your brain and your mind come from? You will be led back to the One Source.

You find yourself on a spiritual, working basis now. It will no longer insult your intelligence to realize that wealth is a state of mind. Take this little phrase; repeat it slowly four or five minutes three or four times a day quietly to yourself, particularly before you go to sleep: "Money is forever circulating freely in my life, and there is always a Divine surplus." As you do this regularly and systematically, the idea of wealth will be conveyed to your deeper mind, and you will develop a wealth consciousness. Idle, mechanical repetition will not succeed in building the consciousness of wealth. Begin to feel the truth of what you affirm. You know what you are doing, and why you are doing it. You know your deeper self is responsive to what you consciously accept as true.

In the beginning people who are in financial difficulties do not get results with such affirmations as, "I am wealthy," "I am prosperous," "I am successful"; such statements may cause their conditions to get worse. The reason is the subconscious mind will only accept the dominant of two ideas, or the dominant mood or feeling. When they say, "I am prosperous," their feeling of lack is greater, and something within them says, "No, you are not prosperous, you are broke." The feeling of lack is dominant so that each affirmation calls forth the mood of lack, and more lack becomes theirs. The way to overcome this for beginners is to affirm what the conscious and subconscious mind will agree on; then there will be no contradiction. Our subconscious mind accepts our beliefs, feelings, convictions, and what we consciously accept as true.

A man could engage the cooperation of his subconscious mind by saying, "I am prospering every day." "I am growing in wealth and in wisdom every day." "Every day my wealth is multiplying." "I am advancing, growing, and moving forward financially." These and similar statements would not create any conflict in the mind.

For instance if a salesman has only ten cents in his pocket, he could easily agree that he would have more tomorrow. If he sold a pair of shoes tomorrow, there is nothing within him which says his sales could not increase. He could use statements, such as, "My sales are increasing every day." "I am advancing and moving forward." He would find these would be sound psychologically, acceptable to his mind, and produce desirable fruit.

The spiritually advanced student who quietly, knowingly, and feelingly says, "I am prosperous," "I am successful," "I am wealthy," gets wonderful results also. Why would this be true? When they think, feel, or say, "I am prosperous," they mean God is All Supply or Infinite Riches, and what is true of God is true of them. When they say, "I am wealthy," they know God is Infinite Supply, the Inexhaustible, Treasure-House, and what is true of God is, therefore, true of them, for God is within them.

Many men get wonderful results by dwelling on three abstract ideas, such as health, wealth, and success. *Health* is a Divine Reality or quality of God. *Wealth* is of God; it is eternal and endless. *Success* is of God; God is always successful in all His undertakings.

The way they produce remarkable results is to stand before a mirror as they shave, and repeat for five or ten minutes: "Health, wealth, and success." They do not say, "I am healthy," or "I am successful"; they create no opposition in their minds. They are quiet and relaxed; thus the mind is receptive and passive; then they repeat these words. Amazing results follow. All they are doing is identifying with truths that are eternal, changeless, and timeless.

You can develop a wealth consciousness. Put the principles enunciated and elaborated on in this book to practice, and your desert will rejoice and blossom as the rose.

I worked with a young boy in Australia many years ago who wanted to become a physician and surgeon, but he had no money; nor had he graduated from high school. For expenses he used to clean out doctors' offices, wash windows, and do odd repair jobs. He told me that every night as he went to sleep, he used to see a diploma on a wall with his name in big, bold letters. He used to clean and shine the diplomas in the medical building where he worked; it was not hard for him to engrave the diploma in his mind and develop it there. I do not know how long he continued this imaging, but it must have been for some months.

Results followed as he persisted. One of the doctors took a great liking to this young boy, and after training him in the art of sterilizing instruments, giving hypodermic injections, and other miscellaneous first aid work, he became a technical assistant in his office. The doctor sent him to high school and also to college at his expense.

Today this man is a prominent doctor in Montreal, Canada. He had a dream! A clear image in his mind! *His wealth was in his mind.*

Wealth is your idea, desire, talent, urge for service, capacity to give to mankind, your ability for usefulness to society, and your love for humanity in general.

This young boy operated a great law unconsciously. Troward says, "Having seen the end, you have willed the means to the realization of the end." The *end* in this boy's case was to be a physician. To imagine, see, and feel the reality of being a doctor now, to live with that idea, sustain it, nourish it, and to love it until through his imagination it penetrated the layers of the subconscious, becoming a conviction, paved the way to the fulfillment of his dreams.

He could have said, "I have no education." "I do not know the right people." "I am too old to go to school now." "I have no money; it would take years, and I am not intelligent." He would then be beaten before he started. His wealth was in his use of the Spiritual Power within him which responded to his thought.

The means or the way in which our prayer is answered is always hidden from us except that occasionally we may intuitively perceive a part of the process. *My ways are past finding out.* The *ways* are not known. The only thing man has to do is to imagine and accept the end in his mind, and leave its unfoldment to the subjective wisdom within.

Oftentimes the question is asked, "What should I do after meditating on the end and accepting my desire in consciousness? The answer is simple: You will be compelled to do whatever is necessary for the unfoldment of your ideal. The law of the subconscious is compulsion. The law of life is action and reaction. What we do is the automatic response to our inner movements of the mind, inner feeling, and conviction.

A few months ago as I went to sleep, I imagined I was reading one of my most popular books, *Magic of Faith* in French. I began to realize and imagine this book going into all French-speaking nations. For several weeks I did this every night, falling asleep with the imaginary French edition of *Magic of Faith* in my hands. Just before Christmas in 1954, I received a letter from a leading publisher in Paris, France, enclosing a contract drawn up, asking me to sign it, giving him permission to publish and promote abroad to all French-speaking countries the French edition of *Magic of Faith*.

You might ask me what did I do about the publishing of this book after prayer? I would have to say, "Nothing!" The subjective wisdom took over, and brought it to pass in its own way, which was a far better way than any method I could consciously desire.

All of our external movements, motions, and actions follow the inner movements of the mind. Inner action precedes all outer action. Whatever steps you take physically, or what you seem to do objectively, will all be a part of a pattern which you were compelled to fulfill.

Accepting the end wills the means to the realization of the end. Believe that you have it now, and you shall receive it.

We must cease denying our good. Realize that the only thing that keeps us from the riches that lie all around us is our mental attitude, or the way we look at God, life, and the world in general. Know, believe, and act on the positive assumption that there is no reason why you cannot have, be, and do whatever you wish to accomplish through the great laws of God.

Your knowledge of how your mind works is your saviour and redeemer. Thought and feeling are your destiny. You possess everything by right of consciousness. The consciousness of health produces health; the consciousness of wealth produces wealth. The world seems to deny or oppose what you pray for; your senses sometimes mock and laugh at you.

If you say to your friend, you are opening up a new business for yourself, he may proceed to give you all the reasons why you are bound to fail. If you are susceptible to his hypnotic spell, he may instill fear of failure in your mind. As you become aware of the spiritual power which is one and indivisible, and responds to your thought, you will reject the darkness and ignorance of the world, and know that you possess all the equipment, power, and knowledge to succeed.

To walk on the Royal Road to Riches, you must not place obstacles and impediments on the pathway of others; neither must you be jealous or envious of others. Actually when you entertain these negative states of mind, you are hurting and injuring yourself, because you are thinking and feeling it. "The suggestion," as Quimby said, "you give to another, you are giving to yourself." This is the reason that the law of the golden rule is a cosmic, divine law.

I am sure you have heard men say, "That fellow has a racket." "He is a racketeer." "He is getting money dishonestly." "He is a faker." "I knew him when he had nothing." "He is crooked, a thief, and a swindler." If you analyze the man who talks like that, he is usually in want or suffering from some financial or physical illness. Perhaps his former, college friends went up the ladder of success and excelled him; now he is bitter and envious of their progress. In many instances this is the cause of his downfall. Thinking negatively of these classmates, and condemning their wealth, causes the wealth and prosperity he is praying for to vanish and flee away. He is condemning the things he is praying for. He is praying two ways. On the one hand he is saying, "God is prospering me," and in the next breath, silently or audibly, he is saying, "I resent that fellow's wealth." Always make it a special point to bless the other person, and rejoice in his prosperity and success; when you do, you bless and prosper yourself.

If you go into the bank, and you see your competitor across the street deposit twenty times more than you do, or you see him deposit ten thousand dollars, rejoice and be exceedingly glad to see God's abundance being manifested through one of his sons. You are then blessing and exalting what you are praying for. What you bless, you multiply. What you condemn, you lose.

If you are working in a large organization, and you are silently thinking and resenting the fact you are underpaid, that you are not appreciated, and that you deserve more money and greater recognition, you are subconsciously severing your ties with that organization. You are setting a law in motion; then the superintendent or manager says to you, "We have to let you go." You dismissed yourself. The manager was simply the instrument through which your own negative, mental state was confirmed. In other words he was a messenger telling you what you conceived as true about yourself. It was an example of the law of action and reaction. The action was the internal movement of your mind; the *reaction* was the response of the outer world to conform to your inner thinking.

Perhaps as you read this, you are thinking of someone who has prospered financially by taking advantage of others, by defrauding them, in selling them unsound investments in property, etc. The answer to this is obvious, because if we rob, cheat, or defraud another, we do the same to ourselves. In reality in this case we are actually hurting or robbing from ourselves. We are in a mood of lack in the first place, which is bound to attract loss to us. The loss may come in many ways; it may come in loss of health, prestige, peace of mind, social status, sickness in the home, or in business. It may not necessarily come in loss of money. We must not be shortsighted and think that the loss has to come just in dollars and cents.

Isn't it a wonderful feeling to place your head on the pillow at night, and feel you are at peace with the whole world, and that your heart is full of goodwill toward all? There are some people who have accumulated money the wrong way, as by tramping on others, trickery, deceit, and chicanery. What is the price? Sometimes it is mental and physical disease, guilt complexes, insomnia, or hidden fears. As one man said to me, "Yes, I rode roughshod over others. I got what I wanted, but I got cancer doing it." He realized he had attained his wealth in the wrong way.

You can be wealthy and prosperous without hurting anyone. Many men are constantly robbing themselves; they steal from themselves: peace of mind, health, joy, inspiration, happiness, and the laughter of God. They may say that they have never stolen, but is it true? Every time we resent another, or are jealous, or envious of another's wealth or success, we are stealing from ourselves. These are the thieves and robbers which Jesus cast out of the temple; likewise you must cast them out incisively and decisively. Do not let them live in your mind. Cut their heads off with the fire of right thought and feeling.

I remember in the early days of the war reading about a woman in Brooklyn, New York, who went around from store to store buying up all the coffee she could. She knew it was going to be rationed; she was full of fear that there would not be enough for her. She bought as much as she could, and stored it in the cellar. That evening she went to church services. When she came home, burglars had broken down the door, stolen not only the coffee, but silverware, money, jewelry, and other things.

This good woman said what they all say: "Why did this happen to me when I was at church? I never stole from anyone."

Is this true? Was she not in the consciousness of lack and fear when she began to hoard supplies of coffee? Her mood and fear of lack was sufficient to bring about loss in her home and possessions. She did not have to put her hand on the cash register or rob a bank; her fear of lack produced lack. This is the reason that many people who are what society calls "good citizens" suffer loss. They are good in the worldly sense; i.e., they pay their taxes; they obey the laws, vote regularly, and are generous to charities, but they are resentful of others' possessions, their wealth, or social position. If they would like to take money when no one was looking, such an attitude is definitely and positively a state of lack, and may cause the person who indulges in such a mental state to attract charlatans or knaves who may swindle or cheat them in some business transaction.

Before the outer thief robs us, we have first robbed ourselves. There must be an inner thief, before the outer one appears.

A man can have a guilt complex, and be accusing himself constantly. I knew such a man; he was very honest as a teller in a bank. He never stole any money, but he had an illicit romance; he was supporting another woman, and denying his family. He lived in fear that he would be discovered; a deep sense of guilt resulted. Fear follows guilt. Fear causes a contraction of the muscles and mucous membranes; acute sinusitis developed. Medication only gave him temporary relief.

I explained to this client the cause of his trouble, and told him the cure was to give up his outside affair. He said he couldn't; she was his soul mate, and that he had tried. He was always condemning and accusing himself.

One day he was accused by one of the officials of the bank of having embezzled some money; it looked serious for him, as the evidence was circumstantial. He became panic stricken, and realized that the only reason he was wrongfully accused was that he had been accusing and condemning himself. He saw how mind operates. Inasmuch as he was always accusing himself on the inner plane, he would be accused on the outer.

He broke off the relationship immediately with the other woman due to the shock of being accused of embezzling, and began to pray for Divine harmony and understanding between himself and the bank official. He began to claim, "There is nothing hidden that is not revealed. The peace of God reigns supreme in the minds and hearts of all concerned."

Truth prevailed. The whole matter was dissolved in the light of truth. Another young man was discovered as the culprit. The bank teller knew that only through prayer was he saved from a jail sentence.

The great law is, "As you would that men should think about you, think you about them in the same manner. As you would that men should feel about you, feel you also about them in like manner."

Say from your heart, "I wish for every man who walks the earth, what I wish for myself. The sincere wish of my heart is, therefore, peace, love, joy, abundance, and God's blessings to all men everywhere. Rejoice and be glad in the progression, advancement, and prosperity of all men. Whatever you claim as true for yourself, claim it for all men everywhere. If you pray for happiness and peace of mind, let your claim be peace and happiness for all. Do not ever try and deprive another of any joy. If you do, you deprive yourself. When the ship comes in for your friend, it comes in for you also.

If someone is promoted in your organization, be glad and happy. Congratulate him, rejoice in his advancement and recognition. If you are angry or resentful, you are demoting yourself. Do not try and withhold from another his God-given birthright to happiness, success, achievement, abundance, and all good things.

Jesus said, "Sow up for yourselves treasures in heaven, where the moth and the rust doth not consume, and where thieves cannot break through and steal." Hatred and resentment rot and corrode the heart causing us to become full of scars, impurities, toxins, and poisons.

The treasures of heaven are the truths of God which we possess in our soul. Fill your minds with peace, harmony, faith, joy, honesty, integrity, loving kindness, and gentleness; then you will be sowing for yourself treasures in the heavens of your own mind.

If you are seeking wisdom regarding investments, or if you are worried about your stocks or bonds, quietly claim, "Infinite Intelligence governs and watches over all my financial transactions, and whatsoever I do shall prosper." Do this frequently and you will find that your investments will be wise; moreover you will be protected from loss, as you will be prompted to sell your securities or holdings before any loss accrues to you.

Let the following prayer be used daily by you regarding your home, business, and possessions: "The overshadowing Presence which guides the planets on their course and causes the sun to shine, watches over all my possessions, home, business, and all things that are mine. God is my fortress and vault. All my possessions are secure in God. It is wonderful." By reminding yourself daily of this great truth, and by observing the laws of Love, you will always be guided, watched over, and prospered in all your ways. You will never suffer from loss; for you have chosen the Most High as your Counsellor and Guide. The envelope of God's Love surrounds, enfolds, and encompasses you at all times. You rest in the Everlasting Arms of God.

All of us should seek an inner guidance for our problems. If you have a financial problem, repeat this before you retire at night: "Now I shall sleep in peace. I have turned this matter over to the God-Wisdom within. It knows only the answer. As the sun rises in the morning, so will my answer be resurrected. I know the sunrise never fails." Then go off to sleep.

Do not fret, fuss, and fume over a problem. Night brings counsel. Sleep on it. Your intellect can not solve all your problems. Pray for the Light that is to come. Remember the dawn always comes; then the shadows flee away. Let your sleep every night be a contented bliss.

You are not a victim of circumstances, except you believe you are. You can rise and overcome any circumstance or condition. You will have different experiences as you stand on the rock of spiritual Truth, steadfast, and faithful to your deeper purposes and desires.

In large stores, the management employs store detectives to prevent people from stealing; they catch a number every day trying to get something for nothing. All such people are living in the consciousness of lack and limitation, and are stealing from themselves, attracting at the same time all manner of loss. These people lack faith in God, and the understanding of how their minds work. If they would pray for true peace, Divine expression, and supply, they would find work; then by honesty, integrity, and perseverence they would become a credit to themselves and society at large.

Jesus said, "For ye have the poor always with you; but me ye have not always." The *poor states* of consciousness are always with us in this sense, that no matter how much wealth you now have, there is something you want with all your heart. It may be a problem of health; perhaps a son or daughter needs guidance, or harmony is lacking in the home. At that moment you are poor.

We could not know what abundance was, except we were conscious of lack. "I have chosen twelve, and one of you is a devil."

Whether it be the king of England or the boy in the slums, we are all born into limitation and into the race belief. It is through these limitations we grow. We could never discover the Inner Power, except through problems and difficulties; these are our *poor states* which prod us in seeking the solution. We could not know what joy was, except we could shed a tear of sorrow. We must be aware of poverty, to seek liberation and freedom, and ascend into God's opulence.

The *poor states,* such as fear, ignorance, worry, lack, and pain are not bad when they cause you to seek the opposite. When you get into trouble, and get kicked around from pillar to post; when you ask negative, heart-rending questions, such as "Why are all these things happening to me?" "Why does there seem to be a jinx following me?" light will come into your mind. Through your suffering, pain, or misery, you will discover the truth which sets you free. "Sweet are the uses of adversity, like a toad ugly and venomous, yet wears a precious jewel on its head."

Through dissatisfaction we are led to satisfaction. All those studying the laws of life have been dissatisfied with something. They have had some problem or difficulty which they could not solve; or they were not satisfied with the man-made answers to life's riddles. They have found their answer in the God-Presence within themselves—the pearl of great price—the precious jewel. The Bible says, "I sought the Lord, and I found him, and He delivered me from all my fears."

When you realize your ambition or desire, you will be satisfied for only a period of brief time; then the urge to expand will come again. This is Life seeking to express Itself at higher levels through you. When one desire is satisfied, another comes, etc. to infinity. You are here to grow. Life is progression; it is not static. You are here to go from glory to glory; there is no end; for there is no end to God's glory.

We are all poor in the sense we are forever seeking more light, wisdom, happiness, and greater joy out of life. God is Infinite, and never in Eternity could you exhaust the glory, beauty, and wisdom which is within; this is how wonderful you are.

In the absolute state all things are finished, but in the relative world we must awaken to that glory which was ours before the world was. No matter how wise you are, you are seeking more wisdom; so you are still poor. No matter how intelligent you are in the field of mathematics, physics, or astronomy, you are only scratching the surface. You are still poor. The journey is ever onward, upward, and Godward. It is really an awakening process, whereby you realize creation is finished. When you know God does not have to learn, grow, expand, or unfold, you begin to gradually awaken from the dream of limitation, and become alive in God. As the scales of fear, ignorance, race belief, and mass hypnosis fall from your eyes, you begin to see as God sees. The blind spots are removed; then you begin to see the world as God made it; for we begin to see it through God's eyes. Now you say, "Behold, the Kingdom of Heaven is at hand!"

Feed the "poor" within you; clothe the naked ideas, and give them form by believing in the reality of the idea, trusting the great Fabricator within to clothe it in form and objectify it. Now your word (idea) shall become flesh (take form). When you are hungry (poor states), you seek food. When worried, you seek peace. When you are sick, you seek health; when you are weak, you seek strength. Your desire for prosperity is the voice of God in you telling you that abundance is yours; therefore, through your poor state, you find the urge to grow, to expand, to unfold, to achieve, and to accomplish your desires.

A pain in your shoulder is a blessing in disguise; it tells you to do something about it at once. If there were no pain and no indication of trouble, your arm might fall off on the street. Your pain is God's alarm system telling you to seek His Peace and His Healing Power, and move from darkness to Light. When cold, you build a fire. When you are hungry, you eat. When you are in lack, enter into the mood of opulence and plenty. Imagine the end; rejoice in it. Having imagined the end, and felt it as true, you have willed the means to the realization of the end.

When you are fearful and worried, feed your mind with the great truths of God that have stood the test of time and will last forever. You can receive comfort by meditating on the great psalms. For example: "The Lord is my shepherd; I shall not want." "God is my refuge, my salvation, whom shall I fear?" "God is an ever-present help in time of trouble." "My God in Him will I trust." "He shall cover me with His feathers, and under His wings shall I rest." "One with God is a majority." "If God be for me, who can be against me?" "I do all things through Christ which strengtheneth me." Let the healing vibrations of these truths flood your mind and heart; then you will crowd out of your mind all your fears, doubts, and worries through this meditative process.

Imbibe another great spiritual truth: "A merry heart maketh a cheerful countenance." "A merry heart hath a continual feast." "A merry heart doeth good like a medicine; a broken spirit drieth the bones." "Therefore I put thee in remembrance that thou stir up the gift of God within thee." Begin *now* to stir up the gift of God by completely rejecting the evidence of senses, the tyranny and despotism of the race mind, and give complete recognition to the spiritual Power within you as the only Cause, the only Power, and the only Presence. Know that it is a responsive and beneficent Power. "Draw nigh unto it, and it will draw nigh unto you." Turn to It devotedly with assurance, trust, and love; it will respond to you as love, peace, guidance, and prosperity.

It will be your Comforter, Guide, Counsellor, and your heavenly Father. You will then say, "God is Love. I have found Him, and He truly has delivered me from all my fears. Furthermore, you will find yourself in green pastures, where abundance and all of God's riches flow freely through you.

Say to yourself freely and joyously during the day, "I walk in the consciousness of the Presence of God all day long." "His fulness flows through me at all times filling up all the empty vessels in my life."

When you are filled full of the feeling of being what you long to be, your prayer is answered. Are all the vessels full in your life? Look under health, wealth, love, and expression. Are you fully satisfied on all levels? Is there something lacking in one of these four? All that you seek, no matter what it is, comes under one of these classifications.

If you say, "All I want is truth or wisdom," you are expressing the desire of all men everywhere. That is what everyone wants, even though he or she may word it differently. Truth or wisdom is the overall desire of every man; this comes under the classification of expression. You wish to express more and more of God here and now.

Through your lack, limitation, and problems, you grow in God's Light, and you discover yourself. There is no other way whereby you could discover yourself.

If you could not use your powers two ways, you would never discover yourself; neither would you ever deduce a law governing you. If you were compelled to be good, or compelled to love, that would not be love. You would then be an automaton. You have freedom to love, because you can give it, or retain it. If compelled to love, there is no love. Aren't you flattered when some woman tells you she loves you and wants you? She has chosen you from all the men in the world. She does not have to love you. If she were forced to love you, you would not be flattered or happy about it.

You have freedom to be a murderer or a Holy man. This is the reason that we praise such men as Lincoln and others. They decided to choose the good; we praise them for their choice. If we believe that circumstances, conditions, events, age, race, religious training, or early environment can preclude the possibility of our attaining a happy, prosperous life, we are thieves and robbers. All that is necessary to express happiness and prosperity is to *feel* happy and prosperous. The feeling of wealth produces wealth. States of consciousness manifest themselves. This is why it is said, "All that ever came before me (feeling) are thieves and robbers." Feeling is the law, and the law is the feeling.

Your desire for prosperity is really the promise of God saying that His riches are yours; accept this promise without any mental reservation.

Quimby likened prayer to that of a lawyer pleading the case before the judge. This teacher of the laws of mind said he could prove the defendant was not guilty as charged, but that the person was a victim of lies and false beliefs. You are the judge; you render your own verdict; then you are set free. The negative thoughts of lack, poverty, and failure are all false; they are all lies; there is nothing to back them up.

You know there is only one spiritual Power, one primal cause, and you, therefore, cease giving power to conditions, circumstances, and opinions of men. Give all Power to the Spiritual Power within you, knowing that It will respond to your thought of abundance and prosperity. Recognizing the supremacy of the Spirit within, and the Power of your own thought or mental image is the way to opulence, freedom, and constant supply. Accept the abundant life in your own mind. Your mental acceptance and expectancy of wealth has its own mathematics and mechanics of expression. As you enter into the mood of opulence, all things necessary for the abundant life will come to pass. You are now the judge arriving at a decision in the courthouse of your mind. You have, like Quimby, produced indisputable evidence showing how the laws of your mind work, and you are now free from fear. You have executed and chopped the heads off all the fear and superstitious thoughts in your mind. Fear is the signal for action; it is not really bad; it tells you to move to the opposite which is faith in God and all positive values.

Let this be your daily prayer; write it in your heart: "God is the source of my supply. That supply is my supply now. His riches flow to me freely, copiously, and abundantly. I am forever conscious of my true worth. I give of my talents freely, and I am wonderfully, divinely compensated. Thank you, Father!"

The Road to Riches

Riches are of the mind. Let us suppose for a moment that a physician's diploma was stolen together with his office equipment. I am sure you would agree that his wealth was in his mind. He could still carry on, diagnose disease, prescribe, operate, and lecture on materia medica. Only his symbols were stolen; he could always get additional supplies. His riches were in his mental capacity, knowledge to help others, and his ability to contribute to humanity in general.

You will always be wealthy when you have an intense desire to contribute to the good of mankind. Your urge for service—i.e., to give of your talents to the world—will always find a response in the heart of the universe.

I knew a man in New York during the financial crisis of 1929, who lost everything he had including his home and all his life's savings. I met him after a lecture which I had given at one of the hotels in the city. This was what he said: "I lost everything. I made a million dollars in four years. I will make it again. All I have lost is a symbol. I can again attract the symbol of wealth in the same way as honey attracts flies."

I followed the career of this man for several years to discover the key to his success. The key may seem strange to you; yet it is a very old one. The name he gave the key was, "Change water into wine!"

He read this passage in the Bible, and he knew it was the answer to perfect health, happiness, peace of mind, and prosperity.

Wine in the Bible always means the realization of your desires, urges, plans, dreams, propositions, etc.; in other words, it is the things you wish to accomplish, achieve, and bring forth.

Water in the Bible usually refers to your mind or consciousness. Water takes the shape of any vessel into which it is poured; likewise whatever you feel and believe as true will become manifest in your world; thus you are always changing water into wine.

The Bible was written by illumined men; it teaches practical, everyday psychology and a way of life. One of the cardinal tenets of the Bible is that you determine, mold, fashion, and shape your own destiny through right thought, feeling, and beliefs. It teaches you that you can solve any problem, overcome any situation, and that you are born to succeed, to win, and to triumph. In order to discover the Royal Road to Riches, and receive the strength and security necessary to advance in life, you must cease viewing the Bible in the traditional way.

The above man who was in a financial crisis used to say to himself frequently during the days when he was without funds, "I can change water into wine!" These words meant to him, "I can exchange the poverty ideas in my mind for the realization of my present desires or needs which are wealth and financial supply."

His mental attitude (water) was, "Once I made a fortune honestly. I will make it again [wine]." His regular affirmation consisted of, "I attracted the symbol [money] once, I am attracting it again. I know this, and feel it is true [wine]."

This man went to work as a salesman for a chemical organization. Ideas for the better promotion of their products came to him; he passed them on to his organization. It was not long until he became vice president. Within four years the company made him president. His constant mental attitude was, "I can change water into wine!"

Look upon the story in John of changing water into wine in a figurative way, and say to yourself as the above-mentioned chemical salesman did: "I can make the invisible ideas, urges, dreams, and desires of mine visible, because I have discovered a simple, universal law of mind.

The law he demonstrated is the law of action and reaction. It means your external world, body, circumstances, environment, and financial status are always a perfect reflection of your inner thinking, beliefs, feelings, and convictions. This being true, you can now change your inner pattern of thought by dwelling on the idea of success, wealth, and peace of mind. As you busy your mind with these latter concepts, these ideas will gradually seep into your mentality like seeds planted in the ground. As all seeds (thoughts and ideas) grow after their kind, so will your habitual thinking and feeling manifest in prosperity, success, and peace of mind. Wise thought (action) is followed by right action (reaction).

You can acquire riches when you become aware of the fact that prayer is a marriage feast. The *feast* is a psychological one; you meditate (mentally eat of) on your good or your desire until you become *one* with it.

I will now cite a case history from my files relating how a young girl performed her first miracle in transforming "water into wine." She operated a very beautiful hair salon. Her mother became ill, and she had to devote considerable time at home neglecting her business. During her absence two of her assistants embezzled funds. She was forced into bankruptcy, losing her home and finding herself deeply in debt. She was unable to pay hospital bills for her mother, and she was now unemployed.

I explained to this woman the magic formula of changing water into wine. Again we made it clear to her that *wine* means answered prayer or the objectification of her ideal.

She was quarreling with the outside world. She said, "Look at the facts: I have lost everything; it is a cruel world. I cannot pay my bills. I do not pray; for I have lost hope." She was so absorbed and engrossed in the material world, that she was completely oblivious to the internal cause of her situation. As we talked, she began to understand that she had to resolve the quarrel in her mind.

No matter what your desire or ideal is as you read this book, you will also find some thought or idea in your mind opposed to it. For example your desire may be for health; perhaps there are several thoughts such as these in your mind simultaneously: "I can't be healed. I have tried, but it is no use; it's getting worse." "I don't know enough about spiritual mind healing."

As you study yourself, don't you have a tug of war in your mind? Like this girl, you find environment and external affairs challenging your desire of expression, wealth, and peace of mind.

True prayer is a mental marriage feast, and it teaches us all how to resolve the mental conflict. In prayer you "write" what you *believe* in your own mind. Emerson said, "A man is what he thinks all day long." By your habitual thinking you make your own mental laws of belief. By repeating a certain train of thought you establish definite opinions and beliefs in the deeper mind called the subconscious; then such mental acceptances, beliefs, and opinions direct and control all the outer actions. To understand this and begin to apply it is the first step in changing "water into wine," or changing lack and limitation into abundance and opulence. The man who is unaware of his own inner, spiritual powers is, therefore, subject to race beliefs, lack, and limitation.

Open your Bible now, and perform your first miracle, as this beauty operator did. You can do it. If you merely read the Bible as a historical event, you will miss the spiritual, mental, scientific view of the laws of mind with which we are concerned in this book.

Let us take this passage: "And the third day there was a marriage in Cana of Galilea; and the mother of Jesus was there." *Galilee* means your mind or consciousness. *Cana* means your desire. The *marriage* is purely mental or the subjective embodiment of your desire. This whole, beautiful drama of prayer is a psychological one in which all the characters are mental states, feelings, and ideas within you.

One of the meanings of *Jesus* is illumined reason. The *mother of Jesus* means the feeling, moods, or emotions which possess us.

"And both Jesus was called, and his disciples, to the marriage." *Your disciples* are your inner powers and faculties enabling you to realize your desires.

"And when they wanted wine, the mother of Jesus saith unto him, They have no wine." *Wine,* as we have stated, represents the answered prayer or the manifestation of your desire and ideals in life. You can now see this is an everyday drama taking place in your own life.

When you wish to accomplish something as this girl did, namely, finding work, supply, and a way out of your problem, suggestions of lack come to you; such as, "There is no hope. All is lost, I can't accomplish it; it is hopeless." This is the voice from the outside world saying to you, "They have no wine," or "Look at the facts." This is your feeling of lack, limitation, or bondage speaking.

How do you meet the challenge of circumstances and conditions? By now you are getting acquainted with the laws of mind which are as follows: "As I think and feel inside, so is my outside world; i.e., my body, finances, environment, social position, and all phases of my external relationship to the world and man. Your internal, mental movements and imagery govern, control, and direct the external plane in your life.

The Bible says, "As he thinketh in his heart, so *is* he." The *heart* is a Chaldean word meaning the subconscious mind. In other words your thought must reach subjective levels by engaging the power of your subliminal self.

Thought and feeling are your destiny. Thought charged with feeling and interest is always subjectified, and becomes manifest in your world. *Prayer* is a marriage of thought and feeling, or your idea and emotion; this is what the marriage feast relates.

Any idea or desire of the mind felt as true comes to pass, whether it is good, bad, or indifferent. Knowing the law now that what you imagine and feel in your mind, you will express, manifest, or experience in the outside, enables you to begin to discipline your mind.

When the suggestion of lack, fear, doubt, or despair (they have no wine) come to your mind, immediately reject it mentally by focusing your attention at once on the answered prayer, or the fulfillment of your desire.

The statement given in the Bible from John 2, "Mine hour is not yet come," and "Woman, what have I to do with thee," are figurative, idiomatic, oriental expressions.

As we paraphrase this quotation, *woman* means the negative feeling that you indulge in. These negative suggestions have no power or reality, because there is nothing to back them up.

A suggestion of lack has no power; the power is resident in your own thought and feeling.

What does God mean to you? *God* is the Name given to the One Spiritual Power. *God* is the One Invisible Source from Which all things flow.

When your thoughts are constructive and harmonious, the spiritual power being responsive to your thought flows as harmony, health, and abundance. Practice the wonderful discipline of completely rejecting every thought of lack by immediately recognizing the availability of the spiritual power, and its response to your constructive thoughts and imagery; then you will be practicing the truth found in these words, "Woman what have I to do with thee?"

We read, "Mine hour is not yet come." This means that while you have not yet reached a conviction or positive state of mind, you know you are on the way mentally, because you are engaging your mind on the positive ideals, goals, and objectives in life. Whatever the mind dwells upon, it multiplies, magnifies, and causes it to grow until finally the mind becomes qualified with the new state of consciousness. You are then conditioned positively, whereas before you were conditioned negatively.

The spiritual man in prayer moves from the mood of lack to the mood of confidence, peace, and trust in the spiritual power within himself. Since his trust and faith are in the Spiritual Power, his mother (moods and feeling) registers a feeling of triumph or victory; this will bring about the solution or the answer to your prayer.

The waterpots in the story from the Bible refer to the mental cycles that man goes through in order to bring about the subjective realization of his desire. The length of time may be a moment, hour, week, or month depending on the faith and state of consciousness of the student.

In prayer we must cleanse our mind of false beliefs, fear, doubt, and anxiety by becoming completely detached from the evidence of senses and the external world. In the peacefulness and quietude of your mind, wherein you have stilled the wheels of your mind, meditate on the joy of the answered prayer until that inner certitude comes, whereby *you know that you know*. When you have succeeded in being *one* with your desire, you have succeeded in the mental marriage—or the union of your feeling with your idea.

I am sure you wish to be married (one with) to health, harmony, success, and achievement in your mind at this moment.

Every time you pray you are trying to perform the *marriage feast of Cana* (realization of your desire or ideas). You want to be mentally identified with the concept of peace, success, well being, and perfect health.

"They filled them up to the brim." *The six waterpots* represent your own mind in the spiritual and mental creative act. You must fill your mind *to the brim,* meaning you must become filled full of the feeling of being what you long to be. When you succeed in filling your mind with the ideal you wish to accomplish or express, you are full to the brim; then you cease praying about it; for you feel its reality in your mind. You *know!* It is a finished state of consciousness. You are at peace about it.

"And he saith unto them Draw out now, and bear unto the governor of the feast." Whatever is impregnated in our subconscious mind is always objectified on the screen of space; consequently when we enter a state of conviction that our prayer is answered, we have given the command, "Bear unto the governor of the feast."

You are always governing your mental feast. During the day thousands of thoughts, suggestions, opinions, sights, and sounds reach your eyes and ears. You can reject them as unfit for mental consumption or entertain them as you choose. Your conscious, reasoning, intellectual mind is the governor of the feast. When you consciously choose to entertain, meditate, feast upon, and imagine your heart's desire as true, it becomes a living embodiment, and a part of your mentality, so that your deeper self gives birth or expression to it. In other words what is impressed subjectively is expressed objectively. Your senses or conscious mind sees the objectification of your good. When the conscious mind becomes aware of "water made into wine," it becomes aware of the answered prayer. *Water* might be called, also, the invisible, formless, spiritual power, unconditioned consciousness. *Wine* is conditioned consciousness, or the mind giving birth to its beliefs and convictions.

The servants which draw the water for you represent the mood of peace, confidence, and faith. According to your faith or feeling, your good is attracted or drawn to you.

Imbibe, cherish, fall in love with these spiritual principles which are discussed in this book. In the first recorded miracle of Jesus, you are told that prayer is a marriage feast, or the mind uniting with its desire.

Love is the fulfilling of the law. Love is really an emotional attachment, a sense of oneness with your good. You must be true to that which you love. You must be loyal to your purpose or to your ideal. We are not being true to the one we love, when we are flirting of mentally entertaining other marriages with fear, doubt, worry, anxiety, or false beliefs. Love is a state of oneness, a state of fulfillment. (Refer to the book by the author, *Love is Freedom*.)

When this simple drama was explained to the beauty operator mentioned about, she became rich mentally. She understood this drama, and she put it into practice in her life. This is how she prayed: She knew that the *water* (her own mind) would flow, and fill up all the *empty vessels* in response to her new way of thinking and feeling.

At night this client became very quiet and still, relaxed her body, and began to use constructive imagery. The steps she used are as follows:

First step: She began to imagine the local bank manager was congratulating her on her wonderful deposits in the bank. She kept imagining that for about five minutes.

The second step: In her imagination she heard her mother saying to her, "I am so happy about your wonderful, new position." She continued to hear her say this in a happy, joyous way for about three to five minutes.

The third step: Vividly she imagined the writer was in front of her performing her marriage ceremony. This woman heard me saying as the officiating minister, "I now pronounce you man and wife." Completing this routine, she went off to sleep feeling filled full, i.e., sensing and feeling within herself the joy of the answered prayer.

Nothing happened for three weeks; in fact things got much worse, but she persevered, refusing to take "No" for her answer. She knew that in order to grow spiritually, she too, had to perform her first miracle by changing her fear to faith, her mood of lack to a mood of opulence and prosperity, by changing consciousness (water) into the conditions, circumstances, and experiences she wished to express.

Consciousness, Awareness, Beingness, Principle, Spirit, or whatever Name you give It is the cause of all; it is the only Presence and Power. The Spiritual Power of Spirit within us is the cause and substance of all things. All things—birds, trees, stars, sun, moon, earth, gold, silver, and platinum—are its manifestations. It is the cause and substance of all things. "There is none else."

Understanding this she knew that *water* (consciousness) could become supply in the form of money, true place, or true expression for herself, health for her mother, as well as companionship and fullness of life. She saw this simple—yet profound—truth in the twinkling of an eye, and said to me, "I *accept* my good."

She knew that nothing is hidden from us; all of God is within us, waiting for our discovery and inquiry.

In less than a month this young girl got married. The writer performed the ceremony. I pronounced the words she heard me say over and over again in her meditative, relaxed state, "I now pronounce you man and wife!"

Her husband gave her a check for $24,000 as a wedding present, as well as a trip around the world. Her new expression as a beauty operator was to beautify her home and garden, and make the desert of her mind rejoice and blossom as the rose.

She changed "water into wine." *Water* or her consciousness became charged or conditioned by her constant, true, happy imagery. These images, when sustained regularly, systematically, and with faith in the developing powers of the deeper mind, will come out of the darkness (subconscious mind) into light (objectified on the screen of space).

There is one important rule: Do not expose this newly developed film to the shattering light of fear, doubt, despondency, and worry. Whenever worry or fear knocks at your door, immediately turn to the picture you developed in your mind, and say to yourself, "A beautiful picture is being developed now in the dark house of my mind." Mentally pour on that picture your feeling of joy, faith, and understanding. You know you have operated a psychological, spiritual law; for what is impressed shall be expressed. It is wonderful!

The following is a sure, certain way for developing and manifesting all the material riches and supply you need all the days of your life. If you apply this formula sincerely and honestly, you should be amply rewarded on the external plane. I will illustrate this by telling you of a man who came to see me in London in desperate financial straits. He was a member of the Church of England, and had studied the working of the subconscious mind to some extent.

I told him to say frequently during the day, "God is the source of my supply, and all my needs are met at every moment of time and point of space." Think also of all the animal life in this world, and in all the galaxies of space which are now being taken care of by an Infinite Intelligence. Notice how nature is lavish, extravagant, and bountiful. Think of the fish of the sea which are all being sustained, as well as the birds of the air!"

He began to realize that since he was born, he had been taken care of; fed by his mother; clothed by his father, and watched over by tender, loving parents. This man got a job and was paid in a wonderful way. He reasoned that it was illogical to assume that the Principle of Life which gave him life, and always took care of him would suddenly cease to respond to him.

He realized that he had cut off his own supply by resenting his employer, self-condemnation, criticism of himself, and by his own sense of unworthiness. He had psychologically severed the cord which joined him to the Infinite Source of all things—the Indwelling Spirit or Life Principle, called by some "Consciousness or Awareness."

Man is not fed like the birds; he must consciously commune with the Indwelling Power and Presence, and receive guidance, strength, vitality, and all things necessary for the fulfillment of his needs.

This is the formula which he used to change water into the wine of abundance and financial success. He realized God or the Spiritual Power within him was the cause of all; furthermore he realized that if he could sell himself the idea that wealth was his by Divine right, he would manifest abundance of supply.

The affirmation he used was, "God is the source of my supply. All my financial and other needs are met at every moment of time and point of space; there is always a divine surplus." This simple statement repeated frequently, knowingly, and intelligently conditioned his mind to a prosperity consciousness.

All he had to do was to sell himself this positive idea, in the same way a good salesman has to sell himself on the merits of his product. Such a person is convinced of the integrity of his company, the high quality of the product, the good service which it will give the customer, and the fact that the price is right, etc.

I told him whenever negative thoughts came to his mind, which would happen, not to fight them, quarrel with them in any way, but simply go back to the spiritual, mental formula, and repeat it quietly and lovingly to himself. Negative thoughts came to him in avalanches at times in the form of a flood of negativity. Each time he met them with the positive, firm, loyal conviction: "God supplies all my needs; there is a Divine surplus in my life."

He said as he drove his car, and went through his day's routine, that a host of sundry, miscellaneous, negative concepts crowded his mind from time to time; such as, "There is no hope." "You are broke." Each time such negative thoughts came, he refused their mental admission by turning to the Eternal Source of wealth, health, and all things which he knew to be his own spiritual awareness. Definitely and positively he claimed, "God is the source of my supply, and that supply is mine now!" Or, "There is a Divine solution. God's wealth is my wealth," and other affirmative, positive statements which charged his mind with hope, faith, expectancy, and ultimately a conviction in an ever-flowing fountain of riches supplying all his needs copiously, joyously, and endlessly.

The negative flood of thoughts came to him as often as fifty times in an hour; each time he refused to open the door of his mind to these gangsters, assassins, and thieves which he knew would only rob him of peace, wealth, success, and all good things. Instead he opened the door of his mind to the idea of God's Eternal Life Principle of supply flowing through him as wealth, health, energy, power, and all things necessary to lead a full and happy life here.

As he continued to do this, the second day not so many thieves knocked at his door; the third day, the flow of negative visitors was less; the fourth day, they came intermittently, hoping for admission, but receiving the same mental response: "No entrance! I accept only thoughts and concepts which activate, heal, bless, and inspire my mind!"

He reconditioned his consciousness or mind to a wealth consciousness. "The prince of this world cometh, and hath nothing in me"—This conveys to your mind: The negative thoughts, such as, fear, lack, worry, anxiety came, but they received no response from his mind. He was now immune; God intoxicated, and seized by a divine faith in an ever-expanding consciousness of abundance and financial supply. This man did not lose everything; neither did he go into bankruptcy; he was given extended credit; his business improved; new doors opened up, and he prospered.

Remember always in the prayer-process, you must be loyal to your ideal, purpose, and objective. Many people fail to realize wealth and financial success, because they pray two ways. They affirm God is their supply, and that they are divinely prospered, but a few minutes later they deny their good by saying, "I can't pay this bill." "I can't afford this, that, or the other things." Or they say to themselves, "A jinx is following me." "I can't ever make ends meet." "I never have enough to go around." All such statements are highly destructive, and neutralize your positive prayers. This is what is called, "praying two ways."

You must be faithful to your plan or your goal. You must be true to your knowledge of the spiritual power. Cease making negative marriages, i.e., uniting with negative thoughts, fears, and worries.

Prayer is like a captain directing the course of his ship. You must have a destination. You must know where you are going. The captain of the ship, knowing the laws of navigation, regulates his course accordingly. If the ship is turned from its course by storms or unruly waves, he calmly redirects it along its true course.

You are the captain on the bridge, and you are giving the orders in the way of thoughts, feelings, opinions, beliefs, moods, and mental tones. Keep your eye on the beam. *You go where your vision is!* Cease, therefore, looking at all the obstacles, delays, and impediments that would cause you to go off your course. Be definite and positive. Decide where you are going. Know that your mental attitude is the ship which will take you from the mood of lack and limitation, to the mood and feeling of opulence, and to the belief in the inevitable law of God working for you.

Quimby, who was a doctor, a wonderful student, and teacher of the mental and spiritual laws of mind, said, "Man acts as he is acted upon." What moves you now? What is it that determines your response to life? The answer is as follows: Your ideas, beliefs, and opinions activate your mind and condition you to the point that you become, as Quimby stated, "An expression of your beliefs." This illustrates the truth of Quimby's statement: "Man is belief expressed."

Another popular statement of Quimby's was, "Our minds mingle like atmospheres, and each person has his identity in that atmosphere." When you were a child, you were subject to the moods, feelings, beliefs, and the general mental atmosphere of the home. The fears, anxieties, superstitions, as well as the religious faith and convictions of the parents were impressed on your mind.

Let us say the child had been brought up in a poverty-stricken home, in which there was never enough to go around, financially speaking; he heard constantly the complaint of lack and limitation.

You could say, like Salter in his conditioned reflex therapy, that the child was conditioned to poverty. The young man may have a poverty complex based on his early experiences, training, and beliefs, but he can rise above any situation, and become free; this is done through the power of prayer.

I knew a young boy aged 17, who was born in a place called Hell's Kitchen, in New York. He listened to some lectures I was giving in Steinway Hall, New York, at the time. This boy realized that he had been the victim of negative, destructive thinking, and that if he did not redirect his mind along constructive channels, the world-mind with its fears, failures, hates, and jealousies would move in and control him. "Man acts as he is acted upon."

It stands to reason, as Quimby knew, that if man will not take charge of his own house (mind), the propaganda, false beliefs, fears, and worries of the phenomenalistic world will act as a hypnotic spell over him.

We are immersed in the race mind which believes in sickness, death, misfortune, accident, failures, disease, and diverse disasters. Follow the Biblical injunction: "Come out from among them, and be separate." Identify yourself mentally and emotionally with the Eternal Verities which have stood the test of time.

This young man decided to think and plan for himself. He decided to take the Royal Road to Riches by accepting God's abundance here and now, and to fill his mind with spiritual concepts and perceptions. He knew, as he did this, he would automatically crowd out of his mind all negative patterns.

He adopted a simple process called, "scientific imagination." He had a wonderful voice, but it was not cultivated or developed. I told him the image he gave attention to in his mind would be developed in his deeper mind and come to pass. He understood this to be a law of mind—a law of action and reaction—i.e., the response of the deeper mind to the mental picture held in the conscious mind.

This young man would sit down quietly in his room at home; relax his whole body, and vividly imagine himself singing before a microphone. He would actually reach out for the "feel" of the instrument. He would hear me congratulate him on his wonderful contract, and tell him how magnificent his voice was. By giving his attention and devotion to this mental image regularly and systematically, a deep impression was made on his subconscious mind.

A short time elapsed, and an Italian voice instructor in New York gave him free lessons several times a week, because he saw his possibilities. He got a contract which sent him abroad to sing in the salons of Europe, Asia, South Africa, and other places. His financial worries were over; for he also received a wonderful salary. His hidden talents and ability to release them were his real riches. These talents and powers within all of us are God-given; let us release them.

Did you ever say to yourself, "How can I be more useful to my fellow creature?" "How can I contribute more to humanity?"

A minister-friend of mine told me that in his early days he and his church suffered financially. His technique or process was this simple prayer which worked wonders for him, "God reveals to me better ways to present the truths of God to my fellow creature." Money poured in; the mortgage was paid in a few years, and he has never worried about money since.

As you read this chapter, you have now learned that the inner feelings, moods, and beliefs of man always control and govern his external world. The inner movements of the mind control the outer movements. To change the outside, you must change the inside. "As in Heaven, so on earth;" or as in my mind or consciousness, so is it in my body, circumstances, and environment.

The Bible says, "There is nothing hidden that shall not be revealed." For example if you are sick, you are revealing a mental and emotional pattern which is the cause. If you are upset, or if you receive tragic news, notice how you reveal it in your face, eyes, gestures, tonal qualities, also in your gait and posture. As a matter of fact your whole body reveals your inner distress. You could, of course, through mental discipline and prayer, remain absolutely poised, serene, and calm, refusing to betray your hidden feelings or mental states. You could order the muscles of your body to relax, be quiet, and be still; they would have to obey you. Your eyes, face, and lips would not betray any sign of grief, anger, or despondency.

On the other hand with a little discipline, through prayer and meditation, you could reverse the entire picture. Even though you had received disturbing news, regardless of its grave nature, you could show and exhibit joy, peace, relaxation, and a vibrant, buoyant nature. No one would ever know that you were the recipient of so-called bad news.

Regardless of what kind of news you received today, you could go to the mirror, look at your face, lips, eyes, and your gestures, as you tell yourself, and imagine you have heard the news of having received a vast fortune. Dramatize it, feel it, thrill to it, and notice how your whole body responds to the inner thrill.

You can reverse any situation through prayer. Busy your mind with the concepts of peace, success, wealth, and happiness. Identify yourself with these ideas mentally, emotionally, and pictorially.

Get a picture of yourself as you want to be; retain that image; sustain it with joy, faith, and expectancy; finally you will succeed in experiencing its manifestation.

I say to people who consult me regarding financial lack to "marry wealth." Some see the point, others do not. As all Bible students know, your *wife* is what you are mentally joined to, united with, or at one with.

In other words what you conceive and believe, you give it conception. If you believe the world is cold, cruel, and harsh, that it is a "dog eat dog" way of life, that is *your* concept; you are married to it, and you will have children or issue by that marriage. The children from such a mental marriage or belief will be your experiences, conditions, and circumstances together with all other events in your life. All your experiences and reactions to life will be the image and likeness of the ideas which fathered them.

Look at the many wives the average man is living with, such

as fear, doubt, anxiety, criticism, jealousy, and anger; these play havoc with his mind. Marry wealth by claiming, feeling, and believing: "God supplies all my needs according to his riches in glory." Or take the following statement, and repeat it over and over again knowingly until your consciousness is conditioned by it, or it becomes a part of your meditation: "I am divinely expressed, and I have a wonderful income." Do not say this in a parrot-like fashion, but know that your train of thought is being engraved in your deeper mind, and it becomes a conditioned state of consciousness. Let the phrase become meaningful to you. Pour life, love, and feeling on it, making it alive.

One of my class-students recently opened a restaurant. He phoned me saying that he got married to a restaurant; he meant that he had made up his mind to be very successful, diligent, and persevering, and to see that his business prospered. This man's *wife* (mental) was his belief in the accomplishment of his desire or wish.

Identify yourself with your aim in life, and cease mental marriages with criticism, self-condemnation, anger, fear, and worry. Give attention to your chosen ideal, being full of faith and confidence in the inevitable law of prosperity and success. You will accomplish nothing by loving your ideal one minute, and denying it the next minute; this is like mixing acid and an alkali; for you will get an inert substance. In going along the Royal Road to Riches, you must be faithful to your chosen ideal (your wife).

We find illustrations in the Bible relating to these same truths. For instance, "Eve came out of Adam's rib." *Your rib* is your concept, desire, idea, plan, goal, or aim in life.

Eve means the emotion, feeling nature, or the inner tone. In other words you must mother the idea. The idea must be mothered, loved, and felt as true, in order to manifest your aim in life.

The *idea* is the father; the *emotion* is the mother; this is the marriage feast which is always taking place in your mind.

Ouspensky spoke of the third element which entered in or was formed following the union of your desire and feeling. He called it the neutral element. We may call it "peace"; for God is Peace.

The Bible says, "And the government shall be on his shoulders." In other words let Divine Wisdom be your guide. Let the subjective Wisdom within you lead, guide, and govern you in all your ways. Turn over your request to this Indwelling Presence knowing in your heart and soul that it will dissipate the anxiety, heal the wound, and restore your soul to equanimity and tranquillity. Open your mind and heart, and say, "God is my pilot. He leads me. He prospers me. He is my counsellor." Let your prayer be night and morning, "I am a channel through which God's riches flow ceaselessly, copiously, and freely." Write that prayer in your heart, inscribe it in your mind. Keep on the beam of God's glory!

The man who does not know the inner workings of his own mind is full of burdens, anxieties, and worries; for he has not learned how to cast his burden on the Indwelling Presence, and go free.

The Zen monk was asked by his disciple, "What is Truth?" He replied in a symbolic way by taking the bag off his back, and placing it on the ground.

The disciple then asked him, "Master, how does it work?"

The Zen monk still silent, placed the bag on his back, and walked on down the road singing to himself. The *bag* is your burden, or your problem. You cast it on the subjective Wisdom which knows all, and has the "know-how" of accomplishment. It knows only the answer.

Placing the bag again on his back means though I still have the problem, I now have mental rest and relief from the burden, because I have invoked the Divine Wisdom on my behalf; therefore I sing the song of triumph, knowing that the answer to my prayer is on the way, and I sing for the joy that is set before me. It is wonderful.

"Every man at the beginning doth set forth good wine; and when men have well drunk, then that which is worse; but thou hast kept the good wine until now." This is true of every man when he first enters a knowledge of the laws of mind. He sets out with high spirits and ambitions. He is the new broom which sweeps clean, and he is full of good intentions; oftentimes he forgets the Source of power. He does not remain faithful to the Principle within him, which is scientific and effectual, that would lift him out of his negative experiences, and set him on the high road to freedom and peace of mind. He begins to indulge mentally and emotionally with ideas and thoughts extraneous to his announced aim and goal. In other words he is not faithful to his ideal or wife.

Know that the subjective or deeper self within you will accept your request, and being the great fabricator, it will bring it to pass in its own way. All you do is release your request with faith and confidence, in the same way you would cast a seed on the ground, or mail a letter to a friend, knowing the answer would come.

Did you ever go between two great rocks and listen to the echo of your voice? This is the way the Life Principle within you answers. *You* will hear the echo of your own voice. Your *voice* is your inner, mental movement of the mind—your inner, psychological journey where you feasted mentally on an idea until you were full; then you rested.

Knowing this law and how to use it, be sure you never become drunk with power, arrogance, pride, or conceit. Use the law to bless, heal, inspire, and lift up others, as well as yourself.

Man misuses the law by selfishly taking advantage of his fellow man; if you do, you hurt and attract loss to yourself. Power, security, and riches are not to be obtained externally. They come from the treasure-house of eternity within. We should realize that the *good wine* is always present, for God is the Eternal Now. Regardless of present circumstances, you can prove your good is ever-present by detaching yourself mentally from the problem, going on the High Watch, and go about your Father's business.

To go on the High Watch is to envision your good, to dwell on the new concept of yourself, to become married to it, and sustain the happy mood by remaining faithful—full of faith every step of the way—knowing that the wine of joy, the answered prayer, is on the way. "Now is the day of salvation." "The kingdom of heaven is at hand." "Thou hast kept the good wine until now."

You can—this moment—travel psychologically in your mind, and enter mentally through divine imagination into any desired state. The wealth, health, or invention you wish to introduce are all invisible first. Everything comes out of the Invisible. You must subjectively possess riches, before you can objectively possess wealth. The feeling of wealth produces wealth; for wealth is a state of consciousness. *A state of consciousness* is how you think, feel, believe, and what you mentally give consent to.

A teacher in California receiving over five or six thousand dollars a year looked in a window at a beautiful ermine coat that was priced at $8,000. She said, "It would take me years to save that amount of money. I could never afford it. Oh, how I want it!" She listened to our lectures on Sunday mornings. By ceasing to marry these negative concepts, she learned that she could have a coat, car, or anything she wished without hurting anybody on the face of the earth.

I told her to imagine she had the coat on, to feel its beautiful fur, and to get the feel of it on her. She began to use the power of her imagination prior to sleep at night. She put the imaginary coat on her, fondled it, caressed it, like a child does with her doll. She continued to do this, and finally felt the thrill of it all.

She went to sleep every night wearing this imaginary coat, and being so happy in possessing it. Three months went by, and nothing happened. She was about to waver, but she reminded herself that it is the sustained mood which demonstrates. "He who perseveres to the end shall be saved." The solution will come to the person who does not waver, but always goes about with the perfume of His Presence with him. The answer comes to the man who walks in the light that "It is done!" You are always using the *perfume of His Presence* when you sustain the happy, joyous mood of expectancy knowing your good is on the way. You saw it on the unseen, and you *know* you will see it in the seen.

The sequel to the teacher's drama of the mind is interesting. One Sunday morning after our lecture, a man accidently stepped on her toe, apologized profusely, asked her where she lived, and offered to drive her home. She accepted gladly. Shortly after he proposed marriage; gave her a beautiful diamond ring, and said to her, "I saw the most wonderful coat; you would simply look radiant wearing it!" It was the coat she admired three months previously. (The salesman said over one hundred wealthy women looked at the coat, admired it immensely, but for some reason always selected another garment.)

Through your capacity to choose, imagine the reality of what you have selected, and through faith and perseverance, *you can* realize your goal in life. All the riches of heaven are here now within you waiting to be released. Peace, joy, love, guidance, inspiration, goodwill, and abundance all exist now. All that is necessary in order to express God's riches is for you to leave the present now (your limitation), enter into the mental vision or picture, and in a happy, joyous mood become one with your ideal. Having seen and felt your good in moments of high exaltation, you know that in a little while you shall see your ideal objectively as you walk through time and space. As within, so without. As above, so below. As in heaven so on earth. In other words you will see your beliefs expressed. Man *is* belief expressed!

ARNOLD BENNETT

How to Live on 24 Hours a Day

Contents

Foreword

How to Live on 24 Hours a Day by Arnold Bennett was originally published in 1910, and has not been out of print since. It has influenced people from all walks of life, all around the world, and sold millions of copies. But what could a book published more than a century ago teach us in the twenty-first century? After all, our lives are busier and more complicated than ever before. In fact, sometimes it feels like time is moving faster and faster. Many people complain that they don't have enough time to do the things they want to do.

As it turns out, life in the twenty-first century, as different on the surface as it seems, isn't that different from life in the early 1900s. The issues of feeling overwhelmed, having too little time, and even procrastination were common themes then. The times may look different now than they did then, but the issue of "time" turns out to be, well, timeless.

How to Live on 24 Hours a Day is remarkably "right on time" with its message. The language and some of the examples the author uses in the book can sound dated, but the concepts haven't aged a bit. Many people might say "time is precious," but Bennett goes one step further and says that time is actually like currency. Every day we get exactly twenty-four hours to spend. Everyone gets the same amount, but not everyone spends their hours the same way.

To maximize our time, Bennett writes, we should divide our time into our work day (eight hours), and our personal day (sixteen hours). Then we take that sixteen hours and budget it, like we would money. Bennett shows how we each can find extra time in our day, what to cut out from our lives, and what to focus on. And what should we do with the extra time that we can find? Bennett urges us to use that time to better ourselves, with great art or actions that make our lives deeper and richer, which in turn allows us to cherish and savor each hour of our day, rather than feel like time is slipping through our fingers. We are in control of our daily allotment of time, rather than feeling helpless.

Who was Arnold Bennett? Born in the UK in 1867, over the course of his life he became a magazine editor, a successful novelist, and even the Director of Propaganda for France during World War I. Many of his novels were worldwide bestsellers. He wrote some nonfiction as well, and *How to Live on 24 Hours a Day* is one of these books. While his novels and other books seem to have gone out of fashion and faded from popularity, *How to Live on 24 Hours a Day* has gone on to reach generation after generation with its practical information.

As you read, pay attention to his ideas and program, rather than to the dated examples. Reading through *How to Live on 24 Hours a Day* doesn't take a long time, but the lessons of this book could have a positive effect on you for the rest of your life.

—*Joel Fotinos*

Preface to This Edition

This preface, though placed at the beginning, as a preface must be, should be read at the end of the book.

I have received a large amount of correspondence concerning this small work, and many reviews of it—some of them nearly as long as the book itself—have been printed. But scarcely any of the comment has been adverse. Some people have objected to a frivolity of tone; but as the tone is not, in my opinion, at all frivolous, this objection did not impress me; and had no weightier reproach been put forward I might almost have been persuaded that the volume was flawless! A more serious stricture has, however, been offered—not in the press, but by sundry obviously sincere correspondents—and I must deal with it. The sentence against which protests have been made is as follows: "In the majority of instances he [the typical man] does not precisely feel a passion for his business; at best he does not dislike it. He begins his business functions with some reluctance, as late as he can, and he ends them with joy, as early as he can. And his engines, while he is engaged in his business, are seldom at their full 'h.p.'"

I am assured, in accents of unmistakable sincerity, that there are many business men—not merely those in high positions or with fine prospects, but modest subordinates with no hope of ever being much better of—who do enjoy their business functions, who do not shirk them, who do not arrive at the office as late as possible and depart as early as possible, who, in a word, put the whole of their force into their day's work and are genuinely fatigued at the end thereof.

I am ready to believe it. I do believe it. I know it. I always knew it. Both in London and in the provinces it has been my lot to spend long years in subordinate situations of business; and the fact did not escape me that a certain proportion of my peers showed what amounted to an honest passion for their duties, and that while engaged in those duties they were really *living* to the fullest extent of which they were capable. But I remain convinced that these fortunate and happy individuals (happier perhaps than they guessed) did not and do not constitute a majority, or anything like a majority. I remain convinced that the majority of decent average conscientious men of business (men with aspirations and ideals) do not as a rule go home of a night genuinely tired. I remain convinced that they put not as much but as little of themselves as they conscientiously can into the earning of a livelihood, and that their vocation bores rather than interests them.

Nevertheless, I admit that the minority is of sufficient importance to merit attention, and that I ought not to have ignored it so completely as I did do. The whole difficulty of the hard-working minority was put in a single colloquial sentence by one of my correspondents. He wrote: "I am just as keen as anyone on doing something to 'exceed my program,' but allow me to tell you that when I get home at six thirty p.m. I am not anything like so fresh as you seem to imagine."

Now I must point out that the case of the minority, who throw themselves with passion and gusto into their daily business task, is infinitely less deplorable than the case of the majority, who go half-heartedly and feebly through their official day. The former are less in need of advice "how to live." At any rate during their official day of, say, eight hours they are really alive; their engines are giving the full indicated "h.p." The other eight working hours of their day may be badly organized, or even frittered away; but it is less disastrous to waste eight hours a day than sixteen hours a day; it is better to have lived a bit than never to have lived at all. The real tragedy is the tragedy of the man who is braced to effort neither in the office nor out of it, and to this man this book is primarily addressed. "But," says the other and more fortunate man, "although my ordinary program is bigger than his, I want to exceed my program too! I am living a bit; I want to live more. But I really can't do another day's work on the top of my official day."

The fact is, I, the author, ought to have foreseen that I should appeal most strongly to those who already had an interest in existence. It is always the man who has tasted life who demands more of it. And it is always the man who never gets out of bed who is the most difficult to rouse.

Well, you of the minority, let us assume that the intensity of your daily money-getting will not allow you to carry out quite all the suggestions in the following pages. Some of the suggestions may yet stand. I admit that you may not be able to use the time spent on the journey home at night; but the suggestion for the journey to the office in the morning is as practicable for you as for anybody. And that weekly interval of forty hours, from Saturday to Monday, is yours just as much as the other man's, though a slight accumulation of fatigue may prevent you from employing the whole of your "h.p." upon it. There remains, then, the important portion of the three or more evenings a week. You tell me flatly that you are too tired to do anything outside your program at night. In reply to which I tell you flatly that if your ordinary day's work is thus exhausting, then the balance of your life is wrong and must be adjusted. A man's powers ought not to be monopolized by his ordinary day's work. What, then, is to be done?

The obvious thing to do is to circumvent your ardor for your ordinary day's work by a ruse. Employ your engines in something beyond the program before, and not after, you employ them on the program itself. Briefly, get up earlier in the morning. You say you cannot. You say it is impossible for you to go earlier to bed of a night—to do so would upset the entire household. I do not think it is quite impossible to go to bed earlier at night. I think that if you persist in rising earlier, and the consequence is insufficiency of sleep, you will soon find a way of going to bed earlier. But my impression is that the consequence of rising earlier will not be an insufficiency of sleep. My impression, growing stronger every year, is that sleep is partly a matter of habit—and of slackness. I am convinced that most people sleep as long as they do because they are at a loss for any other diversion. How much sleep do you think is daily obtained by the powerful healthy man who daily rattles up your street in charge of Carter Paterson's van? I have consulted a doctor on this point. He is a doctor who for twenty-five years has had a large general practice in a large flourishing suburb of London, inhabited by exactly such people as you and me. He is a curt man, and his answer was curt:

"Most people sleep themselves stupid."

He went on to give his opinion that nine men out of ten would have better health and more fun out of life if they spent less time in bed.

Other doctors have confirmed this judgment, which, of course, does not apply to growing youths.

Rise an hour, an hour and a half, or even two hours earlier; and—if you must—retire earlier when you can. In the matter of exceeding programs, you will accomplish as much in one morning hour as in two evening hours. "But," you say, "I couldn't begin without some food, and servants." Surely, my dear sir, in an age when an excellent spirit-lamp (including a saucepan) can be bought for

less than a shilling, you are not going to allow your highest wel-
fare to depend upon the precarious immediate co-operation of a
fellow creature! Instruct the fellow creature, whoever she may be,
at night. Tell her to put a tray in a suitable position over night. On
that tray two biscuits, a cup and saucer, a box of matches and a
spirit-lamp; on the lamp, the saucepan; on the saucepan, the lid—
but turned the wrong way up; on the reversed lid, the small teapot,
containing a minute quantity of tea leaves. You will then have to
strike a match—that is all. In three minutes the water boils, and
you pour it into the teapot (which is already warm). In three more
minutes the tea is infused. You can begin your day while drinking it. These details may seem trivial to the foolish, but to the
thoughtful they will not seem trivial. The proper, wise balancing
of one's whole life may depend upon the feasibility of a cup of tea
at an unusual hour.

—*A. B.*

The Daily Miracle

"Yes, he's one of those men that don't know how to manage. Good situation. Regular income. Quite enough for luxuries as well as needs. Not really extravagant. And yet the fellow's always in difficulties. Somehow he gets nothing out of his money. Excellent flat—half empty! Always looks as if he'd had the brokers in. New suit—old hat! Magnificent necktie—baggy trousers! Asks you to dinner: cut glass—bad mutton, or Turkish coffee—cracked cup! He can't understand it. Explanation simply is that he fritters his income away. Wish I had the half of it! I'd show him—"

So we have most of us criticized, at one time or another, in our superior way.

We are nearly all chancellors of the exchequer: it is the pride of the moment. Newspapers are full of articles explaining how to live on such-and-such a sum, and these articles provoke a correspondence whose violence proves the interest they excite. Recently, in a daily organ, a battle raged round the question whether a woman can exist nicely in the country on £85 a year. I have seen an essay, "How to live on eight shillings a week." But I have never seen an essay, "How to live on twenty-four hours a day." Yet it has been said that time is money. That proverb understates the case. Time is a great deal more than money. If you have time you can obtain money—usually. But though you have the wealth of a cloak-room attendant at the Carlton Hotel, you cannot buy yourself a minute more time than I have, or the cat by the fire has.

Philosophers have explained space. They have not explained time. It is the inexplicable raw material of everything. With it, all is possible; without it, nothing. The supply of time is truly a daily miracle, an affair genuinely astonishing when one examines it. You wake up in the morning, and lo! your purse is magically filled with twenty-four hours of the unmanufactured tissue of the universe of your life! It is yours. It is the most precious of possessions. A highly singular commodity, showered upon you in a manner as singular as the commodity itself!

For remark! No one can take it from you. It is unstealable. And no one receives either more or less than you receive.

Talk about an ideal democracy! In the realm of time there is no aristocracy of wealth, and no aristocracy of intellect. Genius is never rewarded by even an extra hour a day. And there is no punishment. Waste your infinitely precious commodity as much as you will, and the supply will never be withheld from you. No mysterious power will say: "This man is a fool, if not a knave. He does not deserve time; he shall be cut off at the meter." It is more certain than consols, and payment of income is not affected by Sundays. Moreover, you cannot draw on the future. Impossible to get into debt! You can only waste the passing moment. You cannot waste tomorrow; it is kept for you. You cannot waste the next hour; it is kept for you.

I said the affair was a miracle. Is it not?

You have to live on this twenty-four hours of daily time. Out of it you have to spin health, pleasure, money, content, respect, and the evolution of your immortal soul. Its right use, its most effective use, is a matter of the highest urgency and of the most thrilling actuality. All depends on that. Your happiness—the elusive prize that you are all clutching for, my friends!—depends on that. Strange that the newspapers, so enterprising and up-to-date as they are, are not full of "How to live on a given income of time," instead of "How to live on a given income of money"! Money is far commoner than time. When one reflects, one perceives that money is just about the commonest thing there is. It encumbers the earth in gross heaps.

If one can't contrive to live on a certain income of money, one earns a little more—or steals it, or advertises for it. One doesn't necessarily muddle one's life because one can't quite manage on a thousand pounds a year; one braces the muscles and makes it guineas, and balances the budget. But if one cannot arrange that an income of twenty-four hours a day shall exactly cover all proper items of expenditure, one does muddle one's life definitely. The supply of time, though gloriously regular, is cruelly restricted.

Which of us lives on twenty-four hours a day? And when I say "lives," I do not mean exists, nor "muddles through." Which of us is free from that uneasy feeling that the "great spending departments" of his daily life are not managed as they ought to be? Which of us is quite sure that his fine suit is not surmounted by a shameful hat, or that in attending to the crockery he has forgotten the quality of the food? Which of us is not saying to himself—which of us has not been saying to himself all his life: "I shall alter that when I have a little more time"?

We never shall have any more time. We have, and we have always had, all the time there is. It is the realization of this profound and neglected truth (which, by the way, I have not discovered) that has led me to the minute practical examination of daily time-expenditure.

The Desire to Exceed One's Program

"But," someone may remark, with fine English disregard of everything except the point, "what is he driving at with his twenty-four hours a day? I have no difficulty in living on twenty-four hours a day. I do all that I want to do, and still find time to go in for newspaper competitions. Surely it is a simple affair, knowing that one has only twenty-four hours a day, to content one's self with twenty-four hours a day!"

To you, my dear sir, I present my excuses and apologies. You are precisely the man that I have been wishing to meet for about forty years. Will you kindly send me your name and address, and state your charge for telling me how you do it? Instead of me talking to you, you ought to be talking to me. Please come forward. That you exist, I am convinced, and that I have not yet encountered you is my loss. Meanwhile, until you appear, I will continue to chat with my companions in distress—that innumerable band of souls who are haunted, more or less painfully, by the feeling that the years slip by, and slip by, and slip by, and that they have not yet been able to get their lives into proper working order.

If we analyze that feeling, we shall perceive it to be, primarily, one of uneasiness, of expectation, of looking forward, of aspiration. It is a source of constant discomfort, for it behaves like a skeleton at the feast of all our enjoyments. We go to the theater and laugh; but between the acts it raises a skinny finger at us. We rush violently for the last train, and while we are cooling a long age on the platform waiting for the last train, it promenades its bones up and down by our side and inquires: "O man, what hast thou done with thy youth? What art thou doing with thine age?" You may urge that this feeling of continuous looking forward, of aspiration, is part of life itself, and inseparable from life itself. True!

But there are degrees. A man may desire to go to Mecca. His conscience tells him that he ought to go to Mecca. He fares forth, either by the aid of Cook's, or unassisted; he may probably never reach Mecca; he may drown before he gets to Port Said; he may perish ingloriously on the coast of the Red Sea; his desire may remain eternally frustrate. Unfulfilled aspiration may always trouble him. But he will not be tormented in the same way as the man who, desiring to reach Mecca, and harried by the desire to reach Mecca, never leaves Brixton.

It is something to have left Brixton. Most of us have not left Brixton. We have not even taken a cab to Ludgate Circus and inquired from Cook's the price of a conducted tour. And our excuse to ourselves is that there are only twenty-four hours in the day.

If we further analyze our vague, uneasy aspiration, we shall, I think, see that it springs from a fixed idea that we ought to do something in addition to those things which we are loyally and morally obliged to do. We are obliged, by various codes written and unwritten, to maintain ourselves and our families (if any) in health and comfort, to pay our debts, to save, to increase our prosperity by increasing our efficiency. A task sufficiently difficult! A task which very few of us achieve! A task often beyond our skill! Yet, if we succeed in it, as we sometimes do, we are not satisfied; the skeleton is still with us.

And even when we realize that the task is beyond our skill, that our powers cannot cope with it, we feel that we should be less discontented if we gave to our powers, already overtaxed, something still further to do.

And such is, indeed, the fact. The wish to accomplish something outside their formal program is common to all men who in the course of evolution have risen past a certain level.

Until an effort is made to satisfy that wish, the sense of uneasy waiting for something to start which has not started will remain to disturb the peace of the soul. That wish has been called by many names. It is one form of the universal desire for knowledge. And it is so strong that men whose whole lives have been given to the systematic acquirement of knowledge have been driven by it to overstep the limits of their program in search of still more knowledge. Even Herbert Spencer, in my opinion the greatest mind that ever lived, was often forced by it into agreeable little backwaters of inquiry.

I imagine that in the majority of people who are conscious of the wish to live—that is to say, people who have intellectual curiosity—the aspiration to exceed formal programs takes a literary shape. They would like to embark on a course of reading. Decidedly the British people are becoming more and more literary. But I would point out that literature by no means comprises the whole field of knowledge, and that the disturbing thirst to improve one's self—to increase one's knowledge—may well be slaked quite apart from literature. With the various ways of slaking I shall deal later. Here I merely point out to those who have no natural sympathy with literature that literature is not the only well.

Precautions Before Beginning

Now that I have succeeded (if succeeded I have) in persuading you to admit to yourself that you are constantly haunted by a suppressed dissatisfaction with your own arrangement of your daily life; and that the primal cause of that inconvenient dissatisfaction is the feeling that you are every day leaving undone something which you would like to do, and which, indeed, you are always hoping to do when you have "more time"; and now that I have drawn your attention to the glaring, dazzling truth that you never will have "more time," since you already have all the time there is—you expect me to let you into some wonderful secret by which you may at any rate approach the ideal of a perfect arrangement of the day, and by which, therefore, that haunting, unpleasant, daily disappointment of things left undone will be got rid of!

I have found no such wonderful secret. Nor do I expect to find it, nor do I expect that anyone else will ever find it. It is undiscovered. When you first began to gather my drift, perhaps there was a resurrection of hope in your breast. Perhaps you said to yourself, "This man will show me an easy, unfatiguing way of doing what I have so long in vain wished to do." Alas, no! The fact is that there is no easy way, no royal road. The path to Mecca is extremely hard and stony, and the worst of it is that you never quite get there after all.

The most important preliminary to the task of arranging one's life so that one may live fully and comfortably within one's daily budget of twenty-four hours is the calm realization of the extreme difficulty of the task, of the sacrifices and the endless effort which it demands. I cannot too strongly insist on this.

If you imagine that you will be able to achieve your ideal by ingeniously planning out a timetable with a pen on a piece of paper, you had better give up hope at once. If you are not prepared for discouragements and disillusions; if you will not be content with a small result for a big effort, then do not begin. Lie down again and resume the uneasy doze which you call your existence.

It is very sad, is it not, very depressing and somber? And yet I think it is rather fine, too, this necessity for the tense bracing of the will before anything worth doing can be done. I rather like it myself. I feel it to be the chief thing that differentiates me from the cat by the fire.

"Well," you say, "assume that I am braced for the battle. Assume that I have carefully weighed and comprehended your ponderous remarks; how do I begin?" Dear sir, you simply begin. There is no magic method of beginning. If a man standing on the edge of a swimming-bath and wanting to jump into the cold water should ask you, "How do I begin to jump?" you would merely reply, "Just jump. Take hold of your nerves, and jump."

As I have previously said, the chief beauty about the constant supply of time is that you cannot waste it in advance. The next year, the next day, the next hour are lying ready for you, as perfect, as unspoiled, as if you had never wasted or misapplied a single moment in all your career. Which fact is very gratifying and reassuring. You can turn over a new leaf every hour if you choose. Therefore no object is served in waiting till next week, or even until tomorrow. You may fancy that the water will be warmer next week. It won't. It will be colder.

But before you begin, let me murmur a few words of warning in your private ear.

Let me principally warn you against your own ardor. Ardor in well-doing is a misleading and a treacherous thing. It cries out loudly for employment; you can't satisfy it at first; it wants more and more; it is eager to move mountains and divert the course of rivers. It isn't content till it perspires. And then, too often, when it feels the perspiration on its brow, it wearies all of a sudden and dies, without even putting itself to the trouble of saying, "I've had enough of this."

Beware of undertaking too much at the start. Be content with quite a little. Allow for accidents. Allow for human nature, especially your own.

A failure or so, in itself, would not matter, if it did not incur a loss of self-esteem and of self-confidence. But just as nothing succeeds like success, so nothing fails like failure. Most people who are ruined are ruined by attempting too much. Therefore, in setting out on the immense enterprise of living fully and comfortably within the narrow limits of twenty-four hours a day, let us avoid at any cost the risk of an early failure. I will not agree that, in this business at any rate, a glorious failure is better than a petty success. I am all for the petty success. A glorious failure leads to nothing; a petty success may lead to a success that is not petty.

So let us begin to examine the budget of the day's time. You say your day is already full to overflowing. How? You actually spend in earning your livelihood—how much? Seven hours, on the average? And in actual sleep, seven? I will add two hours, and be generous. And I will defy you to account to me on the spur of the moment for the other eight hours.

The Cause of the Trouble

In order to come to grips at once with the question of time-expenditure in all its actuality, I must choose an individual case for examination. I can only deal with one case, and that case cannot be the average case, because there is no such case as the average case, just as there is no such man as the average man. Every man and every man's case is special.

But if I take the case of a Londoner who works in an office, whose office hours are from ten to six, and who spends fifty minutes morning and night in traveling between his house door and his office door, I shall have got as near to the average as facts permit. There are men who have to work longer for a living, but there are others who do not have to work so long.

Fortunately the financial side of existence does not interest us here; for our present purpose the clerk at a pound a week is exactly as well of as the millionaire in Carlton House-terrace.

Now the great and profound mistake which my typical man makes in regard to his day is a mistake of general attitude, a mistake which vitiates and weakens two-thirds of his energies and interests. In the majority of instances he does not precisely feel a passion for his business; at best he does not dislike it. He begins his business functions with reluctance, as late as he can, and he ends them with joy, as early as he can. And his engines while he is engaged in his business are seldom at their full "h.p." (I know that

I shall be accused by angry readers of traducing the city worker; but I am pretty thoroughly acquainted with the City, and I stick to what I say.)

Yet in spite of all this he persists in looking upon those hours from ten to six as "the day," to which the ten hours preceding them and the six hours following them are nothing but a prologue and epilogue. Such an attitude, unconscious though it be, of course kills his interest in the odd sixteen hours, with the result that, even if he does not waste them, he does not count them; he regards them simply as margin.

This general attitude is utterly illogical and unhealthy, since it formally gives the central prominence to a patch of time and a bunch of activities which the man's one idea is to "get through" and have "done with." If a man makes two-thirds of his existence subservient to one-third, for which admittedly he has no absolutely feverish zest, how can he hope to live fully and completely? He cannot.

If my typical man wishes to live fully and completely he must, in his mind, arrange a day within a day. And this inner day, a Chinese box in a larger Chinese box, must begin at 6 p.m. and end at 10 a.m. It is a day of sixteen hours; and during all these sixteen hours he has nothing whatever to do but cultivate his body and his soul and his fellow men. During those sixteen hours he is free; he is not a wage-earner; he is not preoccupied by monetary cares; he is just as good as a man with a private income. This must be his attitude. And his attitude is all important. His success in life (much more important than the amount of estate upon what his executors will have to pay estate duty) depends on it.

What? You say that full energy given to those sixteen hours will lessen the value of the business eight? Not so. On the contrary, it will assuredly increase the value of the business eight. One of the chief things which my typical man has to learn is that the mental faculties are capable of a continuous hard activity; they do not tire like an arm or a leg. All they want is change—not rest, except in sleep.

I shall now examine the typical man's current method of employing the sixteen hours that are entirely his, beginning with his uprising. I will merely indicate things which he does and which I think he ought not to do, postponing my suggestions for "planting" the times which I shall have cleared—as a settler clears spaces in a forest.

In justice to him I must say that he wastes very little time before he leaves the house in the morning at 9:10. In too many houses he gets up at nine, break-fasts between 9:07 and 9:09½, and then bolts. But immediately he bangs the front door his mental faculties, which are tireless, become idle. He walks to the station in a condition of mental coma. Arrived there, he usually has to wait for the train. On hundreds of suburban stations every morning you see men calmly strolling up and down platforms while railway companies unblushingly rob them of time, which is more than money. Hundreds of thousands of hours are thus lost every day simply because my typical man thinks so little of time that it has never occurred to him to take quite easy precautions against the risk of its loss.

He has a solid coin of time to spend every day—call it a sovereign. He must get change for it, and in getting change he is content to lose heavily.

Supposing that in selling him a ticket the company said, "We will change you a sovereign, but we shall charge you three halfpence for doing so," what would my typical man exclaim? Yet that is the equivalent of what the company does when it robs him of five minutes twice a day.

You say I am dealing with minutiae. I am. And later on I will justify myself.

Now will you kindly buy your paper and step into the train?

Tennis and the Immortal Soul

You get into the morning train with your newspaper, and you calmly and majestically give yourself up to your newspaper. You do not hurry. You know you have at least half an hour of security in front of you. As your glance lingers idly at the advertisements of shipping and of songs on the outer pages, your air is the air of a leisured man, wealthy in time, of a man from some planet where there are a hundred and twenty-four hours a day instead of twenty-four. I am an impassioned reader of newspapers. I read five English and two French dailies, and the news-agents alone know how many weeklies, regularly. I am obliged to mention this personal fact lest I should be accused of a prejudice against newspapers when I say that I object to the reading of newspapers in the morning train. Newspapers are produced with rapidity, to be read with rapidity. There is no place in my daily program for newspapers. I read them as I may in odd moments. But I do read them. The idea of devoting to them thirty or forty consecutive minutes of wonderful solitude (for nowhere can one more perfectly immerse one's self in one's self than in a compartment full of silent, withdrawn, smoking males) is to me repugnant. I cannot possibly allow you to scatter priceless pearls of time with such Oriental lavishness. You are not the Shah of time. Let me respectfully remind you that you have no more time than I have. No newspaper reading in trains! I have already "put by" about three-quarters of an hour for use.

Now you reach your office. And I abandon you there till six o'clock. I am aware that you have nominally an hour (often in reality an hour and a half) in the midst of the day, less than half of which time is given to eating. But I will leave you all that to spend as you choose. You may read your newspapers then.

I meet you again as you emerge from your office. You are pale and tired. At any rate, your wife says you are pale, and you give her to understand that you are tired. During the journey home you have been gradually working up the tired feeling. The tired feeling hangs heavy over the mighty suburbs of London like a virtuous and melancholy cloud, particularly in winter. You don't eat immediately on your arrival home. But in about an hour or so you feel as if you could sit up and take a little nourishment. And you do. Then you smoke, seriously; you see friends; you potter; you play cards; you flirt with a book; you note that old age is creeping on; you take a stroll; you caress the piano. . . . By Jove! a quarter past eleven. Time to think about going to bed! You then devote quite forty minutes to thinking about going to bed; and it is conceivable that you are acquainted with a genuinely good whisky. At last you go to bed, exhausted by the day's work. Six hours, probably more, have gone since you left the office—gone like a dream, gone like magic, unaccountably gone!

That is a fair sample case. But you say: "It's all very well for you to talk. A man *is* tired. A man must see his friends. He can't always be on the stretch." Just so. But when you arrange to go to the theater (especially with a pretty woman) what happens? You rush to the suburbs; you spare no toil to make yourself glorious in fine raiment; you rush back to town in another train; you keep yourself on the stretch for four hours, if not five; you take her home; you take yourself home. You don't spend three-quarters of an hour in "thinking about" going to bed. You go. Friends and fatigue have equally been forgotten, and the evening has seemed so exquisitely long (or perhaps too short)! And do you remember that time when you were persuaded to sing in the chorus of the amateur operatic society, and slaved two hours every other night for three months? Can you deny that when you have something definite to look forward to at eventide, something that is to employ all your energy—the thought of that something gives a glow and a more intense vitality to the whole day?

What I suggest is that at six o'clock you look facts in the face and admit that you are not tired (because you are not, you know), and that you arrange your evening so that it is not cut in the middle by a meal. By so doing you will have a clear expanse of at least three hours. I do not suggest that you should employ three hours every night of your life in using up your mental energy. But I do suggest that you might, for a commencement, employ an hour and a half every other evening in some important and consecutive cultivation of the mind. You will still be left with three evenings for friends, bridge, tennis, domestic scenes, odd reading, pipes, gardening, pottering, and prize competitions. You will still have the terrific wealth of forty-four hours between 2 p.m. Saturday and 10 a.m. Monday. If you persevere you will soon want to pass four evenings, and perhaps five, in some sustained endeavor to be genuinely alive. And you will fall out of that habit of muttering to yourself at 11:15 p.m., "Time to be thinking about going to bed." The man who begins to go to bed forty minutes before he opens his bedroom door is bored; that is to say, he is not living.

But remember, at the start, those ninety nocturnal minutes thrice a week must be the most important minutes in the ten thousand and eighty. They must be sacred, quite as sacred as a dramatic rehearsal or a tennis match. Instead of saying, "Sorry I can't see you, old chap, but I have to run off to the tennis club," you must say, ". . . but I have to work." This, I admit, is intensely difficult to say. Tennis is so much more urgent than the immortal soul.

Remember Human Nature

I have incidentally mentioned the vast expanse of forty-four hours between leaving business at 2 p.m. on Saturday and returning to business at 10 a.m. on Monday. And here I must touch on the point whether the week should consist of six days or of seven. For many years—in fact, until I was approaching forty—my own week consisted of seven days. I was constantly being informed by older and wiser people that more work, more genuine living, could be got out of six days than out of seven.

And it is certainly true that now, with one day in seven in which I follow no program and make no effort save what the caprice of the moment dictates, I appreciate intensely the moral value of a weekly rest. Nevertheless, had I my life to arrange over again, I would do again as I have done. Only those who have lived at the full stretch seven days a week for a long time can appreciate the full beauty of a regular-recurring idleness. Moreover, I am aging. And it is a question of age. In cases of abounding youth and exceptional energy and desire for effort I should say unhesitatingly: Keep going, day in, day out.

But in the average case I should say: Confine your formal program (super-program, I mean) to six days a week. If you find yourself wishing to extend it, extend it, but only in proportion to your wish; and count the time extra as a windfall, not as regular income, so that you can return to a six-day program without the sensation of being poorer, of being a backslider.

Let us now see where we stand. So far we have marked for saving out of the waste of days, half an hour at least on six mornings a week, and one hour and a half on three evenings a week. Total, seven hours and a half a week.

I propose to be content with that seven hours and a half for the present. "What?" you cry. "You pretend to show us how to live, and you only deal with seven hours and a half out of a hundred and sixty-eight! Are you going to perform a miracle with your seven hours and a half?" Well, not to mince the matter, I am—if you will kindly let me! That is to say, I am going to ask you to attempt an experience which, while perfectly natural and explicable, has all the air of a miracle. My contention is that the full use of those seven-and-a-half hours will quicken the whole life of the week, add zest to it, and increase the interest which you feel in even the most banal occupations. You practice physical exercises for a mere ten minutes morning and evening, and yet you are not astonished when your physical health and strength are beneficially affected every hour of the day, and your whole physical outlook changed. Why should you be astonished that an average of over an hour a day given to the mind should permanently and completely enliven the whole activity of the mind?

More time might assuredly be given to the cultivation of one's self. And in proportion as the time was longer the results would be greater. But I prefer to begin with what looks like a trifling effort.

It is not really a trifling effort, as those will discover who have yet to essay it. To "clear" even seven hours and a half from the jungle is passably difficult. For some sacrifice has to be made. One may have spent one's time badly, but one did spend it; one did do something with it, however ill-advised that something may have been. To do something else means a change of habits.

And habits are the very dickens to change! Further, any change, even a change for the better, is always accompanied by drawbacks and discomforts. If you imagine that you will be able to devote seven hours and a half a week to serious, continuous effort, and still live your old life, you are mistaken. I repeat that some sacrifice, and an immense deal of volition, will be necessary. And it is because I know the difficulty, it is because I know the almost disastrous effect of failure in such an enterprise, that I earnestly advise a very humble beginning. You must safeguard your self-respect. Self-respect is at the root of all purposefulness, and a failure in an enterprise deliberately planned deals a desperate wound at one's self-respect. Hence I iterate and reiterate: Start quietly, unostentatiously.

When you have conscientiously given seven hours and a half a week to the cultivation of your vitality for three months—then you may begin to sing louder and tell yourself what wondrous things you are capable of doing.

Before coming to the method of using the indicated hours, I have one final suggestion to make. That is, as regards the evenings, to allow much more than an hour and a half in which to do the work of an hour and a half. Remember the chance of accidents. Remember human nature. And give yourself, say, from 9 to 11:30 for your task of ninety minutes.

Controlling the Mind

People say: "One can't help one's thoughts." But one can. The control of the thinking machine is perfectly possible. And since nothing whatever happens to us outside our own brain; since nothing hurts us or gives us pleasure except within the brain, the supreme importance of being able to control what goes on in that mysterious brain is patent. This idea is one of the oldest platitudes, but it is a platitude whose profound truth and urgency most people live and die without realizing. People complain of the lack of power to concentrate, not witting that they may acquire the power, if they choose.

And without the power to concentrate—that is to say, without the power to dictate to the brain its task and to ensure obedience—true life is impossible. Mind control is the first element of a full existence.

Hence, it seems to me, the first business of the day should be to put the mind through its paces. You look after your body, inside and out; you run grave danger in hacking hairs of your skin; you employ a whole army of individuals, from the milkman to the pigkiller, to enable you to bribe your stomach into decent behavior. Why not devote a little attention to the far more delicate machinery of the mind, especially as you will require no extraneous aid? It is for this portion of the art and craft of living that I have reserved the time from the moment of quitting your door to the moment of arriving at your office.

"What? I am to cultivate my mind in the street, on the platform, in the train, and in the crowded street again?" Precisely. Nothing simpler! No tools required! Not even a book. Nevertheless, the affair is not easy.

When you leave your house, concentrate your mind on a subject (no matter what, to begin with). You will not have gone ten yards before your mind has skipped away under your very eyes and is larking round the corner with another subject.

Bring it back by the scruff of the neck. Ere you have reached the station you will have brought it back about forty times. Do not despair. Continue. Keep it up. You will succeed. You cannot by any chance fail if you persevere. It is idle to pretend that your mind is incapable of concentration. Do you not remember that morning when you received a disquieting letter which demanded a very carefully-worded answer? How you kept your mind steadily on the subject of the answer, without a second's intermission, until you reached your office; whereupon you instantly sat down and wrote the answer? That was a case in which *you* were roused by circumstances to such a degree of vitality that you were able to dominate your mind like a tyrant. You would have no trifling. You insisted that its work should be done, and its work was done.

By the regular practice of concentration (as to which there is no secret—save the secret of perseverance) you can tyrannize over your mind (which is not the highest part of *you*) every hour of the day, and in no matter what place. The exercise is a very convenient one. If you got into your morning train with a pair of dumbbells for your muscles or an encyclopedia in ten volumes for your learning, you would probably excite remark. But as you walk in the street, or sit in the corner of the compartment behind a pipe, or "strap-hang" on the Subterranean, who is to know that you are engaged in the most important of daily acts? What asinine boor can laugh at you?

I do not care what you concentrate on, so long as you concentrate. It is the mere disciplining of the thinking machine that counts. But still, you may as well kill two birds with one stone, and concentrate on something useful. I suggest—it is only a suggestion—a little chapter of Marcus Aurelius or Epictetus.

Do not, I beg, shy at their names. For myself, I know nothing more "actual," more bursting with plain common-sense, applicable to the daily life of plain persons like you and me (who hate airs, pose, and nonsense) than Marcus Aurelius or Epictetus. Read a chapter—and so short they are, the chapters!—in the evening and concentrate on it the next morning. You will see.

Yes, my friend, it is useless for you to try to disguise the fact. I can hear your brain like a telephone at my ear. You are saying to yourself: "This fellow was doing pretty well up to his seventh chapter. He had begun to interest me faintly. But what he says about thinking in trains, and concentration, and so on, is not for me. It may be well enough for some folks, but it isn't in my line."

It is for you, I passionately repeat; it is for you. Indeed, you are the very man I am aiming at.

Throw away the suggestion, and you throw away the most precious suggestion that was ever offered to you. It is not my suggestion. It is the suggestion of the most sensible, practical, hard-headed men that have walked the earth. I only give it you at second-hand. Try it. Get your mind in hand. And see how the process cures half the evils of life—especially worry, that miserable, avoidable, shameful disease—worry!

The Reflective Mood

The exercise of concentrating the mind (to which at least half an hour a day should be given) is a mere preliminary, like scales on the piano. Having acquired power over that most unruly member of one's complex organism, one has naturally to put it to the yoke. Useless to possess an obedient mind unless one profits to the furthest possible degree by its obedience. A prolonged primary course of study is indicated.

Now as to what this course of study should be there cannot be any question; there never has been any question. All the sensible people of all ages are agreed upon it. And it is not literature, nor is it any other art, nor is it history, nor is it any science. It is the study of one's self. Man, know thyself. These words are so hackneyed that verily I blush to write them. Yet they must be written, for they need to be written. (I take back my blush, being ashamed of it.) Man, know thyself. I say it out loud. The phrase is one of those phrases with which everyone is familiar, of which everyone acknowledges the value, and which only the most sagacious put into practice. I don't know why. I am entirely convinced that what is more than anything else lacking in the life of the average well-intentioned man of today is the reflective mood.

We do not reflect. I mean that we do not reflect upon genuinely important things; upon the problem of our happiness, upon the main direction in which we are going, upon what life is giving to us, upon the share which reason has (or has not) in determining our actions, and upon the relation between our principles and our conduct.

And yet you are in search of happiness, are you not? Have you discovered it?

The chances are that you have not. The chances are that you have already come to believe that happiness is unattainable. But men have attained it. And they have attained it by realizing that happiness does not spring from the procuring of physical or mental pleasure, but from the development of reason and the adjustment of conduct to principles.

I suppose that you will not have the audacity to deny this. And if you admit it, and still devote no part of your day to the deliberate consideration of your reason, principles, and conduct, you admit also that while striving for a certain thing you are regularly leaving undone the one act which is necessary to the attainment of that thing.

Now, shall I blush, or will you?

Do not fear that I mean to thrust certain principles upon your attention. I care not (in this place) what your principles are. Your principles may induce you to believe in the righteousness of burglary. I don't mind. All I urge is that a life in which conduct does not fairly well accord with principles is a silly life; and that conduct can only be made to accord with principles by means of daily examination, reflection, and resolution. What leads to the permanent sorrowfulness of burglars is that their principles are contrary to burglary. If they genuinely believed in the moral excellence of burglary, penal servitude would simply mean so many happy years for them; all martyrs are happy, because their conduct and their principles agree.

As for reason (which makes conduct, and is not unconnected with the making of principles), it plays a far smaller part in our lives than we fancy. We are supposed to be reasonable; but we are much more instinctive than reasonable. And the less we reflect, the less reasonable we shall be. The next time you get cross with the waiter because your steak is over-cooked, ask reason to step into the cabinet-room of your mind, and consult her. She will probably tell you that the waiter did not cook the steak, and had no control over the cooking of the steak; and that even if he alone was to blame, you accomplished nothing good by getting cross; you merely lost your dignity, looked a fool in the eyes of sensible men, and soured the waiter, while producing no effect whatever on the steak.

The result of this consultation with reason (for which she makes no charge) will be that when once more your steak is over-cooked you will treat the waiter as a fellow-creature, remain quite calm in a kindly spirit, and politely insist on having a fresh steak. The gain will be obvious and solid.

In the formation or modification of principles, and the practice of conduct, much help can be derived from printed books (issued at sixpence each and upwards). I mentioned in my last chapter Marcus Aurelius and Epictetus. Certain even more widely known works will occur at once to the memory. I may also mention Pascal, La Bruyère, and Emerson. For myself, you do not catch me traveling without my Marcus Aurelius. Yes, books are valuable. But no reading of books will take the place of a daily, candid, honest examination of what one has recently done, and what one is about to do—of a steady looking at one's self in the face (disconcerting though the sight may be).

When shall this important business be accomplished? The solitude of the evening journey home appears to me to be suitable for it. A reflective mood naturally follows the exertion of having earned the day's living. Of course if, instead of attending to an elementary and profoundly important duty, you prefer to read the paper (which you might just as well read while waiting for your dinner) I have nothing to say. But attend to it at some time of the day you must. I now come to the evening hours.

Interest in the Arts

Many people pursue a regular and uninterrupted course of idleness in the evenings because they think that there is no alternative to idleness but the study of literature; and they do not happen to have a taste for literature. This is a great mistake.

Of course it is impossible, or at any rate very difficult, properly to study anything whatever without the aid of printed books. But if you desire to understand the deeper depths of bridge or of boat-sailing you would not be deterred by your lack of interest in literature from reading the best books on bridge or boat-sailing. We must, therefore, distinguish between literature, and books treating of subjects not literary. I shall come to literature in due course.

Let me now remark to those who have never read Meredith, and who are capable of being unmoved by a discussion as to whether Mr. Stephen Phillips is or is not a true poet, that they are perfectly within their rights. It is not a crime not to love literature. It is not a sign of imbecility. The mandarins of literature will order out to instant execution the unfortunate individual who does not comprehend, say, the influence of Wordsworth on Tennyson. But that is only their impudence. Where would they be, I wonder, if requested to explain the influences that went to make Tchaikovsky's "Pathetic Symphony"?

There are enormous fields of knowledge quite outside literature which will yield magnificent results to cultivators. For example (since I have just mentioned the most popular piece of high-class music in England today), I am reminded that the Promenade Concerts begin in August. You go to them. You smoke your cigar or cigarette (and I regret to say that you strike your matches during the soft bars of the "Lohengrin" overture), and you enjoy the music. But you say you cannot play the piano or the fiddle, or even the banjo; that you know nothing of music.

What does that matter? That you have a genuine taste for music is proved by the fact that, in order to fill his hall with you and your peers, the conductor is obliged to provide programs from which bad music is almost entirely excluded (a change from the old Covent Garden days!).

Now surely your inability to perform "The Maiden's Prayer" on a piano need not prevent you from making yourself familiar with the construction of the orchestra to which you listen a couple of nights a week during a couple of months! As things are, you probably think of the orchestra as a heterogeneous mass of instruments producing a confused agreeable mass of sound. You do not listen for details because you have never trained your ears to listen to details.

If you were asked to name the instruments which play the great theme at the beginning of the C minor symphony you could not name them for your life's sake. Yet you admire the C minor symphony. It has thrilled you. It will thrill you again. You have even talked about it, in an expansive mood, to that lady—you know whom I mean. And all you can positively state about the C minor symphony is that Beethoven composed it and that it is a "jolly fine thing."

Now, if you have read, say, Mr. Krehbiel's "How to Listen to Music" (which can be got at any bookseller's for less than the price of a stall at the Alhambra, and which contains photographs of all the orchestral instruments and plans of the arrangement of orchestras) you would next go to a promenade concert with an astonishing intensification of interest in it. Instead of a confused mass, the orchestra would appear to you as what it is—a marvelously balanced organism whose various groups of members each have a different and an indispensable function. You would spy out the instruments, and listen for their respective sounds. You would know the gulf that separates a French horn from an English horn, and you would perceive why a player of the hautboy gets higher wages than a fiddler, though the fiddle is the more difficult instrument. You would *live* at a promenade concert, whereas previously you had merely existed there in a state of beatific coma, like a baby gazing at a bright object.

The foundations of a genuine, systematic knowledge of music might be laid. You might specialize your inquiries either on a particular form of music (such as the symphony), or on the works of a particular composer. At the end of a year of forty-eight weeks of three brief evenings each, combined with a study of programs and attendances at concerts chosen out of your increasing knowledge, you would really know something about music, even though you were as far of as ever from jangling "The Maiden's Prayer" on the piano.

"But I hate music!" you say. My dear sir, I respect you.

What applies to music applies to the other arts. I might mention Mr. Clermont Witt's "How to Look at Pictures," or Mr. Russell Sturgis's "How to Judge Architecture," as beginnings (merely beginnings) of systematic vitalizing knowledge in other arts, the materials for whose study abound in London.

"I hate all the arts!" you say. My dear sir, I respect you more and more.

I will deal with your case next, before coming to literature.

Nothing in Life Is Humdrum

Art is a great thing. But it is not the greatest. The most important of all perceptions is the continual perception of cause and effect—in other words, the perception of the continuous development of the universe—in still other words, the perception of the course of evolution. When one has thoroughly got imbued into one's head the leading truth that nothing happens without a cause, one grows not only large-minded, but large-hearted.

It is hard to have one's watch stolen, but one reflects that the thief of the watch became a thief from causes of heredity and environment which are as interesting as they are scientifically comprehensible; and one buys another watch, if not with joy, at any rate with a philosophy that makes bitterness impossible. One loses, in the study of cause and effect, that absurd air which so many people have of being always shocked and pained by the curiousness of life. Such people live amid human nature as if human nature were a foreign country full of awful foreign customs. But, having reached maturity, one ought surely to be ashamed of being a stranger in a strange land!

The study of cause and effect, while it lessens the painfulness of life, adds to life's picturesqueness. The man to whom evolution is but a name looks at the sea as a grandiose, monotonous spectacle, which he can witness in August for three shillings third-class return. The man who is imbued with the idea of development, of continuous cause and effect, perceives in the sea an element which in the day-before-yesterday of geology was vapour, which yesterday was boiling, and which to-morrow will inevitably be ice.

He perceives that a liquid is merely something on its way to be solid, and he is penetrated by a sense of the tremendous, changeful picturesqueness of life. Nothing will afford a more durable satisfaction than the constantly cultivated appreciation of this. It is the end of all science.

Cause and effect are to be found everywhere. Rents went up in Shepherd's Bush. It was painful and shocking that rents should go up in Shepherd's Bush. But to a certain point we are all scientific students of cause and effect, and there was not a clerk lunching at a Lyons Restaurant who did not scientifically put two and two together and see in the (once) Two-penny Tube the cause of an excessive demand for wigwams in Shepherd's Bush, and in the excessive demand for wigwams the cause of the increase in the price of wigwams.

"Simple!" you say, disdainfully. Everything—the whole complex movement of the universe—is as simple as that—when you can sufficiently put two and two together. And, my dear sir, perhaps you happen to be an estate agent's clerk, and you hate the arts, and you want to foster your immortal soul, and you can't be interested in your business because it's so humdrum.

Nothing is humdrum.

The tremendous, changeful picturesqueness of life is marvelously shown in an estate agent's office. What! There was a block of traffic in Oxford Street; to avoid the block people actually began to travel under the cellars and drains, and the result was a rise of rents in Shepherd's Bush! And you say that isn't picturesque! Suppose you were to study, in this spirit, the property question in London for an hour and a half every other evening. Would it not give zest to your business, and transform your whole life?

You would arrive at more difficult problems. And you would be able to tell us why, as the natural result of cause and effect, the longest straight street in London is about a yard and a half in length, while the longest absolutely straight street in Paris extends for miles. I think you will admit that in an estate agent's clerk I have not chosen an example that specially favors my theories.

You are a bank clerk, and you have not read that breathless romance (disguised as a scientific study), Walter Bagehot's "Lombard Street"? Ah, my dear sir, if you had begun with that, and followed it up for ninety minutes every other evening, how enthralling your business would be to you, and how much more clearly you would understand human nature.

You are "penned in town," but you love excursions to the country and the observation of wild life—certainly a heart-enlarging diversion. Why don't you walk out of your house door, in your slippers, to the nearest gas lamp of a night with a butterfly net, and observe the wild life of common and rare moths that is beating about it, and co-ordinate the knowledge thus obtained and build a superstructure on it, and at last get to *know* something about something?

You need not be devoted to the arts, nor to literature, in order to live fully.

The whole field of daily habit and scene is waiting to satisfy that curiosity which means life, and the satisfaction of which means an understanding heart.

I promised to deal with your case, O man who hates art and literature, and I have dealt with it. I now come to the case of the person, happily very common, who *does* "like reading."

Serious Reading

Novels are excluded from "serious reading," so that the man who, bent on self-improvement, has been deciding to devote ninety minutes three times a week to a complete study of the works of Charles Dickens will be well advised to alter his plans. The reason is not that novels are not serious—some of the greatest literature of the world is in the form of prose fiction—the reason is that bad novels ought not to be read, and that good novels never demand any appreciable mental application on the part of the reader. It is only the bad parts of Meredith's novels that are difficult. A good novel rushes you forward like a skiff down a stream, and you arrive at the end, perhaps breathless, but unexhausted. The best novels involve the least strain. Now in the cultivation of the mind one of the most important factors is precisely the feeling of strain, of difficulty, of a task which one part of you is anxious to achieve and another part of you is anxious to shirk; and that feeling cannot be got in facing a novel. You do not set your teeth in order to read "Anna Karenina." Therefore, though you should read novels, you should not read them in those ninety minutes.

Imaginative poetry produces a far greater mental strain than novels. It produces probably the severest strain of any form of literature. It is the highest form of literature. It yields the highest form of pleasure, and teaches the highest form of wisdom. In a word, there is nothing to compare with it. I say this with sad conscious-ness of the fact that the majority of people do not read poetry.

I am persuaded that many excellent persons, if they were con-fronted with the alternatives of reading "Paradise Lost" and going round Trafalgar Square at noonday on their knees in sack-cloth, would choose the ordeal of public ridicule. Still, I will never cease advising my friends and enemies to read poetry before anything.

If poetry is what is called "a sealed book" to you, begin by reading Hazlitt's famous essay on the nature of "poetry in gen-eral." It is the best thing of its kind in English, and no one who has read it can possibly be under the misapprehension that poetry is a medieval torture, or a mad elephant, or a gun that will go off by itself and kill at forty paces. Indeed, it is difficult to imagine the mental state of the man who, after reading Hazlitt's essay, is not urgently desirous of reading some poetry before his next meal. If the essay so inspires you I would suggest that you make a com-mencement with purely narrative poetry.

There is an infinitely finer English novel, written by a woman, than anything by George Eliot or the Brontës, or even Jane Austen, which perhaps you have not read. Its title is "Aurora Leigh," and its author E. B. Browning. It happens to be written in verse, and to contain a considerable amount of genuinely fine poetry. Decide to read that book through, even if you die for it. Forget that it is fine poetry. Read it simply for the story and the social ideas. And when you have done, ask yourself honestly whether you still dislike po-etry. I have known more than one person to whom "Aurora Leigh" has been the means of proving that in assuming they hated poetry they were entirely mistaken.

Of course, if, after Hazlitt, and such an experiment made in the light of Hazlitt, you are finally assured that there is something in you which is antagonistic to poetry, you must be content with history or philosophy. I shall regret it, yet not inconsolably. "The

Decline and Fall" is not to be named in the same day with "Paradise Lost," but it is a vastly pretty thing; and Herbert Spencer's "First Principles" simply laughs at the claims of poetry and refuses to be accepted as aught but the most majestic product of any human mind. I do not suggest that either of these works is suitable for a tyro in mental strains. But I see no reason why any man of average intelligence should not, after a year of continuous reading, be fit to assault the supreme masterpieces of history or philosophy. The great convenience of masterpieces is that they are so astonishingly lucid.

I suggest no particular work as a start. The attempt would be futile in the space at my command. But I have two general suggestions of a certain importance. The first is to define the direction and scope of your efforts. Choose a limited period, or a limited subject, or a single author. Say to yourself: "I will know something about the French Revolution, or the rise of railways, or the works of John Keats." And during a given period, to be settled beforehand, confine yourself to your choice. There is much pleasure to be derived from being a specialist.

The second suggestion is to think as well as to read. I know people who read and read, and for all the good it does them they might just as well cut bread-and-butter. They take to reading as better men take to drink. They fly through the shires of literature on a motor-car, their sole object being motion. They will tell you how many books they have read in a year.

Unless you give at least forty-five minutes to careful, fatiguing reflection (it is an awful bore at first) upon what you are reading, your ninety minutes of a night are chiefly wasted. This means that your pace will be slow.

Never mind.

Forget the goal; think only of the surrounding country; and after a period, perhaps when you least expect it, you will suddenly find yourself in a lovely town on a hill.

Dangers to Avoid

I cannot terminate these hints, often, I fear, too didactic and abrupt, upon the full use of one's time to the great end of living (as distinguished from vegetating) without briefly referring to certain dangers which lie in wait for the sincere aspirant towards life. The first is the terrible danger of becoming that most odious and least supportable of persons—a prig. Now a prig is a pert fellow who gives himself airs of superior wisdom. A prig is a pompous fool who has gone out for a ceremonial walk, and without knowing it has lost an important part of his attire, namely, his sense of humor. A prig is a tedious individual who, having made a discovery, is so impressed by his discovery that he is capable of being gravely displeased because the entire world is not also impressed by it. Unconsciously to become a prig is an easy and a fatal thing.

Hence, when one sets forth on the enterprise of using all one's time, it is just as well to remember that one's own time, and not other people's time, is the material with which one has to deal; that the earth rolled on pretty comfortably before one began to balance a budget of the hours, and that it will continue to roll on pretty comfortably whether or not one succeeds in one's new role of chancellor of the exchequer of time. It is as well not to chatter too much about what one is doing, and not to betray a too-pained sadness at the spectacle of a whole world deliberately wasting so many hours out of every day, and therefore never really living. It will be found, ultimately, that in taking care of one's self one has quite all one can do.

Another danger is the danger of being tied to a program like a slave to a chariot. One's program must not be allowed to run away with one. It must be respected, but it must not be worshiped as a fetish. A program of daily employ is not a religion.

This seems obvious. Yet I know men whose lives are a burden to themselves and a distressing burden to their relatives and friends simply because they have failed to appreciate the obvious. "Oh, no," I have heard the martyred wife exclaim, "Arthur always takes the dog out for exercise at eight o'clock and he always begins to read at a quarter to nine. So it's quite out of the question that we should . . ." etc., etc. And the note of absolute finality in that plaintive voice reveals the unsuspected and ridiculous tragedy of a career.

On the other hand, a program is a program. And unless it is treated with deference it ceases to be anything but a poor joke. To treat one's program with exactly the right amount of deference, to live with not too much and not too little elasticity, is scarcely the simple affair it may appear to the inexperienced.

And still another danger is the danger of developing a policy of rush, of being gradually more and more obsessed by what one has to do next. In this way one may come to exist as in a prison, and one's life may cease to be one's own. One may take the dog out for a walk at eight o'clock, and meditate the whole time on the fact that one must begin to read at a quarter to nine, and that one must not be late.

And the occasional deliberate breaking of one's program will not help to mend matters. The evil springs not from persisting without elasticity in what one has attempted, but from originally attempting too much, from filling one's program till it runs over. The only cure is to reconstitute the program, and to attempt less.

But the appetite for knowledge grows by what it feeds on, and there are men who come to like a constant breathless hurry of endeavor. Of them it may be said that a constant breathless hurry is better than an eternal doze.

In any case, if the program exhibits a tendency to be oppressive, and yet one wishes not to modify it, an excellent palliative is to pass with exaggerated deliberation from one portion of it to another; for example, to spend five minutes in perfect mental quiescence between chaining up the St. Bernard and opening the book; in other words, to waste five minutes with the entire consciousness of wasting them.

The last, and chiefest danger which I would indicate, is one to which I have already referred—the risk of a failure at the commencement of the enterprise.

I must insist on it.

A failure at the commencement may easily kill outright the newborn impulse towards a complete vitality, and therefore every precaution should be observed to avoid it. The impulse must not be over-taxed. Let the pace of the first lap be even absurdly slow, but let it be as regular as possible.

And, having once decided to achieve a certain task, achieve it at all costs of tedium and distaste. The gain in self-confidence of having accomplished a tiresome labor is immense.

Finally, in choosing the first occupations of those evening hours, be guided by nothing whatever but your taste and natural inclination.

It is a fine thing to be a walking encyclopedia of philosophy, but if you happen to have no liking for philosophy, and to have a liking for the natural history of street-cries, much better leave philosophy alone, and take to street-cries.

PETER B. KYNE

The Go-Getter

This little book is dedicated to the memory of my dead chief, Brigadier-General Leroy S. Lyon, sometime commander of the 65th field artillery brigade, 40th division, United States Army.

He practiced and preached a religion of loyalty to the country and the appointed task, whatever it might be.

Contents

Foreword

"It shall be done!"

These words frame the main theme from *The Go-Getter,* a parable written by Peter B. Kyne. *The Go-Getter* is one of the most successful and influential books from the earliest twentieth century. It has been said to have influenced some of the most successful people in the last century. People from entry-level positions all the way to CEOs have used the ideas in this book to further their careers and their lives. Even today, *The Go-Getter* is taught by successful financiers, entrepreneurs, and success consultants.

What about this parable has captured the attention of so many millions in the last hundred years? *The Go-Getter* tells the story of Bill Peck, a young war veteran who begins to work for Ricks Logging & Lumbering Company. His boss, Cappy Ricks, is impressed by Peck's work, but skeptical about him at the same time. He decides to give Peck the ultimate test to determine whether or not Peck is up to the task: find the blue vase. Peck's answer at all times: "It shall be done." Despite hardships, Peck's dedication serves as a template for readers on how to succeed.

The themes in this book include how to have faith in yourself, how to be determined despite the odds, how not to take "no" for an answer, how to maintain a positive attitude, how to take control of your career, and how to prepare yourself to succeed. While this parable has caught the attention of the business community, the principles can be used in every area of our lives, with any goal we might have. These themes are underscored in *A Message to Garcia,* the powerful story by Elbert Hubert that is also included in this volume.

The author, Peter B. Kyne, was a successful novelist from San Francisco, California. His many novels were turned into films—over one hundred, in fact—but over time, his novels seemed to have faded from popularity. His slim parable, however, has never gone out of print, and has continued to inspire and motivate generation after generation.

And now it's your turn. No matter what your circumstances, read this book, and then look at your goals and say, "It shall be done" . . . and then go do it!

—*Joel Fotinos*

1

Mr. Alden P. Ricks, known in Pacific Coast wholesale lumber and shipping circles as Cappy Ricks, had more troubles than a hen with ducklings. He remarked as much to Mr. Skinner, president and general manager of the Ricks Logging & Lumbering Company, the corporate entity which represented Cappy's vast lumber interests; and he fairly barked the information at Captain Matt Peasley, his son-in-law and also president and manager of the Blue Star Navigation Company, another corporate entity which represented the Ricks interest in the American mercantile marine.

Mr. Skinner received this information in silence. He was not related to Cappy Ricks. But Matt Peasley sat down, crossed his legs and matched glares with his mercurial father-in-law.

"*You* have troubles!" he jeered, with emphasis on the pronoun. "Have you got a misery in your back, or is Herbert Hoover the wrong man for Secretary of Commerce?"

"Stow your sarcasm, young feller," Cappy shrilled. "You know dad-blamed well it isn't a question of health or politics. It's the fact that in my old age I find myself totally surrounded by the choicest aggregation of mental duds since Ajax defied the lightning."

"Meaning whom?"

"You and Skinner."

"Why, what have we done?"

"You argued me into taking on the management of twenty-five

of those infernal Shipping Board freighters, and no sooner do we have them allocated to us than a near panic hits the country, freight rates go to glory, marine engineers go on strike and every infernal young whelp we send out to take charge of one of our offices in the Orient promptly gets the swelled head and thinks he's divinely ordained to drink up all the synthetic Scotch whiskey manufactured in Japan for the benefit of thirsty Americans. In my old age you two have forced us into the position of having to fire folks by cable. Why? Because we're breaking into a game that can't be played on the home grounds. A lot of our business is so far away we can't control it."

Matt Peasley leveled an accusing finger at Cappy Ricks. "We never argued you into taking over the management of those Shipping Board boats. We argued me into it. I'm the goat. You have nothing to do with it. You retired ten years ago. All the troubles in the marine end of this shop belong on my capable shoulders, old settler."

"Theoretically—yes. Actually—no. I hope you do not expect me to abandon mental as well as physical effort. Great Wampus Cats! Am I to be denied a sentimental interest in matters where I have a controlling financial interest? I admit you two boys are running my affairs and ordinarily you run them rather well, but—but—ahem! Harumph-h-h! What's the matter with you, Matt? And you, also, Skinner? If Matt makes a mistake, it's your job to remind him of it before the results manifest themselves, is it not? And vice versa. Have you two boobs lost your ability to judge men, or did you ever have such ability?"

"You're referring to Henderson, of the Shanghai office, I dare say," Mr. Skinner cut in.

"I am, Skinner. And I'm here to remind you that if we'd stuck to our own game, which is coastwise shipping, and had left the trans-Pacific field with its general cargoes to others, we wouldn't have any Shanghai office at this moment and we would not be pestered by the Hendersons of this world."

"He's the best lumber salesman we've ever had," Mr. Skinner defended. "I had every hope that he would send us orders for many a cargo for Asiatic delivery."

"And he had gone through every job in this office, from office boy to sales manager in the lumber department and from freight clerk to passenger agent in the navigation company," Matt Peasley supplemented.

"I admit all of that. But did you consult me when you decided to send him out to China on his own?"

"Of course not. I'm boss of the Blue Star Navigation Company, am I not? The man was in charge of the Shanghai office before you ever opened your mouth to discharge your cargo of free advice."

"I told you then that Henderson wouldn't make good, didn't I?"

"You did."

"And now I have an opportunity to tell you the little tale you didn't give me an opportunity to tell you before you sent him out. Henderson *was* a good man—a crackerjack man—when he had a better man over him. But—I've been twenty years reducing a tendency on the part of that fellow's head to bust his hat-band. And now he's gone south with a hundred and thirty thousand taels of our Shanghai bank account."

"Permit me to remind you, Mr. Ricks," Mr. Skinner cut in coldly, "that he was bonded to the extent of a quarter of a million dollars."

"Not a peep out of you, Skinner. Not a peep. Permit me to remind *you* that I'm the little genius who placed that insurance unknown to you and Matt. And I recall now that I was reminded by you, Matthew, my son, that I had retired ten years ago and please, would I quit interfering in the internal administration of your office."

"Well, I must admit your far-sightedness in that instance will keep the Shanghai office out of the red ink this year," Matt Peasley replied. "However, we face this situation, Cappy. Henderson has drunk and gambled and signed chits in excess of his salary. He hasn't attended to business and he's capped his inefficiency by absconding with our bank account. We couldn't foresee that. When we send a man out to the Orient to be our manager there, we have to trust him all the way or not at all. So there is no use weeping over spilled milk, Cappy. Our job is to select a successor to Henderson and send him out to Shanghai on the next boat."

"Oh, very well, Matt," Cappy replied magnanimously, "I'll not rub it into you. I suppose I'm far from generous, bawling you out like this. Perhaps, when you're my age and have had a lot of mental and moral cripples nip you and draw blood as often as they've drawn it on me you'll be a better judge than I of men worthy of the weight of responsibility. Skinner, have you got a candidate for this job?"

"I regret to say, sir, I have not. All of the men in my department are quite young—too young for the responsibility."

"What do you mean—young?" Cappy blazed.

"Well, the only man I would consider for the job is Andrews and he is too young—about thirty, I should say."

"About thirty, eh? Strikes me you were about twenty-eight when I threw ten thousand a year at you in actual cash, and a couple of million dollars' worth of responsibility."

"Yes, sir, but then Andrews has never been tested———"

"Skinner," Cappy interrupted in his most awful voice, "it's a constant source of amazement to me why I refrain from firing you. You say Andrews has never been tested. Why hasn't he been tested? Why are we maintaining untested material in this shop, anyhow? Eh? Answer me that. Tut, tut, tut! Not a peep out of you, sir. If you had done your Christian duty, you would have taken a year's vacation when lumber was selling itself in 1919 and 1920, and you would have left Andrews sitting in at your desk to see the sort of stuff he's made of."

"It's a mighty lucky thing I didn't go away for a year," Skinner protested respectfully, "because the market broke—like that—and if you don't think we have to hustle to sell sufficient lumber to keep our own ships busy freighting it——"

"Skinner, how dare you contradict me? How old was Matt Peasley when I turned over the Blue Star Navigation Company to him, lock, stock and barrel? Why, he wasn't twenty-six years old. Skinner, you're a dodo! The killjoys like you who have straddled the neck of industry and throttled it with absurd theories that a man's back must be bent like an ox-bow and his locks snowy white before he can be entrusted with responsibility and a living wage, have caused all of our wars and strikes. This is a young man's world, Skinner, and don't you ever forget it. The go-getters of this world are under thirty years of age. Matt," he concluded, turning to his son-in-law, "what do you think of Andrews for that Shanghai job?"

"I think he'll do."

"Why do you think he'll do?"

"Because he ought to do. He's been with us long enough to have acquired sufficient experience to enable him——"

"Has he acquired the courage to tackle the job, Matt?" Cappy interrupted. "That's more important than this doggoned experience you and Skinner prate so much about."

"I know nothing of his courage. I assume that he has force and initiative. I know he has a pleasing personality."

"Well, before we send him out we ought to know whether or no he has force and initiative."

"Then," quoth Matt Peasley, rising, "I wash my hands of the job of selecting Henderson's successor. You've butted in, so I suggest you name the lucky man."

"Yes, indeed," Skinner agreed. "I'm sure it's quite beyond my poor abilities to uncover Andrews' force and initiative on such short notice. He does possess sufficient force and initiative for his present job, but——"

"But will he possess force and initiative when he has to make a quick decision six thousand miles from expert advice, and stand or fall by that decision? That's what we want to know, Skinner."

"I suggest, sir," Mr. Skinner replied with chill politeness, "that you conduct the examination."

"I accept the nomination, Skinner. By the Holy Pink-toed Prophet! The next man we send out to that Shanghai office is going to be a go-getter. We've had three managers go rotten on us and that's three too many."

And without further ado, Cappy swung his aged legs up on to his desk and slid down in his swivel chair until he rested on his spine. His head sank on his breast and he closed his eyes.

"He's framing the examination for Andrews," Matt Peasley whispered, as he and Skinner made their exits.

2

The President emeritus of the Ricks interests was not destined to uninterrupted cogitation, however. Within ten minutes his private exchange operator called him to the telephone.

"What is it?" Cappy yelled into the transmitter.

"There is a young man in the general office. His name is Mr. William E. Peck and he desires to see you personally."

Cappy sighed. "Very well," he replied. "Have him shown in."

Almost immediately the office boy ushered Mr. Peck into Cappy's presence. The moment he was fairly inside the door the visitor halted, came easily and naturally to "attention" and bowed respectfully, while the cool glance of his keen blue eyes held steadily the autocrat of the Blue Star Navigation Company.

"Mr. Ricks, Peck is my name, sir—William E. Peck. Thank you, sir, for acceding to my request for an interview."

"Ahem! Hum-m-m!" Cappy looked belligerent. "Sit down, Mr. Peck."

Mr. Peck sat down, but as he crossed to the chair beside Cappy's desk, the old gentleman noticed that his visitor walked with a slight limp, and that his left forearm had been amputated half way to the elbow. To the observant Cappy, the American Legion button in Mr. Peck's lapel told the story.

"Well, Mr. Peck," he queried gently, "what can I do for you?"

"I've called for my job," the veteran replied briefly.

"By the Holy Pink-toed Prophet!" Cappy ejaculated, "you say that like a man who doesn't expect to be refused."

"Quite right, sir. I do not anticipate a refusal."

"Why?"

Mr. William E. Peck's engaging but somewhat plain features rippled into the most compelling smile Cappy Ricks had ever seen. "I am a salesman, Mr. Ricks," he replied. "I know that statement to be true because I have demonstrated, over a period of five years, that I can sell my share of anything that has a hockable value. I have always found, however, that before proceeding to sell goods I had to sell the manufacturer of those goods something, to-wit— myself! I am about to sell myself to you."

"Son," said Cappy smilingly, "you win. You've sold me already. When did they sell you a membership in the military forces of the United States of America?"

"On the morning of April 7th, 1917, sir."

"That clinches our sale. I soldiered with the Knights of Co- lumbus at Camp Kearny myself, but when they refused to let me go abroad with my division my heart was broken, so I went over the hill."

That little touch of the language of the line appeared to warm Mr. Peck's heart considerably, establishing at once a free masonry between them.

"I was with the Portland Lumber Company, selling lumber in the Middle West before the war," he explained. "Uncle Sam gave me my sheepskin at Letterman General Hospital last week, with half disability on my ten thousand dollars' worth of government insurance. Whittling my wing was a mere trifle, but my broken leg was a long time mending, and now it's shorter than it really ought to be. And I developed pneumonia with influenza and they found some T. B. indications after that. I've been at the government tu- berculosis hospital at Fort Bayard, New Mexico, for a year. However, what's left of me is certified to be sound. I've got five inches chest expansion and I feel fine."

"Not at all blue or discouraged?" Cappy hazarded.

"Oh, I got off easy, Mr. Ricks. I have my head left—and my right arm. I can think and I can write, and even if one of my wheels is flat, I can hike longer and faster after an order than most. Got a job for me, Mr. Ricks?"

"No, I haven't, Mr. Peck. I'm out of it, you know. Retired ten years ago. This office is merely a headquarters for social frivolity—a place to get my mail and mill over the gossip of the street. Our Mr. Skinner is the chap you should see."

"I have seen Mr. Skinner, sir," the erstwhile warrior replied, "but he wasn't very sympathetic. I think he jumped to the conclusion that I was attempting to trade him my empty sleeve. He informed me that there wasn't sufficient business to keep his present staff of salesmen busy, so then I told him I'd take anything, from stenographer up. I'm the champion one-handed typist of the United States Army. I can tally lumber and bill it. I can keep books and answer the telephone."

"No encouragement, eh?"

"No, sir."

"Well, now, son," Cappy informed his cheerful visitor confidentially, "you take my tip and see my son-in-law, Captain Peasley. He's high, low and jack-in-the-game in the shipping end of our business."

"I have also interviewed Captain Peasley. He was very kind. He said he felt that he owed me a job, but business is so bad he couldn't make a place for me. He told me he is now carrying a dozen ex-service men merely because he hasn't the heart to let them go. I believe him."

"Well, my dear boy—my dear young friend! Why do you come to me?"

"Because," Mr. Peck replied smilingly, "I want you to go over their heads and give me a job. I don't care a hoot what it is, provided I can do it. If I can do it, I'll do it better than it was ever done before, and if I can't do that I'll quit to save you the embarrassment of firing me. I'm not an object of charity, but I'm scarcely the man I used to be and I'm four years behind the procession and have to catch up. I have the best of references——"

"I see you have," Cappy cut in blandly, and pressed the push-button on his desk. Mr. Skinner entered. He glanced disapprovingly at William E. Peck and then turned inquiring eyes toward Cappy Ricks.

"Skinner, dear boy," Cappy purred amiably, "I've been thinking over the proposition to send Andrews out to the Shanghai office, and I've come to this conclusion. We'll have to take a chance. At the present time that office is in charge of a stenographer, and we've got to get a manager on the job without further loss of time. So I'll tell you what we'll do. We'll send Andrews out on the next boat, but inform him that his position is temporary. Then if he doesn't make good out there we can take him back into this office, where he is a most valuable man. Meanwhile—ahem! hum-m-m! Harumph!—meanwhile, you'd oblige me greatly, Skinner, my dear boy, if you would consent to take this young man into your office and give him a good work-out to see the stuff he's made of. As a favor to me, Skinner, my dear boy, as a favor to me."

Mr. Skinner, in the language of the sporting world, was down for the count—and knew it. Young Mr. Peck knew it too, and smiled graciously upon the general manager, for young Mr. Peck had been in the army, where one of the first great lessons to be assimilated is this: that the commanding general's request is always tantamount to an order.

"Very well, sir," Mr. Skinner replied coldly. "Have you arranged the compensation to be given Mr. Peck?"

Cappy threw up a deprecating hand. "That detail is entirely up to you, Skinner. Far be it from me to interfere in the internal administration of your department. Naturally you will pay Mr. Peck what he is worth and not a cent more." He turned to the triumphant Peck. "Now, you listen to me, young feller. If you think you're slipping gracefully into a good thing, disabuse your mind of that impression right now. You'll step right up to the plate, my son, and you'll hit the ball fairly on the nose, and you'll do it early and often. The first time you tip a foul, you'll be warned. The second time you do it you'll get a month's lay-off to think it over, and the third time you'll be out—for keeps. Do I make myself clear?"

"You do, sir," Mr. Peck declared happily. "All I ask is fighting room and I'll hack my way into Mr. Skinner's heart. Thank you, Mr. Skinner, for consenting to take me on. I appreciate your action very, very much and shall endeavor to be worthy of your confidence."

"Young scoundrel! In-fer-nal young scoundrel!" Cappy murmured to himself. "He has a sense of humor, thank God! Ah, poor old narrow-gauge Skinner! If that fellow ever gets a new or unconventional thought in his stodgy head, it'll kill him overnight. He's hopping mad right now, because he can't say a word in his own defense, but if he doesn't make hell look like a summer holiday for Mr. Bill Peck, I'm due to be mercifully chloroformed. Good Lord, how empty life would be if I couldn't butt in and raise a little riot every once in so often."

Young Mr. Peck had risen and was standing at attention. "When do I report for duty, sir?" he queried of Mr. Skinner.

"Whenever you're ready," Skinner retorted with a wintry smile. Mr. Peck glanced at a cheap wrist watch. "It's twelve o'clock now," he soliloquized aloud. "I'll pop out, wrap myself around some rations and report on the job at one P. M. I might just as well knock out half a day's pay." He glanced at Cappy Ricks and quoted:

*"Count that day lost whose low descending sun
Finds prices shot to glory and business done for fun."*

Unable to maintain his composure in the face of such levity during office hours, Mr. Skinner withdrew, still wrapped in his sub-Antarctic dignity. As the door closed behind him, Mr. Peck's eyebrows went up in a manner indicative of apprehension.

"I'm off to a bad start, Mr. Ricks," he opined.

"You only asked for a start," Cappy piped back at him. "I didn't guarantee you a *good* start, and I wouldn't because I can't. I can only drive Skinner and Matt Peasley so far—and no farther. There's always a point at which I quit—er—ah—William."

"More familiarly known as Bill Peck, sir."

"Very well, Bill." Cappy slid out to the edge of his chair and peered at Bill Peck balefully over the top of his spectacles. "I'll have my eye on you, young feller," he shrilled. "I freely acknowledge our indebtedness to you, but the day you get the notion in your head that this office is an old soldiers' home—" He paused thoughtfully. "I wonder what Skinner *will* pay you?" he mused. "Oh, well," he continued, "whatever it is, take it and say nothing and when the moment is propitious—and provided you've earned it—I'll intercede with the danged old relic and get you a raise."

"Thank you very much, sir. You are most kind. Good-day, sir."

And Bill Peck picked up his hat and limped out of The Presence. Scarcely had the door closed behind him than Mr. Skinner re-entered Cappy Ricks' lair. He opened his mouth to speak, but Cappy silenced him with an imperious finger.

"Not a peep out of you, Skinner, my dear boy," he chirped amiably. "I know exactly what you're going to say and I admit your right to say it, but—ah—ahem! Harumph-h-h!—now, Skinner, listen to reason. How the devil could you have the heart to reject that crippled ex-soldier? There he stood, on one sound leg, with his left sleeve tucked into his coat pocket and on his homely face the grin of an unwhipped, unbeatable man. But you—blast your cold, unfeeling soul, Skinner!—looked him in the eye and turned him down like a drunkard turns down near-beer. Skinner, how *could* you do it?"

Undaunted by Cappy's admonitory finger, Mr. Skinner struck a distinctly defiant attitude.

"There is no sentiment in business," he replied angrily. "A week ago last Thursday the local posts of the American Legion commenced their organized drive for jobs for their crippled and unemployed comrades, and within three days you've sawed off two hundred and nine such jobs on the various corporations that you control. The gang you shipped up to the mill in Washington has already applied for a charter for a new post to be known as Cappy Ricks Post No. 534. And you had experienced men discharged to make room for these ex-soldiers."

"You bet I did," Cappy yelled triumphantly. "It's always Old Home Week in every logging camp and saw-mill in the Northwest for I. W. W.'s and revolutionary communists. I'm sick of their unauthorized strikes and sabotage, and by the Holy Pink-toed Prophet, Cappy Ricks Post No. 534, American Legion, is the only sort of back-fire I can think of to put the Wobblies on the run."

"Every office and ship and retail yard could be run by a first-sergeant," Skinner complained. "I'm thinking of having reveille and retreat and bugle calls and Saturday morning inspections. I tell you, sir, the Ricks interests have absorbed all the old soldiers possible and at the present moment those interests are overflowing with glory. What we want are workers, not talkers. These ex-soldiers spend too much time fighting their battles over again."

"Well, Comrade Peck is the last one I'll ask you to absorb, Skinner," Cappy promised contritely. "Ever read Kipling's Barrack Room Ballads, Skinner?"

"I have no time to read," Mr. Skinner protested.

"Go up town this minute and buy a copy and read one ballad entitled 'Tommy,'" Cappy barked. "For the good of your immortal soul," he added.

"Well, Comrade Peck doesn't make a hit with me, Mr. Ricks. He applied to me for a job and I gave him his answer. Then he went to Captain Matt and was refused, so, just to demonstrate his bad taste, he went over our heads and induced you to pitchfork him into a job. He'll curse the day he was inspired to do that."

"Skinner! Skinner! Look me in the eye! Do you know why I asked you to take on Bill Peck?"

"I do. Because you're too tender-hearted for your own good."

"You unimaginative dunderhead! You jibbering jackdaw! How could I reject a boy who simply would not be rejected? Why, I'll bet a ripe peach that Bill Peck was one of the doggondest finest soldiers you ever saw. He carries his objective. He sized you up just like that, Skinner. He declined to permit you to block him. Skinner, that Peck person has been opposed by experts. Yes, sir— experts! What kind of a job are you going to give him, Skinner, my dear boy?"

"Andrews' job, of course."

"Oh, yes, I forgot. Skinner, dear boy, haven't we got about half a million feet of skunk spruce to saw off on somebody?" Mr. Skinner nodded and Cappy continued with all the naïve eagerness of one who has just made a marvelous discovery, which he is confident will revolutionize science. "Give him that stinking stuff to peddle, Skinner, and if you can dig up a couple of dozen carloads of red fir or bull pine in transit, or some short or odd-length stock, or some larch ceiling or flooring, or some hemlock random stock—in fact, anything the trade doesn't want as a gift—you get me, don't you, Skinner?"

Mr. Skinner smiled his swordfish smile. "And if he fails to make good—*au revoir*, eh?"

"Yes, I suppose so, although I hate to think about it. On the other hand, if he makes good he's to have Andrews' salary. We must be fair, Skinner. Whatever our faults we must always be fair." He rose and patted the general manager's lean shoulder. "There, there, Skinner, my boy. Forgive me if I've been a trifle—ah—ahem!—precipitate and—er—harumph-h-h! Skinner, if you put a prohibitive price on that skunk fir, by the Holy Pink-toed Prophet, I'll fire you! Be fair, boy, be fair. No dirty work, Skinner. Remember, Comrade Peck has half of his left forearm buried in France."

3

At twelve-thirty, as Cappy was hurrying up California Street to luncheon at the Commercial Club, he met Bill Peck limping down the sidewalk. The ex-soldier stopped him and handed him a card.

"What do you think of that, sir?" he queried. "Isn't it a neat business card?"

Cappy read:

RICKS LUMBER & LOGGING COMPANY
Lumber and its products
248 California St.
San Francisco.
Represented by
William E. Peck
If you can drive nails in it—we have it!

Cappy Ricks ran a speculative thumb over Comrade Peck's business card. It was engraved. And copper plates or steel dies are not made in half an hour!

"By the Twelve Ragged Apostles!" This was Cappy's most terrible oath and he never employed it unless rocked to his very foundations. "Bill, as one bandit to another—come clean. When did you first make up your mind to go to work for us?"

"A week ago," Comrade Peck replied blandly.

"And what was your grade when Kaiser Bill went A. W. O. L.?"

"I was a buck."

"I don't believe you. Didn't anybody ever offer you something better?"

"Frequently. However, if I had accepted I would have had to resign the nicest job I ever had. There wasn't much money in it, but it was filled with excitement and interesting experiments. I used to disguise myself as a Christmas tree or a box car and pick off German sharp-shooters. I was known as Peck's Bad Boy. I was often tempted to quit, but whenever I'd reflect on the number of American lives I was saving daily, a commission was just a scrap of paper to me."

"If you'd ever started in any other branch of the service you'd have run John J. Pershing down to lance corporal. Bill, listen! Have you ever had any experience selling skunk spruce?"

Comrade Peck was plainly puzzled. He shook his head. "What sort of stock is it?" he asked.

"Humboldt County, California, spruce, and it's coarse and stringy and wet and heavy and smells just like a skunk directly after using. I'm afraid Skinner's going to start you at the bottom— and skunk spruce is it."

"Can you drive nails in it, Mr. Ricks?"

"Oh, yes."

"Does anybody ever buy skunk spruce, sir?"

"Oh, occasionally one of our bright young men digs up a half-wit who's willing to try anything once. Otherwise, of course, we would not continue to manufacture it. Fortunately, Bill, we have very little of it, but whenever our woods boss runs across a good tree he hasn't the heart to leave it standing, and as a result, we always have enough skunk spruce on hand to keep our salesmen humble."

"I can sell anything—at a price," Comrade Peck replied unconcernedly, and continued on his way back to the office.

4

For two months Cappy Ricks saw nothing of Bill Peck. That enterprising veteran had been sent out into the Utah, Arizona, New Mexico and Texas territory the moment he had familiarized himself with the numerous details regarding freight rates, weights and the mills he represented, all things which a salesman should be familiar with before he starts out on the road. From Salt Lake City he wired in an order for two carloads of larch rustic and in Ogden he managed to inveigle a retail yard with which Mr. Skinner had been trying to do business for years, into sampling a carload of skunk spruce boards, random lengths and grades, at a dollar above the price given him by Skinner. In Arizona he worked up some new business in mining timbers, but it was not until he got into the heart of Texas that Comrade Peck really commenced to demonstrate his selling ability. Standard oil derricks were his specialty and he shot the orders in so fast that Mr. Skinner was forced to wire him for mercy and instruct him to devote his talent to the disposal of cedar shingles and siding, Douglas fir and redwood. Eventually he completed his circle and worked his way home, via Los Angeles, pausing, however, in the San Joaquin Valley to sell two more carloads of skunk spruce. When this order was wired in, Mr. Skinner came to Cappy Ricks with the telegram.

"Well, I must admit Comrade Peck can sell lumber," he announced grudgingly. "He has secured five new accounts and here is an order for two more carloads of skunk spruce. I'll have to raise his salary about the first of the year."

"My dear Skinner, why the devil wait until the first of the year? Your pernicious habit of deferring the inevitable parting with money has cost us the services of more than one good man. You know you have to raise Comrade Peck's salary sooner or later, so why not do it now and smile like a dentifrice advertisement while you're doing it? Comrade Peck will feel a whole lot better as a result, and who knows? He may conclude you're a human being, after all, and learn to love you?"

"Very well, sir. I'll give him the same salary Andrews was getting before Peck took over his territory."

"Skinner, you make it impossible for me to refrain from showing you who's boss around here. He's better than Andrews, isn't he?"

"I think he is, sir."

"Well then, for the love of a square deal, pay him more and pay it to him from the first day he went to work. Get out. You make me nervous. By the way, how is Andrews getting along in his Shanghai job?"

"He's helping the cable company pay its income tax. Cables about three times a week on matters he should decide for himself. Matt Peasley is disgusted with him."

"Ah! Well, I'm not disappointed. And I suppose Matt will be in here before long to remind me that I was the bright boy who picked Andrews for the job. Well, I did, but I call upon you to remember, Skinner, when I'm assailed, that Andrews' appointment was temporary."

"Yes, sir, it was."

"Well, I suppose I'll have to cast about for his successor and beat Matt out of his cheap 'I told you so' triumph. I think Comrade Peck has some of the earmarks of a good manager for our Shanghai office, but I'll have to test him a little further." He looked up humorously at Mr. Skinner. "Skinner, my dear boy," he continued, "I'm going to have him deliver a blue vase."

Mr. Skinner's cold features actually glowed. "Well, tip the chief of police and the proprietor of the store off this time and save yourself some money," he warned Cappy. He walked to the window and looked down into California Street. He continued to smile.

"Yes," Cappy continued dreamily, "I think I shall give him the thirty-third degree. You'll agree with me, Skinner, that if he delivers the blue vase he'll be worth ten thousand dollars a year as our Oriental manager?"

"I'll say he will," Mr. Skinner replied slangily.

"Very well, then. Arrange matters, Skinner, so that he will be available for me at one o'clock, a week from Sunday. I'll attend to the other details."

Mr. Skinner nodded. He was still chuckling when he departed for his own office.

5

A week from the succeeding Saturday, Mr. Skinner did not come down to the office, but a telephone message from his home informed the chief clerk that Mr. Skinner was at home and somewhat indisposed. The chief clerk was to advise Mr. Peck that he, Mr. Skinner, had contemplated having a conference with the latter that day, but that his indisposition would prevent this. Mr. Skinner hoped to be feeling much better to-morrow, and since he was very desirous of a conference with Mr. Peck before the latter should depart on his next selling pilgrimage, on Monday, would Mr. Peck be good enough to call at Mr. Skinner's house at one o'clock Sunday afternoon? Mr. Peck sent back word that he would be there at the appointed time and was rewarded with Mr. Skinner's thanks, via the chief clerk.

Promptly at one o'clock the following day, Bill Peck reported at the general manager's house. He found Mr. Skinner in bed, reading the paper and looking surprisingly well. He trusted Mr. Skinner felt better than he looked. Mr. Skinner did, and at once entered into a discussion of the new customers, other prospects he particularly desired Mr. Peck to approach, new business to be investigated, and further details without end. And in the midst of this conference Cappy Ricks telephoned.

A portable telephone stood on a commode beside Mr. Skinner's bed, so the latter answered immediately. Comrade Peck watched

Skinner listen attentively for fully two minutes, then heard him say:

"Mr. Ricks, I'm terribly sorry. I'd love to do this errand for you, but really I'm under the weather. In fact, I'm in bed as I speak to you now. But Mr. Peck is here with me and I'm sure he'll be very happy to attend to the matter for you."

"By all means," Bill Peck hastened to assure the general manager. "Who does Mr. Ricks want killed and where will he have the body delivered?"

"Hah-hah! Hah-hah!" Mr. Skinner had a singularly annoying, mirthless laugh, as if he begrudged himself such an unheard-of indulgence. "Mr. Peck says," he informed Cappy, "that he'll be delighted to attend to the matter for you. He wants to know whom you want killed and where you wish the body delivered. Hah-hah! Hah! Peck, Mr. Ricks will speak to you."

Bill Peck took the telephone. "Good-afternoon, Mr. Ricks."

"Hello, old soldier. What are you doing this afternoon?"

"Nothing—after I conclude my conference with Mr. Skinner. By the way, he has just given me a most handsome boost in salary, for which I am most appreciative. I feel, however, despite Mr. Skinner's graciousness, that you have put in a kind word for me with him, and I want to thank you——"

"Tut, tut. Not a peep out of you, sir. Not a peep. You get nothing for nothing from Skinner or me. However, in view of the fact that you're feeling kindly toward me this afternoon, I wish you'd do a little errand for me. I can't send a boy and I hate to make a messenger out of you—er—ah—ahem! That is, harumph-h-h——!"

"I have no false pride, Mr. Ricks."

"Thank you, Bill. Glad you feel that way about it. Bill, I was prowling around town this forenoon, after church, and down in a store on Sutter Street, between Stockton and Powell Street, on the right hand side as you face Market Street, I saw a blue vase in a window. I have a weakness for vases, Bill. I'm a sharp on them, too. Now, this vase I saw isn't very expensive as vases go—in fact, I wouldn't buy it for my collection—but one of the finest and sweetest ladies of my acquaintance has the mate to that blue vase I saw in the window, and I know she'd be prouder than Punch if she had two of them—one for each side of her drawing room mantel, understand?

"Now, I'm leaving from the Southern Pacific depot at eight o'clock to-night, bound for Santa Barbara to attend her wedding anniversary to-morrow night. I forget what anniversary it is, Bill, but I have been informed by my daughter that I'll be very much *de trop* if I send her any present other than something in porcelain or China or Cloisonné—well, Bill, this crazy little blue vase just fills the order. Understand?"

"Yes, sir. You feel that it would be most graceful on your part if you could bring this little blue vase down to Santa Barbara with you to-night. You have to have it to-night, because if you wait until the store opens on Monday the vase will reach your hostess twenty-four hours after her anniversary party."

"Exactly, Bill. Now, I've simply got to have that vase. If I had discovered it yesterday I wouldn't be asking you to get it for me to-day, Bill."

"Please do not make any explanations or apologies, Mr. Ricks. You have described the vase—no you haven't. What sort of blue is it, how tall is it and what is, approximately, its greatest diameter? Does it set on a base, or does it not? Is it a solid blue, or is it figured?"

"It's a Cloisonné vase, Bill—sort of old Dutch blue, or Delft, with some Oriental funny-business on it. I couldn't describe it exactly, but it has some birds and flowers on it. It's about a foot tall and four inches in diameter and sets on a teak-wood base."

"Very well, sir. You shall have it."

"And you'll deliver it to me in stateroom A, car 7, aboard the train at Third and Townsend Streets, at seven fifty-five to-night?"

"Yes, sir."

"Thank you, Bill. The expense will be trifling. Collect it from the cashier in the morning, and tell him to charge it to my account." And Cappy hung up.

At once Mr. Skinner took up the thread of the interrupted conference, and it was not until three o'clock that Bill Peck left his house and proceeded down-town to locate Cappy Ricks' blue vase.

He proceeded to the block in Sutter Street between Stockton and Powell Streets, and although he walked patiently up one side of the street and down the other, not a single vase of any description showed in any shop window, nor could he find a single shop where such a vase as Cappy had described might, perchance, be displayed for sale.

"I think the old boy has erred in the co-ordinates of the target," Bill Peck concluded, "or else I misunderstood him. I'll telephone his house and ask him to repeat them."

He did, but nobody was at home except a Swedish maid, and all she knew was that Mr. Ricks was out and the hour of his return was unknown. So Mr. Peck went back to Sutter Street and scoured once more every shop window in the block. Then he scouted two blocks above Powell and two blocks below Stockton. Still the blue vase remained invisible.

So he transferred his search to a corresponding area on Bush Street, and when that failed, he went painstakingly over four blocks of Post Street. He was still without results when he moved one block further west and one further south and discovered the blue vase in a huge plate-glass window of a shop on Geary Street near Grant Avenue. He surveyed it critically and was convinced that it was the object he sought.

He tried the door, but it was locked, as he had anticipated it would be. So he kicked the door and raised an infernal racket, hoping against hope that the noise might bring a watchman from the rear of the building. In vain. He backed out to the edge of the sidewalk and read the sign over the door:

B. COHEN'S ART SHOP

This was a start, so Mr. Peck limped over to the Palace Hotel and procured a telephone directory. By actual count there were nineteen B. Cohens scattered throughout the city, so before commencing to call the nineteen, Bill Peck borrowed the city directory from the hotel clerk and scanned it for the particular B. Cohen who owned the art shop. His search availed him nothing. B. Cohen was listed as an art dealer at the address where the blue vase reposed in the show window. That was all.

"I suppose he's a commuter," Mr. Peck concluded, and at once proceeded to procure directories of the adjacent cities of Berkeley, Oakland and Alameda. They were not available, so in despair he changed a dollar into five cent pieces, sought a telephone booth and commenced calling up all the B. Cohens in San Francisco. Of the nineteen, four did not answer, three were temporarily disconnected, six replied in Yiddish, five were not the B. Cohen he sought, and one swore he was Irish and that his name was spelled Cohan and pronounced with an accent on both syllables.

The B. Cohens resident in Berkeley, Oakland, Alameda, San Rafael, Sausalito, Mill Valley, San Mateo, Redwood City and Palo

Alto were next telephoned to, and when this long and expensive task was done, Ex-Private Bill Peck emerged from the telephone booth wringing wet with perspiration and as irritable as a clucking hen. Once outside the hotel he raised his haggard face to heaven and dumbly queried of the Almighty what He meant by saving him from quick death on the field of honor only to condemn him to be talked to death by B. Cohens in civil life.

It was now six o'clock. Suddenly Peck had an inspiration. Was the name spelled Cohen, Cohan, Cohn, Kohn or Coen?

"If I have to take a Jewish census again tonight I'll die," he told himself desperately, and went back to the art shop.

The sign read: B. COHN'S ART SHOP.

"I wish I knew a bootlegger's joint," poor Peck complained. "I'm pretty far gone and a little wood alcohol couldn't hurt me much now. Why, I could have sworn that name was spelled with an E. It seems to me I noted that particularly."

He went back to the hotel telephone booth and commenced calling up all the B. Cohns in town. There were eight of them and six of them were out, one was maudlin with liquor and the other was very deaf and shouted unintelligibly.

"Peace hath its barbarities no less than war," Mr. Peck sighed. He changed a twenty-dollar bill into nickels, dimes and quarters, returned to the hot, ill-smelling telephone booth and proceeded to lay down a barrage of telephone calls to the B. Cohns of all towns of any importance contiguous to San Francisco Bay. And he was lucky. On the sixth call he located the particular B. Cohn in San Rafael, only to be informed by Mr. Cohn's cook that Mr. Cohn was dining at the home of a Mr. Simon in Mill Valley.

There were three Mr. Simons in Mill Valley, and Peck called them all before connecting with the right one. Yes, Mr. B. Cohn was there. Who wished to speak to him? Mr. Heck? Oh, Mr. Lake!

A silence. Then—"Mr. Cohn says he doesn't know any Mr. Lake and wants to know the nature of your business. He is dining and doesn't like to be disturbed unless the matter is of grave importance."

"Tell him Mr. Peck wishes to speak to him on a matter of very great importance," wailed the ex-private.

"Mr. Metz? Mr. Ben Metz?"

"No, no, no. Peck—p-e-c-k."

"D-e-c-k?"

"No, P."

"C?"

"P."

"Oh, yes, E. E—what?"

"C-K——"

"Oh, yes, Mr. Eckstein."

"Call Cohn to the 'phone or I'll go over there on the next boat and kill you, you damned idiot," shrieked Peck. "Tell him his store is on fire."

That message was evidently delivered for almost instantly Mr. B. Cohn was puffing and spluttering into the 'phone.

"Iss dot der fire marshal?" he managed to articulate.

"Listen, Mr. Cohn. Your store is not on fire, but I had to say so in order to get you to the telephone. I am Mr. Peck, a total stranger to you. You have a blue vase in your shop window on Geary Street in San Francisco. I want to buy it and I want to buy it before seven forty-five to-night. I want you to come across the bay and open the store and sell me that vase."

"Such a business! Vot you think I am? Crazy?"

"No, Mr. Cohn, I do not. I'm the only crazy man talking. I'm crazy for that vase and I've got to have it right away."

"You know vot dot vase costs?" Mr. B. Cohn's voice dripped syrup.

"No, and I don't give a hoot what it costs. I want what I want when I want it. Do I get it?"

"Ve-ell, lemme see. Vot time iss it?" A silence while B. Cohn evidently looked at his watch. "It iss now a quarter of seven, Mr. Eckstein, und der nexd drain from Mill Valley don't leaf until eight o'clock. Dot vill get me to San Francisco at eight-fifty—und I am dining mit friends und haf just finished my soup."

"To hell with your soup. I want that blue vase."

"Vell, I tell you, Mr. Eckstein, if you got to have it, call up my head salesman, Herman Joost, in der Chilton Apardments— Prospect three—two—four—nine, und tell him I said he should come down right avay qvick und sell you dot blue vase. Good-bye, Mr. Eckstein."

And B. Cohn hung up.

Instantly Peck called Prospect 3249 and asked for Herman Joost. Mr. Joost's mother answered. She was desolated because Herman was not at home, but vouchsafed the information that he was dining at the country club. Which country club? She did not know. So Peck procured from the hotel clerk a list of the country clubs in and around San Francisco and started calling them up. At eight o'clock he was still being informed that Mr. Juice was not a member, that Mr. Luce wasn't in, that Mr. Coos had been dead three months and that Mr. Boos had played but eight holes when he received a telegram calling him back to New York. At the other clubs Mr. Joust was unknown.

"Licked," murmured Bill Peck, "but never let it be said that I didn't go down fighting. I'm going to heave a brick through that show window, grab the vase and run with it."

He engaged a taxicab and instructed the driver to wait for him at the corner of Geary and Stockton Streets. Also, he borrowed from the chauffeur a ball peen hammer. When he reached the art shop of B. Cohn, however, a policeman was standing in the doorway, violating the general orders of a policeman on duty by surreptitiously smoking a cigar.

"He'll nab me if I crack that window," the desperate Peck decided, and continued on down the street, crossed to the other side and came back. It was now dark and over the art shop B. Cohn's name burned in small red, white and blue electric lights.

And lo, it was spelled B. Cohen!

Ex-Private William E. Peck sat down on a fire hydrant and cursed with rage. His weak leg hurt him, too, and for some damnable reason, the stump of his left arm developed the feeling that his missing hand was itchy.

"The world is filled with idiots," he raved furiously. "I'm tired and I'm hungry. I skipped luncheon and I've been too busy to think of dinner."

He walked back to his taxicab and returned to the hotel where, hope springing eternal in his breast, he called Prospect 3249 again and discovered that the missing Herman Joost had returned to the bosom of his family. To him the frantic Peck delivered the message of B. Cohn, whereupon the cautious Herman Joost replied that he would confirm the authenticity of the message by telephoning to Mr. Cohn at Mr. Simon's home in Mill Valley. If Mr. B. Cohn or Cohen confirmed Mr. Kek's story he, the said Herman Joost, would be at the store sometime before nine o'clock, and if Mr. Kek cared to, he might await him there.

Mr. Kek said he would be delighted to wait for him there.

At nine-fifteen Herman Joost appeared on the scene. On his way down the street he had taken the precaution to pick up a policeman and bring him along with him. The lights were switched on in the store and Mr. Joost lovingly abstracted the blue vase from the window.

"What's the cursed thing worth?" Peck demanded.

"Two thousand dollars," Mr. Joost replied without so much

as the quiver of an eyelash. "Cash," he added, apparently as an afterthought.

The exhausted Peck leaned against the sturdy guardian of the law and sighed. This was the final straw. He had about ten dollars in his possession.

"You refuse, absolutely, to accept my check?" he quavered.

"I don't know you, Mr. Peck," Herman Joost replied simply.

"Where's your telephone?"

Mr. Joost led Peck to the telephone and the latter called up Mr. Skinner.

"Mr. Skinner," he announced, "this is all that is mortal of Bill Peck speaking. I've got the store open and for two thousand dollars—cash—I can buy the blue vase Mr. Ricks has set his heart upon."

"Oh, Peck, dear fellow," Mr. Skinner purred sympathetically. "Have you been all this time on that errand?"

"I have. And I'm going to stick on the job until I deliver the goods. For God's sake let me have two thousand dollars and bring it down to me at B. Cohen's Art Shop on Geary Street near Grant Avenue. I'm too utterly exhausted to go up after it."

"My dear Mr. Peck, I haven't two thousand dollars in my house. That is too great a sum of money to keep on hand."

"Well, then, come down-town, open up the office safe and get the money for me."

"Time lock on the office safe, Peck. Impossible."

"Well then, come down-town and identify me at hotels and cafés and restaurants so I can cash my own check."

"Is your check good, Mr. Peck?"

The flood of invective which had been accumulating in Mr. Peck's system all the afternoon now broke its bounds. He screamed at Mr. Skinner a blasphemous invitation to betake himself to the lower regions.

"To-morrow morning," he promised hoarsely, "I'll beat you to death with the stump of my left arm, you miserable, cold-blooded, lazy, shiftless slacker."

He called up Cappy Ricks' residence next, and asked for Captain Matt Peasley, who, he knew, made his home with his father-in-law. Matt Peasley came to the telephone and listened sympathetically to Peck's tale of woe.

"Peck, that's the worst outrage I ever heard of," he declared. "The idea of setting you such a task. You take my advice and forget the blue vase."

"I can't," Peck panted. "Mr. Ricks will feel mighty chagrined if I fail to get the vase to him. I wouldn't disappoint him for my right arm. He's been a dead game sport with me, Captain Peasley."

"But it's too late to get the vase to him, Peck. He left the city at eight o'clock and it is now almost half past nine."

"I know, but if I can secure legal possession of the vase I'll get it to him before he leaves the train at Santa Barbara at six o'clock to-morrow morning."

"How?"

"There's a flying school out at the Marina and one of the pilots there is a friend of mine. He'll fly to Santa Barbara with me and the vase."

"You're crazy."

"I know it. Please lend me two thousand dollars."

"What for?"

"To pay for the vase."

"Now I know you're crazy—or drunk. Why, if Cappy Ricks ever forgot himself to the extent of paying two hundred dollars for a vase he'd bleed to death in an hour."

"Won't you let me have two thousand dollars, Captain Peasley?"

"I will not, Peck, old son. Go home and to bed and forget it."

"Please. You can cash your checks. You're known so much better than I, and it's Sunday night———"

"And it's a fine way you keep holy the Sabbath day," Matt Peasley retorted and hung up.

"Well," Herman Joost queried, "do we stay here all night?"

Bill Peck bowed his head. "Look here," he demanded suddenly, "do you know a good diamond when you see it?"

"I do," Herman Joost replied.

"Will you wait here until I go to my hotel and get one?"

"Sure."

Bill Peck limped painfully away. Forty minutes later he returned with a platinum ring set with diamonds and sapphires.

"What are they worth?" he demanded.

Herman Joost looked the ring over lovingly and appraised it conservatively at twenty-five hundred dollars.

"Take it as security for the payment of my check," Peck pleaded. "Give me a receipt for it and after my check has gone through clearing I'll come back and get the ring."

Fifteen minutes later, with the blue vase packed in excelsior and reposing in a stout cardboard box, Bill Peck entered a restaurant and ordered dinner. When he had dined he engaged a taxi and was driven to the flying field at the Marina. From the night watchman he ascertained the address of his pilot friend and at midnight, with his friend at the wheel, Bill Peck and his blue vase soared up into the moonlight and headed south.

An hour and a half later they landed in a stubble field in the Salinas Valley and, bidding his friend good-bye, Bill Peck trudged across to the railroad track and sat down. When the train bearing Cappy Ricks came roaring down the valley, Peck twisted a Sunday paper with which he had provided himself, into an improvised torch, which he lighted. Standing between the rails he swung the flaming paper frantically.

The train slid to a halt, a brakeman opened a vestibule door and Bill Peck stepped wearily aboard.

"What do you mean by flagging this train?" the brakeman demanded angrily, as he signaled the engineer to proceed. "Got a ticket?"

"No, but I've got the money to pay my way. And I flagged this train because I wanted to change my method of travel. I'm looking for a man in stateroom A of car 7, and if you try to block me there'll be murder done."

"That's right. Take advantage of your half-portion arm and abuse me," the brakeman retorted bitterly. "Are you looking for that little old man with the Henry Clay collar and the white mutton-chop whiskers?"

"I certainly am."

"Well, he was looking for you just before we left San Francisco. He asked me if I had seen a one-armed man with a box under his good arm. I'll lead you to him."

A prolonged ringing at Cappy's stateroom door brought the old gentleman to the entrance in his nightshirt.

"Very sorry to have to disturb you, Mr. Ricks," said Bill Peck, "but the fact is there were so many Cohens and Cohns and Cohans, and it was such a job to dig up two thousand dollars, that I failed to connect with you at seven forty-five last night, as per orders. It was absolutely impossible for me to accomplish the task within the time limit set, but I was resolved that you should not be disappointed. Here is the vase. The shop wasn't within four blocks of where you thought it was, sir, but I'm sure I found the right vase. It ought to be. It cost enough and was hard enough to get, so it should be precious enough to form a gift for any friend of yours."

Cappy Ricks stared at Bill Peck as if the latter were a wraith.

"By the Twelve Ragged Apostles!" he murmured. "By the Holy Pink-toed Prophet! We changed the sign on you and we stacked the Cohens on you and we set a policeman to guard the shop to keep you from breaking the window, and we made you dig up two thousand dollars on Sunday night in a town where you are practically unknown, and while you missed the train at eight o'clock, you overtake it at two o'clock in the morning and deliver the blue vase. Come in and rest your poor old game leg, Bill. Brakeman, I'm much obliged to you."

Bill Peck entered and slumped wearily down on the settee. "So it was a plant?" he cracked, and his voice trembled with rage. "Well, sir, you're an old man and you've been good to me, so I do not begrudge you your little joke, but Mr. Ricks, I can't stand things like I used to. My leg hurts and my stump hurts and my heart hurts——"

He paused, choking, and the tears of impotent rage filled his eyes. "You shouldn't treat me that way, sir," he complained presently. "I've been trained not to question orders, even when they seem utterly foolish to me; I've been trained to obey them—on time, if possible, but if impossible, to obey them anyhow. I've been taught loyalty to my chief—and I'm sorry my chief found it necessary to make a buffoon of me. I haven't had a very good time the past three years and—and—you can—pa-pa-pass your skunk spruce and larch rustic and short odd length stock to some slacker like Skinner—and you'd better—arrange—to replace—Skinner, because he's young—enough to—take a beating—and I'm going to—give it to him—and it'll be a hospital—job—sir——"

Cappy Ricks ruffled Bill Peck's aching head with a paternal hand.

"Bill, old boy, it was cruel—damnably cruel, but I had a big job for you and I had to find out a lot of things about you before I entrusted you with that job. So I arranged to give you the Degree of the Blue Vase, which is the supreme test of a go-getter. You thought you carried into this stateroom a two thousand dollar vase, but between ourselves, what you really carried in was a ten thousand dollar job as our Shanghai manager."

"Wha—what!"

"Every time I have to pick out a permanent holder of a job worth ten thousand dollars, or more, I give the candidate the Degree of the Blue Vase," Cappy explained. "I've had two men out of a field of fifteen deliver the vase, Bill."

Bill Peck had forgotten his rage, but the tears of his recent fury still glistened in his bold blue eyes. "Thank you, sir. I forgive you—and I'll make good in Shanghai."

"I know you will, Bill. Now, tell me, son, weren't you tempted to quit when you discovered the almost insuperable obstacles I'd placed in your way?"

"Yes, sir, I was. I wanted to commit suicide before I'd finished telephoning all the C-o-h-e-n-s in the world. And when I started on the C-o-h-n-s—well, it's this way, sir. I just couldn't quit because that would have been disloyal to a man I once knew."

"Who was he?" Cappy demanded, and there was awe in his voice.

"He was my brigadier, and he had a brigade motto: It shall be done. When the divisional commander called him up and told him to move forward with his brigade and occupy certain territory, our brigadier would say: 'Very well, sir. It shall be done.' If any officer in his brigade showed signs of flunking his job because it appeared impossible, the brigadier would just look at him once—and then that officer would remember the motto and go and do his job or die trying.

"In the army, sir, the *esprit de corps* doesn't bubble up from the bottom. It filters down from the top. An organization is what its commanding officer is—neither better nor worse. In my company, when the top sergeant handed out a week of kitchen police to a buck, that buck was out of luck if he couldn't muster a grin and say: 'All right, sergeant. It shall be done.'

"The brigadier sent for me once and ordered me to go out and get a certain German sniper. I'd been pretty lucky—some days I got enough for a mess—and he'd heard of me. He opened a map and said to me: 'Here's about where he holes up. Go get him, Private Peck.' Well, Mr. Ricks, I snapped into it and gave him a rifle salute, and said, 'Sir, it shall be done'—and I'll never forget the look that man gave me. He came down to the field hospital to see me after I'd walked into one of those Austrian 88's. I knew my left wing was a total loss and I suspected my left leg was about to leave me, and I was downhearted and wanted to die. He came and bucked me up. He said: 'Why, Private Peck, you aren't half dead. In civil life you're going to be worth half a dozen live ones—aren't you?' But I was pretty far gone and I told him I didn't believe it, so he gave me a hard look and said: 'Private Peck will do his utmost to recover and as a starter he will smile.' Of course, putting it in the form of an order, I had to give him the usual reply, so I grinned and said: 'Sir, it shall be done.' He was quite a man, sir, and his brigade had a soul—his soul——"

"I see, Bill. And his soul goes marching on, eh? Who was he, Bill?"

Bill Peck named his idol.

"By the Twelve Ragged Apostles!" There was awe in Cappy Ricks' voice, there was reverence in his faded old eyes. "Son," he continued gently, "twenty-five years ago your brigadier was a candidate for an important job in my employ—and I gave him the Degree of the Blue Vase. He couldn't get the vase legitimately, so he threw a cobble-stone through the window, grabbed the vase and ran a mile and a half before the police captured him. Cost me a lot of money to square the case and keep it quiet. But he was too good, Bill, and I couldn't stand in his way; I let him go forward to his destiny. But tell me, Bill. How did you get the two thousand dollars to pay for this vase?"

"Once," said ex-Private Peck thoughtfully, "the brigadier and I were first at a dug-out entrance. It was a headquarters dug-out and they wouldn't surrender, so I bombed them and then we went down. I found a finger with a ring on it—and the brigadier said if I didn't take the ring somebody else would. I left that ring as security for my check."

"But how could you have the courage to let me in for a two thousand dollar vase? Didn't you realize that the price was absurd and that I might repudiate the transaction?"

"Certainly not. You are responsible for the acts of your servant. You are a true blue sport and would never repudiate my action. You told me what to do, but you did not insult my intelligence by telling me how to do it. When my late brigadier sent me after the German sniper he didn't take into consideration the probability that the sniper might get me. He told me to get the sniper. It was my business to see to it that I accomplished my mission and carried my objective, which, of course, I could not have done if I had permitted the German to get me."

"I see, Bill. Well, give that blue vase to the porter in the morning. I paid fifteen cents for it in a five, ten and fifteen cent store. Meanwhile, hop into that upper berth and help yourself to a well-earned rest."

"But aren't you going to a wedding anniversary at Santa Barbara, Mr. Ricks?"

"I am not. Bill, I discovered a long time ago that it's a good idea for me to get out of town and play golf as often as I can. Besides which, prudence dictates that I remain away from the office for a week after the seeker of blue vases fails to deliver the goods and—by the way, Bill, what sort of a game do you play? Oh, forgive me, Bill. I forgot about your left arm."

"Say, look here, sir," Bill Peck retorted, "I'm big enough and ugly enough to play one-handed golf."

"But, have you ever tried it?"

"No, sir," Bill Peck replied seriously, "but—it shall be done!"

ELBERT HUBBARD

A Message
to Garcia

In all this Cuban business there is one man stands out on the horizon of my memory like Mars at perihelion. When war broke out between Spain & the United States, it was very necessary to communicate quickly with the leader of the Insurgents, Garcia was somewhere in the mountain vastness of Cuba—no one knew where. No mail nor telegraph message could reach him. The President must secure his cooperation, and quickly.

What to do!

Some one said to the President, "There's a fellow by the name of Rowan will find Garcia for you, if anybody can."

Rowan was sent for and given a letter to be delivered to Garcia. How "the fellow by the name of Rowan" took the letter, sealed it up in an oil-skin pouch, strapped it over his heart, in four days landed by night off the coast of Cuba from an open boat, disappeared into the jungle, & in three weeks came out on the other side of the Island, having traversed a hostile country on foot, and delivered his letter to Garcia, are things I have no special desire now to tell in detail.

The point I wish to make is this: McKinley gave Rowan a letter to be delivered to Garcia; Rowan took the letter and did not ask, "Where is he at?" By the Eternal! there is a man whose form should be cast in deathless bronze and the statue placed in every college of the land. It is not book-learning young men need, nor instruction about this and that, but a stiffening of the vertebrae which will cause them to be loyal to a trust, to act promptly, concentrate their energies: do the thing—"Carry a message to Garcia!"

General Garcia is dead now, but there are other Garcias.

No man, who has endeavored to carry out an enterprise where many hands were needed, but has been well nigh appalled at times by the imbecility of the average man—the inability or unwillingness to concentrate on a thing and do it. Slip-shod assistance, foolish inattention, dowdy indifference, & half-hearted work seem the rule; and no man succeeds, unless by hook or crook, or threat, he forces or bribes other men to assist him; or mayhap, God in His goodness performs a miracle, & sends him an Angel of Light for an assistant. You, reader, put this matter to a test: You are sitting now in your office—six clerks are within call.

Summon any one and make this request: "Please look in the encyclopedia and make a brief memorandum for me concerning the life of Correggio."

Will the clerk quietly say, "Yes, sir," and go do the task?

On your life, he will not. He will look at you out of a fishy eye and ask one or more of the following questions:

- Who was he?
- Which encyclopedia?
- Where is the encyclopedia?
- Was I hired for that?
- Don't you mean Bismarck?
- What's the matter with Charlie doing it?
- Is he dead?
- Is there any hurry?
- Shan't I bring you the book and let you look it up yourself?
- What do you want to know for?

And I will lay you ten to one that after you have answered the questions, and explained how to find the information, and why you want it, the clerk will go off and get one of the other clerks to help him try to find Garcia—and then come back and tell you there is no such man. Of course I may lose my bet, but according to the Law of Average, I will not.

Now if you are wise you will not bother to explain to your "assistant" that Correggio is indexed under the C's, not in the K's, but you will smile sweetly and say, "Never mind," and go look it up yourself.

And this incapacity for independent action, this moral stupidity, this infirmity of the will, this unwillingness to cheerfully catch hold and lift, are the things that put pure Socialism so far into the future. If men will not act for themselves, what will they do when the benefit of their effort is for all? A first-mate with knotted club seems necessary; and the dread of getting "the bounce" Saturday night, holds many a worker to his place.

Advertise for a stenographer, and nine out of ten who apply, can neither spell nor punctuate—and do not think it necessary to.

Can such a one write a letter to Garcia?

"You see that bookkeeper," said the foreman to me in a large factory.

"Yes, what about him?"

"Well he's a fine accountant, but if I'd send him up town on an errand, he might accomplish the errand all right, and on the other hand, might stop at four saloons on the way, and when he got to Main Street, would forget what he had been sent for."

Can such a man be entrusted to carry a message to Garcia?

We have recently been hearing much maudlin sympathy expressed for the "down-trodden denizen of the sweat-shop" and the "homeless wanderer searching for honest employment," & with it all often go many hard words for the men in power.

Nothing is said about the employer who grows old before his time in a vain attempt to get frowsy ne'er-do-wells to do intelligent work; and his long patient striving with "help" that does nothing but loaf when his back is turned. In every store and factory there is a constant weeding-out process going on. The employer is constantly sending away "help" that have shown their incapacity to further the interests of the business, and others are being taken on. No matter how good times are, this sorting continues, only if times are hard and work is scarce, the sorting is done finer—but out and forever out, the incompetent and unworthy go.

It is the survival of the fittest. Self-interest prompts every employer to keep the best—those who can carry a message to Garcia.

I know one man of really brilliant parts who has not the ability to manage a business of his own, and yet who is absolutely worthless to any one else, because he carries with him constantly the insane suspicion that his employer is oppressing, or intending to oppress him. He cannot give orders; and he will not receive them. Should a message be given him to take to Garcia, his answer would probably be, "Take it yourself."

Tonight this man walks the streets looking for work, the wind whistling through his threadbare coat. No one who knows him dare employ him, for he is a regular fire-brand of discontent. He is impervious to reason, and the only thing that can impress him is the toe of a thick-soled No. 9 boot.

Of course I know that one so morally deformed is no less to be pitied than a physical cripple; but in our pitying, let us drop a tear, too, for the men who are striving to carry on a great enterprise, whose working hours are not limited by the whistle, and whose hair is fast turning white through the struggle to hold in line dowdy indifference, slip-shod imbecility, and the heartless ingratitude, which, but for their enterprise, would be both hungry & homeless.

Have I put the matter too strongly? Possibly I have; but when all the world has gone a-slumming I wish to speak a word of sympathy for the man who succeeds—the man who, against great odds has directed the efforts of others, and having succeeded, finds there's nothing in it: nothing but bare board and clothes.

I have carried a dinner pail & worked for day's wages, and I have also been an employer of labor, and I know there is something to be said on both sides. There is no excellence, per se, in poverty; rags are no recommendation; & all employers are not rapacious and high-handed, any more than all poor men are virtuous.

My heart goes out to the man who does his work when the "boss" is away, as well as when he is at home. And the man who, when given a letter for Garcia, quietly takes the missive, without asking any idiotic questions, and with no lurking intention of chucking it into the nearest sewer, or of doing aught else but deliver it, never gets "laid off," nor has to go on a strike for higher wages. Civilization is one long anxious search for just such individuals. Anything such a man asks shall be granted; his kind is so rare that no employer can afford to let him go. He is wanted in every city, town and village—in every office, shop, store and factory. The world cries out for such: he is needed, & needed badly—the man who can carry a message to Garcia.

About the Authors

Florence Scovel Shinn (1871–1940) was an American artist and book illustrator. After the publication of her first book, *The Game of Life and How to Play It*, in 1925, she became a popular lecturer and writer.

Napoleon Hill was born in 1883 in a one-room cabin on the Pound River in Wise County, Virginia. He is the author of the motivational classics *The Laws of Success* and *Think and Grow Rich*. Hill passed away in November 1970 after a long and successful career writing, teaching, and lecturing about the principles of success. His lifework continues under the direction of The Napoleon Hill Foundation.

Emmet Fox (1886–1951) was a leader of the New Thought movement and one of the most influential spiritual leaders of the twentieth century. His transformational message—that our reality can be shaped by our thoughts—has empowered millions. His work has impacted spiritual writers such as Wayne Dyer, Esther Hicks, and Louise Hay.

Dr. Joseph Murphy was a major figure in the human potential movement, the spiritual heir to writers like James Allen, Dale Carnegie, Napoleon Hill, and Norman Vincent Peale and a precursor and inspirer of contemporary motivational writers and speakers like Tony Robbins, Zig Ziglar, and Earl Nightingale. He was one of the best-selling authors in the mid-twentieth century. His book *The Power of the Subconscious Mind* has sold millions of copies and has been translated into seventeen languages.

Arnold Bennett was a prolific English novelist and leading realist author during the early twentieth century. In addition to his fictional work, he also wrote selected nonfiction and criticism, including his insightful book *How to Live on 24 Hours a Day*.

Peter B. Kyne, a native of San Francisco, was a prolific screenwriter and the author of the 1920 bestseller *Kindred of the Dust*. His stories of Cappy Ricks and the Ricks Logging & Lumbering Company were serialized in *The Saturday Evening Post* and William Randolph Hearst's *Cosmopolitan* magazine. He died in 1957.

Elbert Hubbard was born in 1856 in Bloomington, Illinois. He was a writer, publisher, and artist who was an influential member of the Arts and Craft movement. His best-known work is the short publication *A Message to Garcia*.